GWR/BR (WR) CASTLE CLASS

Nos 4073–7037 (including 2, 3 & 4 Row Superheater Versions)

COVER CUTAWAY
Castle Class Locomotive Schematic. *(Author's Drawing)*

First published in December 2014

A catalogue record for this book is available
from the British Library.

ISBN 978 0 85733 271 4

Library of Congress control no. 2014935023

Published by Haynes Publishing,
Sparkford, Yeovil,
Somerset BA22 7JJ, UK.
Tel: 01963 442030 Fax: 01963 440001
Int. tel: +44 1963 442030
Int. fax: +44 1963 440001
E-mail: sales@haynes.co.uk
Website: www.haynes.co.uk

Haynes North America Inc.,
861 Lawrence Drive, Newbury Park,
California 91320, USA.

Printed in the USA by Odcombe Press LP,
1299 Bridgestone Parkway, La Vergne,
TN 37086.

Acknowledgements

The book you hold only exists because of the friendship, help
and training I have received from my fellow volunteers at Didcot.
Special thanks go to Laurence Walters and Frank Dumbleton from
the Great Western Society for finding the vast majority of the pictures
you are looking at; and the Great Western Society & Trust and the
many private individuals, including Sir William McAlpine, who allowed
all of these photographs to be used free of charge to promote No
4079, and so that Haynes could donate this book's photo budget
to the No 4079 project. I also have to thank my legion of fact and
language checkers that I have used, including my father Trevor
(cheers Dad!), Alisdair Mathews, Peter Gransden, Peter Chatman,
Laurence Walters, Karl Buckingham, Ciran Johnson and Leigh Drew.
I am also in debt to the No 5029 *Nunney Castle* support crew from
Locomotive Services who graciously took me out on the main line
and treated me as if I had always been a part of their support crew.

This book is dedicated to my team at Didcot that help me look
after the engines under my care in general and No 4079 in particular,
to the memory of those few who have served on the restoration
of No 4079 but sadly did not live long enough to see her finished,
and to my family, who have supported and encouraged me in both
writing this book and restoring the locomotives. This is especially
true of my wonderful and long-suffering partner Selena, who willingly
shares me with over 130 tons of frustrating, cantankerous, but
equally beautiful and inspiring antique metal, and has to put up with
living with a true geek.

Drew Fermor

GWR/BR (WR) CASTLE CLASS

Haynes

Nos 4073–7030 (including 2, 3 & 4 Row Superheater Versions)

Owners' Workshop Manual

A guide to the history and operation of Britain's most successful express passenger steam locomotive type

Drew Fermor

Contents

⎯(●)⎯

OPPOSITE No 5051 *Earl Bathurst* on shed at Didcot.

(Frank Dumbleton)

Foreword

By Richard Croucher,
Chairman, Great Western Society

For over a third of a century the Castle Class were the backbone of the Great Western passenger fleet and its successor, handling a wide variety of duties; masters of whatever they were asked to do, they were more than adequate substitutes for the more powerful King Class with which they shared many characteristics.

In total 155 Castles 'proper' were built over 27 years to August 1950, whilst a further 15 Stars were rebuilt at various times to the Castle Class configuration. In addition the Great Western's one and only Pacific, which was built in 1908 and ran on an extended Star frame, was rebuilt as a Castle in 1924 when its boiler needed renewal, making a class total of 171 Castles overall. The full complement only ran for just over a year, as the first two Castles – both

rebuilt Stars – were withdrawn in September 1951. Apart from a few other rebuilds, it was 1959 before the first Castle 'proper' was withdrawn from service.

The Castles have their genesis in Churchward's four-cylinder 4-6-0 Star Class which were introduced in 1906. By the end of the 1910s the need for a more powerful boiler had been identified, which led in the end to the application of a larger boiler on a slightly extended Star frame and the introduction of the Castle Class in 1923. Of the three separate Classes (Star, Castle and King) to use the four-cylinder frame, arguably the Castles – with their larger boiler and bigger cab – were the most balanced and best-looking 4-6-0s. Although the frames were built for the No 1 boiler as carried by the Stars they seemed proportionally more correct carrying the No 8 boiler.

Although the Castles were built over a long timescale, gradual improvements to the design

BELOW 1 May 2010, No 5029 joins the fleet at Didcot for a gala appearance.
(Frank Dumbleton)

RIGHT The great traveller – No 4037. This early view shows her pretty much as built in December 1910 as a Star Class machine. She was rebuilt as a Castle Class loco in June 1926 and renamed *The South Wales Borderers* in April 1937. She worked until withdrawn in September 1962.
(GWT Collection)

continued to be introduced over the years and the railway preservation movement is fortunate that examples of various stages of development have survived. Two of the eight survivors are the earliest examples, including the class pioneer, 4073 *Caerphilly Castle*, and 4079 *Pendennis Castle*, which the Great Western chose to be its representative on away metals during the 1925 trials with Sir Nigel Gresley's A3 Pacifics on the London & North Eastern Railway, where the Castle excelled, prompting changes to LNER locomotive practice. Two of the other survivors, 5043 *Earl of Mount Edgcumbe* and 7029 *Clun Castle*, carry the final development of the boiler with four-row superheater and double chimney plus mechanical lubricator, whilst 7027 *Thornbury Castle* – which has not been restored as yet – carries the three-row superheater boiler introduced after the end of the Second World War when construction of Castles resumed. The other three survivors (5029 *Nunney Castle*, 5051 *Earl Bathurst/Drysllwyn Castle* and 5080 *Defiant*) are basically examples of the 1930s construction.

The longest-surviving Castle was 4037, which had a 52-year lifespan and ran 2,429,722 miles – the highest recorded by any Great Western locomotive. Built in 1910 as Star *Queen Philippa*, it was rebuilt in 1926 and eventually became *The South Wales Borderers*, one of the Great Western's longest nameplates. Growing up in Taunton in the 1950s, 4037 was a regular visitor and I often wondered how

LEFT Richard Croucher addresses the press conference for the handover of No 4079 from Rio Tinto to the Great Western Society. Richard played a major part in her repatriation in 1999–2000.
(Adrian Knowles/GWS)

RIGHT On 9 February 2008, a photo charter at Didcot turned the shed into Laira Depot for a few days. Here we see No 5051 *Earl Bathurst* masquerading as her long-scrapped sister No 5058 *Earl of Clancarty*, in the company of another of Didcot's treasures, the sole surviving Swindon-built saddle tank locomotive No 1363.
(Frank Dumbleton/GWS)

much of the original locomotive remained.

Pendennis Castle survived in its original condition for over 40 years. To be chosen as the flagship for the away leg of the 1925 trials she must have been amongst the best of the first batch; but what is even more amazing is that in the selection process of eight Castle Class 4-6-0s in 1964 for a special run from Paddington to Plymouth and back to commemorate the 60th Anniversary of the 102.7mph run by *City of Truro* down Wellington Bank in 1904, No 4079 was considered the best against all her younger classmates covering all the various stages of subsequent development. As a result 4079 was chosen for the first leg of the run to Taunton, but unfortunately (or fortunately, probably, as things turned out), fate was to take a hand, and, in all the enthusiasm to have a superb run, she dropped her fire just before Westbury and was abandoned there; but for this she may well have gone the way of the others, but this gave time for *Pendennis* to be preserved.

Her unique history does not end there, because by another quirk of fate 4079 then made the journey to the outback of northern Western Australia in 1977, when she was purchased by Hamersley Iron & Steel, a subsidiary of Rio Tinto, where she remained until 2000 making occasional journeys inland on Hamersley's private railway in midwinter when the temperature dropped to a cool 30°! The Great Western Society is grateful to Hamersley

and Rio Tinto for their decision to repatriate No 4079 to home soil and safe keeping at Didcot Railway Centre, where it has undergone its first heavy general overhaul since 1959.

They say a locomotive is identified by its frames, and despite its age No 4079's frames are the originals, and the Great Western Society is lucky to have an original Castle Class 4-6-0 in its collection. During any major overhaul, almost everything other than the frames and cylinders are completely dismantled, and so it has been with No 4079's overhaul and restoration at Didcot Railway Centre; and in the course of such an exercise many items have been identified which have been carried on other four-cylinder locomotives, not just the Castles – such is the benefit of standardisation as practised by the Great Western Railway!

What better way to learn how a steam locomotive works than to take one to pieces and then put it back together again? This is what Drew Fermor and the team of Great Western Society volunteers have done with No 4079, and the experience and knowledge gained in so doing has led to this manual, which will be appreciated by all enthusiasts interested in how a steam railway locomotive comes together, especially those interested in the workings of Great Western four-cylinder locomotives.

Richard Croucher
Chairman, Great Western Society
Didcot, Oxon, January 2014

Introduction

The Castle Class locomotive – so what?

The mighty Kings were the best thing that ever happened to the Great Western Railway (GWR). Their sheer power, brute force and rugged good looks make them the ultimate in GWR express passenger locomotives. The greatest of the greats in the GWR stud.

But hang on, this is a Castle Class manual, and in any case, how do we measure greatness? If we go by power alone, of course the Kings win – hands down. Only the likes of the LNER/BR A2 Class really beat them to any great degree for express passenger engines. But there has to be more to it than just power alone. The design brief for the Kings has to be one of the oddest in the history of railway engineering – to beat the tractive effort of another company's machine! The Castles, however, were born out of genuine need from the traffic department. Passenger numbers increased dramatically after the First World War, so a little more power and efficiency

was required from the engines that pulled these trains.

The Castles answered that need and then some. They proved an instant hit, taking on and beating all comers in the power and efficiency stakes. The engines could do all that was required of them and more. Their reign at the top of the GWR pile was relatively short-lived, but their efficiency and solidity of design and construction not only saw 171 built or converted from other designs (as opposed to only 30 Kings) but also enabled them to remain relevant enough as a design that British Railways Western Region were still building them in 1950 – a span of some 27 years, only interrupted by WW2.

To my eyes at least, the Castles are by far a more elegant machine, perfectly balanced and proportioned with the whole ensemble seeming to 'fit'. In the looks stakes the Kings appear as they are, a design pushed to the

BELOW On 2 April 2011 the Great Western Society was proud to launch King Class No 6023 *King Edward II* to traffic after a 20+ year restoration from 'mission impossible' scrapyard condition. From right to left are No 5051 *Earl Bathurst*, No 6023 *King Edward II* and visitors No 5043 *Earl of Mount Edgcumbe* and Hall Class No 4965 *Rood Ashton Hall*, from our fellow preservationists at Tyseley.
(Frank Dumbleton/GWS)

ABOVE Big, bigger and biggest. The three stalwarts of the GWR main line have been put on show for the official GWR photographer. Left to right we have King, Castle and Star, showing the development of the four-cylinder design. *(GWS/GWT)*

limit. They are just a bit too 'butch' for me. In addition, compared to the Castles they had many more issues that needed resolving and updating throughout their lives. The Castles benefited from Churchward's work on the Stars and pretty much worked straight out of the box. This is not to say that the Castles themselves were unchanged – as we shall see – but the modifications tended to be as a result of changing circumstances and improvement in production methods rather than any inherent weakness in the basic concept of their four-cylinder 4-6-0 design.

The Kings took the really heavy trains as their extra power dictated, but their usefulness was restricted by their limited route availability. The Castles were more fleet of foot and far more a 'go anywhere' type of machine. Minor infrastructure upgrades led to them being able to traverse the vast majority of the principle and secondary lines of the GWR/BR (WR) network. For more than 40 years they did everything asked of them and more. As an investment, that cannot be ignored. We often forget that the objects of our affection, the prized things of beauty and reverence that we see steam locomotives as today, were simply tools – designed to do a specific job of work in a commercial environment. In this respect the Castles were a very good purchase indeed. As

author Ian Sixsmith once wrote: "[The Castles were] an express design that was in every respect pre-grouping [but] was still being built by the nationalised British Railways which, after all, built only 55 Britannias! It was all really a bit remarkable."

I am obviously biased here and I don't expect that everyone (or indeed anyone) will agree with me, but I am a Castle man, through and through. I have been involved in a torrid affair with one of them for nearly ten years now. My long-suffering and very supportive partner affectionately refers to *Pendennis Castle* as 'the other woman'! I started work on her as a raw recruit, but in the intervening years I have risen to the giddy heights of project manager, and this obsession seems set to continue. I can't see myself giving up my interest or passion for this particular machine any time soon.

There is a reason why otherwise rational and seemingly intelligent people such as I drag themselves out of bed on a cold winter's morning to don overalls and work on what are now obsolete machines: to bring them back to life and run them for an appreciative public. This is because, for me and my fantastic, loyal and hard-working team of volunteers and friends, there is just something magical about steam engines in general and *Pendennis Castle* in particular. A

magic that pushes us to raise tens of thousands of pounds and work in sometimes difficult, frustrating and dirty circumstances for a mere ten-year boiler certificate. I don't know precisely what that magic is, and it varies from person to person. I wish I could define it or bottle it! For me it is the pleasure that comes from reviving what was once described as an almost elemental beast, born of the earth and brought to life with fire and water. A machine that is, in its own way, very close to having a personality and a soul. It's almost like having your own pet dragon. It is also a tangible and tactile connection with history in a way that is impossible to obtain from simply watching it thunder past or riding as a passenger behind it. That is all great, of course, until the last fire is dropped, the feared shape of the boiler inspector* shakes his head and you have to pick yourself up, dust yourself down and start it all over again...

It is this passion and effort of the countless steam volunteers up and down the country that I wish to impart to the reader. This is the driving force that keeps the magnificent steam locomotive survivors of this country (Kings included – I really do like them a great deal too!) performing for the benefit, entertainment, education and inspiration of generations past, present and future.

So, without further ado, I want to tell you a story...

Drew Fermor,
4079 *Pendennis Castle* Restoration Project Manager
Great Western Society, Didcot Railway Centre
July 2014

---

* With apologies to 4079's boiler inspector – I'm being metaphorical, honest!

Chapter One

The Castle story

Collett by name, Churchward by nature

As odd as it may seem to the casual reader, the story of the Castle Class is actually one that starts nearly 20 years before the first of them was built. Their origins lie with arguably the greatest steam locomotive engineer of the early part of the 20th century – George Jackson Churchward.

OPPOSITE No 40 *North Star* – the locomotive that started it all. This view is after she was named in 1906 but before her renumbering into the Star series in 1912 as No 4000. *(GWS/GWT)*

ABOVE No 100 was completed in March 1902, and although she was designed under the Dean regime, she was most certainly an enterprise by Churchward. She begins to illustrate some of the features later to become standard GWR practice, such as a dome-less boiler and Belpaire firebox. She still has the features of older machines, the most obvious of these being the parallel boiler barrel. *(GWS/GWT)*

His big plan for the GWR loco fleet was twofold. Firstly, as far as was possible, he wanted to standardise the locomotives. The practice of standardisation of components on the GWR was far from alien, but Churchward took it a stage further. He gave the GWR a 'kit' of parts from which, with the minimum of effort and additional drawings, any locomotive could be produced – the design of the famous and ubiquitous 'Churchward Moguls' (like Didcot's No 5322) being an excellent case in point. This was a design born almost entirely out of standard parts. It wasn't in Churchward's original standard loco plan but required only a few extra drawings to enable the shop floor to get on with building the prototype. The Moguls grew to be so useful that they became the most numerous tender engine design on the GWR, with 342 machines being constructed.

Secondly, the parts and engineering behind GWR's locomotives had to be absolutely first rate. To this end, Churchward and his staff scoured the globe looking for excellent engineering practice and wherever possible bringing it home and improving on it. In the majority of cases these improvements also had the benefit of nullifying any patents and the attendant fees that may have applied to that technology! Churchward took notice of what was going on in the world about him – this was a far cry from the normally quite insular (on an international basis at least) outlook of British locomotive engineers at the time.

Boiler design was a major focus of Churchward's interest. Many prototypes that

BELOW No 100 out on the GWR main line in the very early 20th century with a wonderful collection of clerestory passenger stock preceded by a Dean full brake not unlike the restored example (Diagram K.14, No 933) at Didcot. *(GWS/GWT)*

He was born in 1857 and became an apprentice to the locomotive superintendent on the South Devon Railway at the age of 16. He transferred to the same office but with the GWR at the age of 19, and from then on this brilliant engineer made a stratospheric rise through the ranks. By the age of 45 he was chief assistant to the GWR locomotive superintendent, William Dean. By the turn of the 20th century Dean was in ill health and was beginning to wind down to retirement. Churchward, on the other hand, was just getting into his stride, and by the time he officially succeeded Dean in 1902 he was in full force.

were built in the very early part of the 20th century carried several different shapes and styles of boiler throughout their developmental phase. Eventually a number of key design features were identified. The firebox chosen was the Belpaire type that had a pinched-in lower section that enabled the firebox sides to fit between the frames, and above this it opened out to a more square cross-section type with a flat 'roof'. This is unlike the more traditional Dean type that simply had a rolled round top which, in cross-section, looked much like the covered wagons of Wild West fame. The new fireboxes had the advantage of a narrow sloping grate that aided the combustion of fuel, and larger water spaces to produce more steam at the hottest end of the boiler. The boiler barrels also came under scrutiny. The standard Dean design was to have this formed into a parallel-sided tube; however, experimentation showed that a conical or tapered section put more water closer to the source of heat (the fire) and also had the benefit of reducing the weight on the front end, allowing for larger and heavier cylinders. Churchward tried a number of half-cone designs, but in the end he found that putting a long taper on the barrel was by far the best method.

Superheating was the final piece of the steam generation puzzle. Superheating is the secondary heating of steam in a series of 'elements' that go back through the hot gasses coming off the fire after leaving the regulator (the engine's throttle). This improves the thermal efficiency of the locomotive over a long run with sustained high-power outputs. This is why it is not usually fitted to smaller,

shunting locomotives, as the maintenance costs outweigh any fuel savings. A number of commercial designs were tried out which refined the GWR engineers' thinking. The final GWR design wasn't completed until 1909 but is included here as it fits in under the current topic of discussion. There were three successive Swindon superheater designs that ended with the less than imaginatively titled Swindon No 3. This was far more effective, and each element was simply fitted with a single attachment point that made a great improvement in both operation and maintenance. This saw its debut on Star Class loco No 4021 *King Edward* when it was completed in June 1909. From this point all relevant locos were either retrofitted with this system or had it fitted as new. By the time this had been completed, apart from the few classes of smallest engines that retained parallel barrels, the basic boiler concept only had to be scaled up or down to suit a locomotive type and its use.

The other thing that had been a major preoccupation for Churchward's studies was the valves used to distribute the steam to either side of the piston to drive a locomotive. He had been engaged in a protracted period of experimentation on a single-cylinder stationary engine. The results of all this led him to conclude that in order to get the steam in, for it to do its work (*ie* expand to its fullest) and then be released after it was spent – so as not to cause back-pressure which would rob the machine of its hard-won efforts – a large piston-type valve had to be used. The older type of slide valve (a design whereby a sliding plate was used as the valve, and which can be found in locomotives such as pannier tanks on the GWR) was all very well in shunting locomotives, but as the demands placed upon engines increased a more efficient way of using the steam had to be found. In order to increase this efficiency a combination of large-diameter valves and ports were tried, and Churchward settled upon a system that involved long travel on the valves and an increase in lap – 'lap' being the amount by which a valve overhangs the port, thus increasing the amount of time that the valve covers either the exhaust or live steam port in its cycle. The type of lap used was dependent on the locomotive's duties. The amount used by

Churchward was a 50% increase on common British practice at the time.

Churchward postulated that he could run the Great Western with about a dozen standard locomotive types, using his standardised boilers, wheels, cylinders, motion and tenders. When looking at the designs for the big mixed traffic and express engines, Churchward was even bolder with his experiments. He decided to go to the extent of arranging a set of trials that involved the purchase of a number of French De Glehn-designed 4-4-2 locos, and converting some of his two-cylinder 4-6-0 prototypes as they were being built to matching 4-4-2s. This was so that he could compare and contrast the merits of compound (using the steam twice over progressively larger cylinders) versus the traditional British simple expansion (one 'chuff' and out) machines that were the mainstay of the UK locomotive fleet. This raised more than a few eyebrows across the British engineering world in general, and within the GWR in particular.

These trials led to the conclusion that compounding, while improving efficiency, did not merit the resultant increase in maintenance costs and, it has to be said, the training of crews. The distances involved on the GWR main lines were simply not great enough for

BELOW AND RIGHT Two interesting views of the concept model of the 'scissors'-style valve gear designed by GWR draughtsman W.H. Pearce. Contemporary sources say that it was very difficult to set up after removal from the locomotive, so, given its issues with patents, it is not hard to see why it was discontinued. *(GWS/GWT)*

the economies to balance out. This decided, Churchward built one last prototype. This was an impressively modern-looking machine. Like its trials cousins, it was a 4-4-2 simple expansion design, but in line with the French locos it possessed four cylinders. The idea of this was to get the same or indeed more power from a similar-size engine but with far smaller reciprocating and rotating masses in the mechanism. This made not only a smoother ride on the locomotive but also made it more manageable for the crews at high speeds. Even more importantly, the reduced stresses meant that wear and tear on the machine was also reduced, consequently reducing maintenance costs. In addition it reduced stress on the track.

This engine was not originally bestowed with a name but was simply known as No 40. However, it soon gained the title *North Star*. As a very traditionalist organisation, the GWR liked to remember its glorious past and this was the name given to one of the earliest broad-gauge locomotives from the tenure of the Victorian luminaries, Isambard Kingdom Brunel and Daniel Gooch. The engine had an unusual 'scissor type' valve gear that is reported to have got Churchward and its designer, W.H. Pearce, into a bit of a close run thing with patent infringement. It seems that this time, though, it was a genuine case of convergent evolution, and although the case was dropped all subsequent locos of this type were built with a Swindon-developed inside (between the frames) version of the famous valve gear designed by

Belgian engineer Egide Walschaerts. Almost all the later 20th-century GWR two-cylinder designs have an inside version of the equally familiar Stephenson-type gear.

No 40 proved to be a fairly competent machine, but was not – in terms of the power it could apply to the track – any better than the simpler and cheaper two-cylinder 4-6-0 Saint Class engine, although the ride for the crew was far superior. One last modification was needed and the trailing wheel set was done away with in favour of another coupled set of driving wheels. This put No 40 into a different league, and soon after a production run of similar machines – the first ten of which were also named after the original broad gauge Star Class – was being built. The first of these was No 4001 *Dog Star* in 1907. They all received names that conjured up mystique, majesty and a regal air. Some of these most impressive names include such absolute crackers as No 4016 *Knight of the Golden Fleece* and No 4018 *Knight of the Grand Cross*. Poor old No 4014, however, was given the name *Knight of the Bath* and was forever known to her crews simply as *Friday Night* (think about it). In all, 72 of these very elegant Edwardian machines were built and served with distinction until the early 1950s, by when the railwaymen were very sorry to see their beloved 'small forties', as they were known, go for scrap.

The Stars did very well, serving with distinction through the First World War and up to the beginning of the 1920s. By this time,

ABOVE An impressive study of No 40 *North Star* on shed. The loco was slowly rebuilt to a more or less Star configuration but retained her scissors valve gear until conversion into a Castle in 1929. She retained her higher-than-standard running plate until scrapped in July 1957. *(GWS/GWT)*

LEFT No 4007 ably demonstrates the longevity of the Star Class by being an express loco in British Railways livery despite having been built in 1907. She was originally named *Rising Star* but was renamed *Swallowfield Park* in 1937. She also displays the curious arrangement of having a reporting number frame mounted on the smokebox door, but they obviously ran out of numbers, as the actual number has been chalked on the upper left smokebox door! She remained in service until September 1951. *(GWS/GWT)*

RIGHT AND BELOW
Thankfully, BR recognised the significance of the Star Class and decided to place No 4003 *Lode Star* in Swindon Museum. Subsequently the locomotive was absorbed into the National Collection. She is the sole preserved Star Class machine and was overhauled and restored by Swindon works before being placed on display.
(Author)

however, the power they could generate was being tested. Traffic levels had increased to the point whereby every day performances of crews and machines were being stretched beyond reasonable expectations. By 1922 Churchward had retired too. In his place was his principal assistant, Charles Benjamin Collett, and the approach of these two figures could not have been more different. Where Churchward was an extrovert, often being seen in the works with his hands-on approach to

BELOW The somewhat enigmatic figure of Charles Benjamin Collett. He is maligned by some, but in many ways is quite misunderstood. He deserves a better appreciation and needs to be regarded as a superb production engineer rather than gauged against his erstwhile predecessor as a locomotive man. *(GWS/GWT)*

solving difficult problems with a gregarious and upfront manner, Collett preferred to manage in a more detached manner. Churchward was a great innovator whereas Collett understood and appreciated the programme of standardisation his predecessor had instigated and used it to its utmost, preferring not to innovate but to build instead on past success. Collett is often criticised for this approach, but there were sound reasons – technical, personal and financial – that made his chosen course of action sensible initially. Unusually, in terms of 20th-century chief mechanical engineers (CME) (the GWR changed the title in line with other railways during Churchward's reign), Collett was not a railwayman.

He was born in 1871 and had shown a particular aptitude for technical and scientific study. This was despite the early death of both his brother and his father whilst he was still a child. This may go some way to explaining his somewhat insular character and lack of interest in generating interpersonal relationships with his co-workers, something that Churchward did with consummate ease. Collett was apprenticed to the firm of Maudsley, Sons & Field, designing marine engines and pumps. Only in 1898 did he join the drawing office at Swindon locomotive works and, following a similar meteoric rise to his predecessor, he became CME. His background with Churchward had meant that he was part of the standardisation process and a fervent believer in it. He was also a highly skilled production engineer, and what he lacked in locomotive experience he more than made up for with factory-floor knowledge. He wasn't liked by the workers at Swindon in the same way as Churchward was, but he was certainly respected as a generally fair and even-handed boss when compared against others of the era, if a little prickly and aloof.

His policy of improving upon the standard designs of his predecessor was actually a very sound one for the GWR both financially and practically. Again the old chestnut of 'stagnation' of loco design is usually trotted out by opponents of Swindon practice, and from a certain point of view this is true; but it must be remembered that at the start of the Collett era, the locos being built by GWR were probably the best in the UK, and indeed the

world, and it made little sense to design a machine that was completely new. It can be argued, however, that towards the beginning of the 1930s the company's lead had begun to be lost, and Collett should have been looking at other avenues by taking a fresh approach in line with the London North Eastern Railway (LNER) and London Midland and Scottish Railway (LMS) developments, but by then the Great Depression was in full swing; and then a little international disagreement had erupted, which, as we all know, boiled over in 1939 into something really unpleasant, following which everyone knew that there just wasn't the time for such niceties as design improvements.

The design for a replacement for the Stars in the top link was a clear example. The principles inherent in the design were sound, but it just needed quickly updating to suit the new demands of the traffic and publicity departments, and that is what Collett did. The first order of business was to make the cylinders larger to achieve extra power. The Stars had started with 14½in cylinders and a modification had been made to bore them out to 15in. To provide the extra punch Collett's new cylinder block had 16in bores. This, in combination with the Star's existing 6ft 8½in driving wheels, increased the tractive effort of the new engine by more than 10% – the difference being felt in BR days, when the Stars were rated as power class five locomotives whereas the Castles were rated as class seven!

There was a problem, however: the use of larger cylinders meant that the power plant, in the form of the boiler, needed to be uprated too – if it was not, the engine was far more likely to run out of steam. There were various thoughts about the boiler, including using one from the standard range available; but Collett was hamstrung by the need to keep the individual axle loads down to below the 20-ton limit in force by the civil engineers on the GWR. Nothing quite worked to give either the correct axle load or large enough reserves of steam. The only candidate was the No 7, as fitted to the late, lamented and highly praised (and, with the advent of the GWS 4709 project, phoenix-like) 47XX class fast goods locos; but it was just too heavy. As a result a new standard boiler – the standard No 8 – was

designed especially for the Castles. This may sound a bit like an oxymoron, but considering the number of Castles built it turned out to be a good decision. This was a very efficient steam generator that built upon the fantastic and methodical work undertaken by Churchward earlier that century.

The engine also received the new Collett-style cab that furnished the crew with such hitherto unknown luxuries as a roof capable of keeping the rain out, and side sheets so wide that they actually needed windows; this necessitated making the main frames a foot (305mm) or so longer at the rear. There were other minor differences. In essence, what stood before them on the drawing board was the

Castle Class. It has to be said, though, that this wasn't exactly the case. As the drawings for the new class were so similar – apart from those for the boiler – the drawing office simply made alterations to the plans for the Star Class in red pencil, and sent them back to the shop floor. It was only later when more significant modifications were made to the class that a full set of drawings was produced.

The first Castle was completed in 1923, and the numbering sequence reflected the close relationship they had with the Stars by simply carrying on where the latter left off. No 4073 *Caerphilly Castle* was hailed by the GWR publicity department as a sensation of the age, and they wasted no time in whipping up a media storm around the machine that would have impressed even some of today's publicists. Thousands of special commemorative booklets were printed, and were so successful that they quickly sold out and had to be reprinted several times. The claims of engine power and efficiency made by the GWR were astounding and caused much consternation in railway circles, but that is a

BELOW AND RIGHT Two very different views of the pioneer of the Castle Class, No 4073 *Caerphilly Castle*. Below we see her in her works portrait in photographic grey livery. What is not generally realised about these pictures is that the lining and insignia were out of regular stocks and in full colour! *(GWS/GWT)* Right she is seen lying in state in Swindon museum, where she was moved after being on display at the Science Museum in South Kensington for many years. *(Author)*

RIGHT AND CENTRE The ultimate Paddington Bear? The 72 Stars and No 4000 were not the only four-cylinder express passenger locomotives built to a pure Churchward design. One other was completed in 1908, and she was a real giant. No 111 was named *The Great Bear* in line with the other Star titles applied to the first batch of top link 4-6-0s. No 111 was the United Kingdom's first 4-6-2 or Pacific-type locomotive. *(GWS/GWT)*

story for another chapter. Suffice to say that trials on the LNER in 1925 and the LMS in 1926 further demonstrated not only their power and great efficiency but also their surefooted stance that made them far less prone to slipping (wheelspin, to the uninitiated). The LMS were so impressed that they actually tried to buy a fleet of Castles, but Swindon politely (and probably with some amusement) declined.

A number of other locomotives were converted to Castle Class standards fairly soon afterwards, the most notable being the GWR's sole Pacific-type machine, No 111 *The Great Bear* (which kept its number; it was renamed *Viscount Churchill*). No 4000 (which had originally been rebuilt to a Star configuration) received the upgrade, as did a number of other Stars. The last batch of Stars (named after Abbeys) was also converted, the last of these conversions taking place in 1938. The Castles were not top of the heap for long, however, as just three years after the triumphant emergence of the 4073 class a new kid was in town. This monster 4-6-0 was built right to the limits of what the Star design and the loading gauge would allow.

The Castles were famed for being the most powerful express passenger locos in the kingdom, but when a new upstart in the Southern Railway came up with their Lord Nelson Class it was felt at Paddington that something really ought to be done to counter this less than agreeable situation. Collett and his team were instructed to take the Castle design with its tractive effort of 31,625lb (14,344.8kg) and put it through an intensive body-building course. The Lord Nelsons had a tractive effort of 33,500lb (15,195.4kg), but Paddington didn't want the Southern just beaten – they wanted

BELOW No 111 was really a showpiece, as she didn't have any obvious advantages over the existing Stars and in fact had several drawbacks. The biggest of these was her weight restriction. The *Bear* was heavy, with an axle load of over 20 tons, and as a result she was restricted to the London/Bristol main line. She was very capable when in the right hands and in good condition, but understandably, at that time, people with experience of Pacific Locomotives were a bit thin on the ground! Despite being the GWR's flagship until the advent of No 4073 *Caerphilly Castle*, the decision to rebuild her into a member of the Castle fleet in 1924 wasn't a hard one when it became clear that her unique boiler was beyond economic repair. *(GWS/GWT)*

ABOVE The reign of the Kings began with the completion of No 6000 *King George V* in June 1927. Looking at the locomotive's cab sides, you can see the medals she was awarded at the Baltimore & Ohio Centenary celebrations, so it can be assumed that this view is one taken upon her return. You will also notice that, due to the medals, the unique-to-class double red weight restrictions are placed under the number plates on this locomotive. *(GWS/GWT)*

it smashed and scattered to the winds. They ordered that the new GWR engine should have a tractive effort of more than 40,000lb (18,143.6kg). This leap in power was made possible by uprating various bridges and other structures on the principal routes to take 22½-ton axle loads, increasing cylinder size and decreasing the wheel diameter to 6ft 6in. It also meant designing another, even larger, boiler in the shape of the increasingly inaccurately named standard No 12. The design shows its extreme proportions in the front bogie, with its highly unusual arrangement of outside bearings at the front and inside bearings at the rear.

This became the King Class, of which the first – No 6000 *King George V* – was completed in time to be sent to the centenary of the Baltimore & Ohio Railroad in the USA, where it greatly impressed all who saw it. These new engines were only used on the principal routes as they were restricted by their sheer weight, and although they were designed almost on a whim they did have a use on the heaviest express trains – a role they dominated until they were withdrawn en masse in 1963. Their more limited usefulness saw just 30 of these purposeful-looking machines built.

Tragedy struck Swindon in 1933 when

RIGHT The hero of that long ago hour. No 5006 *Tregenna Castle* is recorded at Hayes in the late BR period. *(Frank Dumbleton Collection)*

engineering pioneer George Jackson Churchward was killed. Despite retiring in 1922, he had been a frequent visitor to the works and kept his finger on the pulse of activities. He had been a bachelor all his life, and his life was the Great Western. In the intervening years his hearing and eyesight had deteriorated, but his wit and intelligence were as sharp as ever. One foggy evening in December, he was making his way across the line near the loco works when he thought he spotted a defective sleeper in the track-work of the down through line. A railway servant to the end, and obviously mindful of the potential hazard to the safety of all concerned, he went to examine it. As he was doing so, he was struck down and killed by a Paddington to Fishguard express. Ironically it was being pulled by No 4085 *Berkeley Castle* – the offspring of his magnificent Stars. He was buried in the graveyard of Christ Church in Old Town, Swindon, where he rests to this day.

The Castles soon settled down to life at the sharp end of express passenger work and breaking records. This came to a head with the service known to legend as the Cheltenham Flyer. This was the Great Western's fastest train and laid claim to being the fastest schedule in the world, with demanding timings that – whilst well within the capabilities of the Castles – demanded skilled handling by the crews. It was introduced in 1923 and the 77.3-mile non-stop service between Paddington and Cheltenham was originally timed at 75 minutes.

ABOVE **To the great delight of railway enthusiasts, on 11 May 2013 Bob Meanly and his crew at Tyseley Locomotive Works re-ran the Cheltenham Flyer with their famous preserved machine No 5043 *Earl of Mount Edgcumbe*. She ran non-stop thanks to the clever expedient of using a BR-era GUV van equipped with additional water tanks to compensate for the lack of water troughs on the modern national network.** *(Frank Dumbleton)*

This gave it the 'Fastest in Britain' crown; but, ever hungry for more, the GWR cut this to 70 minutes in 1929, to claim the world title. In 1931 the Canadians briefly held the record until, after slashing another three minutes from the schedule, making it a 67-minute trip, the

LEFT **A Cheltenham Flyer of another era – a mid-1930s view of No 5040 *Stokesay Castle* at speed. Despite the fact that more modern forms of traction were at work on other UK railways, the Flyer records go to illustrate just how good the GWR four-cylinder 4-6-0s were – even at this point when the design was nearly 30 years old.** *(GWS/GWT)*

ABOVE Wartime warrior. No 5078 was originally named *Lamphey Castle*, but to celebrate the defeat of the Luftwaffe in the Battle of Britain engines Nos 5071–5082 were renamed after RAF aircraft in late 1940 and early 1941. Here, in unlined green but with her cab side windows restored (indicating a post-war but pre-nationalisation date for this image), No 5078 proudly displays her new name *Beaufort*, derived from the twin-engine Bristol Type 152 bomber that saw use with Costal Command during the conflict. *(GWS/GWT)*

GWR claimed the honour back. The schedule lost a further two minutes in 1932, but the performance to remember was given by 5006 *Tregenna Castle* when she reached an average over the run of 81.7mph and was in Paddington in 57 minutes! The record finally fell to the LNER in 1937, but it clearly demonstrates the fact that time and again these engines were called upon to do more, and they achieved it with ease.

All the glamour of 1930s rail travel came to a screeching halt both figuratively and literally in 1939 with the outbreak of the Second World War. All the highly stylish coaches with their

RIGHT An echo of a future from the past – the body shell and bogies of the Brown–Boveri gas turbine locomotive No 18000. This type of traction was to feature heavily in post-war GWR thinking, and their book *Next Station* outlines what could have been, and makes for interesting reading. *(Author)*

intricate and beautiful interiors were put away. Speed limits were imposed, and the game became not one of whisking your passengers from A to B in the maximum of comfort and efficiency, but rather a process to get the biggest volume of war materials and personnel to where they were needed ASAP. The glitz was gone, replaced by severe austerity. Plain black paint was the order of the day for all UK locomotives, but Swindon supposedly couldn't bring themselves to do this to their beloved Castles and Kings. From what must have been a secret (!) reserve of paint, they remained (albeit without lining) in green, with just a few Castles proving to be the exceptions to the rule. To comply with the blackout regulations they had their side windows removed and plated over, and heavy canvas screens fitted to the cab of the engine. At Didcot, the Heavy Freight Group (affectionately known as 'The Mob') have reproduced a set of these screens for the society's 2884 class 2-8-0 No 3822, which is presented in its wartime livery. The fire in a steam engine gives off intense light – especially when it is working hard – which would provide an excellent marker for enemy aircraft searching for a target to drop their bombs on.

Whilst these measures were excellent at blocking out the light, they did have serious knock-on effects for the crews, because as well as trapping the light in the cab they also trapped the heat. The resultant temperature in the cab was so high that crews were seriously affected by it. The screens also significantly restricted the crew's view. The next opportunity you get to

stand on the footplate of a large tender engine, take a look through the front cab windows and imagine they were your ONLY view of the world. Pictures of No 3822 working at the centre with these screens in place are understandably rare; and when operating on the demonstration line, invariably it is the side of the engine that you can't see that is likely to have the sheet missing! It is little understood by the public just what railwaymen in general and locomotive crews in particular went through in WW2. Crews were in a reserve occupation, so they were not eligible to be signed up for military service. Instead they worked in conditions that went from unpleasant to unbearable, and their shifts could last up to and indeed much more than 24 hours – all this on the meagre home-front rations. A fireman still had to put huge amounts of coal on the fire when the engine was working hard, and the driver had to remain alert to not only the normal hazards of the railway but also the threat that enemy action might have destroyed the track or other important infrastructure that he was traversing. In all, railway crews have received little public recognition for the vital war work they undertook, and there was no medal and little or no thanks or recognition from the government. Lest we forget, they also served.

Another casualty of the war, in a way, was Collett. He had lost his wife Ethelwyn shortly before the launch of the Castles, and it was a tragedy from which he never really recovered. He became even more introverted as a result, and his final four years in service were not, K.J. Cook asserts, the best of his career and

ABOVE No 7008 *Swansea Castle* on the turntable. She was the first Castle built under the direction of British Railways Western Region. Despite the fact that the photograph is not in the greatest condition it is included as a previously unseen view that shows the locomotive in very early condition, with welded Hawksworth tender and what is sometimes referred to as 'intermediate' livery. This was essentially the late GWR scheme but with the BRITISH RAILWAYS text on the tank in the GWR's Egyptian Serif font. *(GWS/GWT)*

the GWR was not 'in the best interests of the department'. It seems his departure from the post was rather more enforced than entirely voluntary. He hung on until 1941, when, just short of his 70th birthday, he retired. The reins were handed over to his assistant Fredrick Hawksworth. Unlike Churchward, Collett withdrew from life at the works immediately and went to live at the home in Wimbledon, London, which he had kept secret from all but his closest confidants. He resigned his membership of every engineering institution of which he was a member. In retirement he became instead deeply involved with the metaphysical and psychical research movements. Collett died on 5 April 1952. His funeral was, unlike that of his predecessor, attended by only a small gathering, which included Hawksworth and Sir William Stanier (who was his assistant at Swindon before being head-hunted to lead the LMS loco department). One supposes he felt that he was going to rejoin his beloved wife.

The war also interrupted the Castle production line, and the last two in the number sequence up to 6000 where the Kings started (Nos 5098 and 5099) were eventually built after the conflict ended. The build programme restarted in 1946 to replace the rapidly ageing Stars. However, things were very different now. The railways had been mercilessly hammered by the war and had taken a big hit both financially and in terms of infrastructure. The Great Western was not in great shape but could have probably survived; it was even looking to the future in the form of orders for prototype gas turbine locomotives from Metropolitan-Vickers in the UK and Brown-Boveri of Switzerland. (The Swiss machine, No 18000 – sadly minus its power plant – is on display at Didcot.) The other Big Four companies were not in such a robust position. To prevent the financial collapse of major parts of the rail network, the post-war government took the decision to nationalise the entire system. This came into effect on 1 January 1948 and was heralded in by all locomotives then in steam blowing their whistles. A new age had begun.

Swindon, despite now being part of a nationalised company, retained its independent spirit and continued constructing GWR locomotive types and doing its own thing,

essentially carrying on much as they had done for nearly a century. Castles were still the mainstay of the express motive power fleet and they were still being built into August 1950, when the last one, No 7037, was appropriately and simply named *Swindon* by the then Princess Elizabeth, later Her Majesty Queen Elizabeth II. The total number of Castles built was 171, but this number did not exist in service all at the same time, because as No 7037 *Swindon* was rolled out the ex-Star which was curiously named and numbered No 100 A1 *Lloyds* was withdrawn in May of the same year.

The Western Region of British Railways, as the GWR became, reintroduced a number of named trains in an effort to rekindle the pre-war spirit, and to some extent they were successful; but this could not hide the fact that, going into the 1960s, we had a Victorian railway system still being driven by labour-intensive and outdated forms of motive power. Not only that, it was becoming increasingly expensive and difficult in the era of 'white heat of technology' to get people to want to work in what were filthy, almost Dickensian conditions (I should

RIGHT HRH Princess Elizabeth unveils the *Swindon* nameplate of No 7037 on 15 November 1950. The engine carried a small brass plate to commemorate the event. Although completed in August of that year she did not carry a name until after the ceremony. She was actually in store between 9 September and 8 November of that year before being released to traffic at Swindon shed, where she spent the vast majority of her working life. *(GWS/GWT)*

know – but I do it for fun!). Even an influx of immigrants didn't help, but it did paper over the cracks for a time.

The last main-line steam locomotive, No 92220, had been completed at Swindon in full Great Western style with copper-capped chimney and full BR passenger green livery (not bad for a humble 9F class freight locomotive). In a special ceremony on 18 March 1960 she was named *Evening Star*. The name was chosen by the employees at Swindon works and reflected the ending of a story that started in the 1840s with the Gooches' broad-gauge Star Class, went through the turn of the 20th century with Churchward's Star Class machine No 4002, and now ended here with No 92220.

Modernisation was now in full swing, and the days of steam as the prime mover on Britain's railways were numbered. Slowly the sheds filled with lines of withdrawn steam engines as the new diesels made their mark. Many of the sheds simply closed as well – the new diesels simply didn't need the level of servicing that the steam engines did. It was a traumatic time for the industry, with hundreds

of highly skilled men suddenly finding out that the skill they had learnt over decades wasn't required or relevant any more. It is usually bad enough for railway enthusiasts to think of their beloved machines going for scrap, but few thoughts are normally spared for the social consequences resulting from the end of steam, in the form of hundreds of men nationwide with skill sets that were now worth nothing. Steam did have a last laugh, though, as many of the new diesels were rushed into service before they were ready – some not being fit for service at all – and there is many a photograph of an almost embarrassed-looking diesel (so far as it is possible for a diesel loco to look embarrassed) and its train being rescued by a steam engine!

BELOW A wonderful late study of No 7033 *Hartlebury Castle* on the Torbay Express. Judging by the pile of coal in the tender and the feather of steam at the safety valve, she is ready to go rather than at the end of a trip. This locomotive is a perfect illustration of the waste in the steam-to-diesel changeover – a loco that was built in July 1950, fitted with a double chimney in July 1959 and yet sent for scrap in January 1963. The design life of this engine was at least 35 years and she was scrapped at less than 13. (GWS/GWT)

RIGHT A filthy No 5007 *Rougemont Castle* ambles through Southall in the early 1960s. The woebegone condition of the locomotive, with steam escaping from the centre cylinder valve covers, is typical of the period. *(Frank Dumbleton Collection)*

After a final fling in 1962 for the Kings and 1964 for the Castles, the steam fleet went into decline. Some engines saw over 40 years' service and were verging on worn-out when withdrawn, whereas others had seen only 13. It has to be said that the scandal of how much money was wasted in either building steam locos with a design life that far exceeded their actual working lifespan, or ordering replacement forms of traction untested and straight off the drawing board that either required further development or were laughably inadequate for the job they were supposed to do, was a scandal that seems not to have touched public consciousness.

The last honours went to No 7029 *Clun Castle*, when she hauled the Western Region's last official steam train out of Paddington to Banbury on 11 June 1965. No 7029 was officially withdrawn in December 1965 and is believed by historians to have been the last Castle in service. From 1923 to 1965 there had been Castles in service on the Great Western

RIGHT Despite being withdrawn in February 1962, whoever dropped the last fire on No 5023 *Brecon Castle* cared enough and was professional enough to put a sack over her chimney – an act that was designed to help preserve a stored engine. It was all in vain, however, as she was cut up not far from where she is standing, here at Swindon, just a few months later. *(Frank Dumbleton)*

main lines. They became the most numerous express passenger types in the country and their design became a classic. For 59 years a four-cylinder beat of one sort or another echoed in and out of Paddington, and, as the old epithet goes, we will not see their like again.

At least, that was BR's plan. The preservationists, however, thought otherwise. The prototype machine, No 4073 *Caerphilly Castle*, had been saved (albeit as a static exhibit in the Science Museum, London, and later at the Steam Museum, Swindon), and No 7029 had been saved by Patrick Whitehouse during the humble beginnings of an organisation that was to become our good friends at Tyseley Locomotive Works. Five more had gone to slumber by the sea in Wales, at Barry scrapyard, biding their time waiting for 'their' enthusiasts to gather funds and come to liberate them. The last one definitely rescued from oblivion, however, had been bought by the unlikeliest of saviours – a bookseller. She was none other than No 4079 *Pendennis Castle*, and she has a very interesting story to tell.

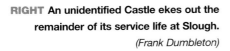

RIGHT An unidentified Castle ekes out the remainder of its service life at Slough.
(Frank Dumbleton)

Chapter Two

Pendennis Castle

Fame, fortune and far-flung places

In February 1924 an ordinary thing happened in Wiltshire: a new locomotive was put through its paces by a Swindon crew. As was the custom, before being released to traffic a new or newly overhauled machine would be tested on local trains. The engine they were preparing today was the latest in steam engine technology.

OPPOSITE *Pendennis Castle* storms through Didcot. On 4 March 1967 two trains ran to commemorate the last through working from Paddington to Birkenhead. The first train was the Birkenhead Flyer, which was worked by No 4079, and the second was the Zulu, which was worked by No 7029 *Clun Castle*. *(Frank Dumbleton)*

ABOVE In an image taken from an old postcard we see the works portrait of Castle Class machine No 4079 *Pendennis Castle*. It is quite remarkable that preserved original Castles No 4079 and No 4073 both remained relatively unchanged in their service lives. This is Castle Class number 7, completed in February 1924, just six months after No 4073 and a year after the last Star. Part of the appeal of the early Castles is that while they have all the mechanical improvements over the Stars, they still have the stylistic cues of their Edwardian predecessors. A perfect blend of power and style! *(GWS/GWT)*

BELOW The subject of the 1924 paper and one of only two Castles completed in 1923, No 4074 *Caldicot Castle*. Unlike her more famous sister she was radically altered throughout her life, receiving a double chimney in 1959. She was withdrawn in May 1962, having travelled at least 1.8 million miles (2.8 million km). Although the engine is in fairly early condition here the picture is not of an early date, as she appears to have a Collett 4,000-gallon tender, and her sanders are in an arrangement only introduced after the building of No 5013 in 1932. *(GWS/GWT)*

After 13 weeks' hard work and a cost of £5,565 for the engine and boiler and another £1,250 for her tender, she was rolled out of the works. It was the seventh such machine built. She was named *Pendennis Castle*. She was soon noted as a fine performer and was released to traffic at the Old Oak Common shed. This could have been her lot, quietly serving the railway until an ignominious meeting with the scrap-man's torch sometime in the 1960s; but fate decreed otherwise.

Her rise to fame started in 1924 at two events. The first was a paper read by Collett to fellow engineers at the First World Power Conference, which was entitled 'Testing of Locomotives on the Great Western Railway'. The paper claimed that while on test,

locomotive No 4074 *Caldicot Castle* had achieved some amazing performance figures. Chief among these was her efficiency. The figure most noted was the fairly impenetrable sounding pounds of coal per drawbar horsepower per hour (!). The best locos elsewhere in the country were able to achieve a figure of somewhere between 4–6lb (1.81–2.72kg). The non-superheated Stars were able to manage 3½lb (1.58kg) at the turn of the century, but the Castles had set the benchmark at 2.83lb (1.28kg). This was on the higher-heat Welsh steam coals used by the GWR, but even factoring in the use of hard Yorkshire coals, this put the figure at 3lb (1.36kg)! This prompted a somewhat incredulous reaction from Collett's peers. Many refused to believe that the figures were genuine.

The second event was a far more public one. The Empire Exhibition of 1924, held at Wembley, was a showcase of the latest and greatest technology and innovation from all over the empire. The Power Hall presented an A1 Pacific in the form of No 4472 *Flying Scotsman* and a Castle Class engine, No 4073 *Caerphilly Castle*. In itself this wasn't so much of a problem, but the sign in front of No 4073 was. It declared her to be 'The most powerful Express Passenger Locomotive in Britain'. To the casual observer, this was a wild claim. The sheer bulk and size of the A1 Pacific surely meant (to the layman observer, perhaps)

that this engine was the one to hold that crown? Opinion, both professional and public, began to turn to the idea of a test of some sort to ascertain the veracity of this claim. The GWR and LNER boards were keen too, and as a result the 1925 Interchange Trials were organised.

The trials were, as much as anything else, to verify the claims of efficiency of each type of locomotive. There were to be two rounds to the trials, run simultaneously over the week beginning 27 April and concluding on 2 May 1925. The GWR round was to be held between London Paddington and Plymouth and featured locomotives No 4074 *Caldicot Castle* and No 4474 *Victor Wild*, and the LNER round was between No 4079 *Pendennis Castle* and No 2555 (later named *Centenary*). The LNER route alternated between London King's Cross and either Doncaster or Grantham. The engines were to burn the lines' native fuel, so No 4474 was to use soft Welsh coal and No 4079 was to use the hard Yorkshire variety. Nothing was left to chance – despite her youth, No 4079 went to Swindon for a full overhaul, and a few weeks before the trial she returned to Old Oak Common, where her selected crew of driver Young and fireman Pearce (chosen because of their top position on the efficiency league called the 'coal sheet') fired and drove her on the new fuel to get its measure. The crew and engine made their way to the LNER, where

BELOW This is the classic view of the 1925 trials that exists in several formats, indicating that there could have been a number of photographers on hand to record the event. It shows No 4079 *Pendennis Castle* and A1 Class No 4475 *Flying Fox* alongside each other at the famous King's Cross 'Top Shed'. Behind No 4079 is the N2 Class No 4724. This particular version is a scanned postcard and has been included as it was given to the author with the tale that it had been found at Doncaster Locomotive works after closure, and the reverse lists the crews of the trials locomotives in pencil. *(GWS/GWT)*

BELOW The mighty
No 4079 doing what
she does best. The
proceedings are
obviously of great
interest, as there are
quite a few heads
hanging out of the
coach windows. It
is hoped they knew
about the upcoming
tunnel… One of the
crew (possibly fireman
Pearce) can be seen
checking the road ahead
in the cab. The exhaust
from the chimney is
going straight up, so
she is obviously working
hard, and the famous
'Western Bark' must
be echoing all over
King's Cross! Pendennis
Castle is sporting the
beautiful 'Garter crest'
livery, tall chimney and
safety valve bonnet,
and for reasons as yet
unexplained – despite
your author's best
efforts – a number of
latching dogs to seal the
smokebox door shut.
(GWS/GWT)

route learning on both the big Pacific types and the Castle was undertaken. Somewhat unsurprisingly, Pearce struggled a little with the wide firebox of the A1s to begin with and this, along with the comparatively small size of the Castle, gave rise to local opinion that they didn't stand a chance in this competition. A certain amount of pity was shown towards them, and the legend goes that much money was laid down at King's Cross 'Top Shed' to support the notion that not only would the GWR lose but that poor old No 4079 wouldn't even be able to haul itself and its train up the fearsome climb from King's Cross to Potter's Bar. The honour of the whole GWR rested on the shoulders of Young, Pearce and Pendennis Castle.

On the morning of the first day of the trials, the top brass of the LNER were assembled on King's Cross platform in order to witness what they felt was going to be the undoing of the Castles. There had been attempts to get driver Young to accept a banking engine to help push him up through the steep tunnels that lead away from King's Cross. He had refused, on the basis that he didn't want to be pushed out on to an unfamiliar main line with no way of stopping, although you have to suppose that there was probably more than a little bit of both company and personal pride behind that decision too. So there stood No 4079, at the head of a heavy train on a very demanding stretch of line that even the local machines couldn't manage without slipping and sliding.

As the crowd watched a very remarkable

thing happened. Pendennis Castle simply romped away with her train. No slipping, no sliding. What was discussed on that platform as the train disappeared into the distance is not recorded, but it can be guessed at. The ability to dismiss the notorious Gas Works and Copenhagen tunnel climbs with both grace and power was typical of the runs that week. Only once was the slightest hint of slipping noticed, but the times to Finsbury Park were all below six minutes. This was a full minute less than any of the Pacific machines could do at their best. At times Young was reining in Pendennis Castle to avoid the accumulation of excessive amounts of time and arriving at their destination far too early! Remarkably, the top speed of the engine recorded was just 83½mph (134.4kph), but speed wasn't the point of this trial and it was the smooth, efficient performance of the Castle and her crew that stood out.

For the LNER, things went from bad to worse. No 2555 Centenary failed and No 2545 (later named Diamond Jubilee) took its place. It had a number of poor runs culminating in a situation where the steam sanding gear failed, leaving it to slip and slide its way up to Finsbury Park, and it continued to lose time throughout the journey. The situation on the GWR main line proved almost farcical when a trial of efficiency almost became a race. No 4474 performed admirably, gathering an impressive total of four early minutes over the fortnight the trials lasted, and no late minutes. No 4074, however, had collected 48½ minutes early and no minutes late! They arrived on 27 April a full 14½ minutes early... The results in terms of timekeeping on the LNER were more sober, but the A1s were only able to produce 2½ early minutes and 50½ minutes late on the schedule. No 4079, however, whilst accruing four late minutes on the schedule had a total of 14½ early minutes. No 4079 was performing at this impressive rate and yet burning 3.7lb (approx 1.7kg) of coal per mile less than the A1s.

So why did Pendennis Castle (and Caldicot Castle, for that matter) seem to romp away to victory? Well, there are several reasons that contributed to their win, all acting in combination. It has to be said from the start that the LNER did suffer a great deal of bad luck on their own main line. The failure of

ABOVE No 4079 out on the East Coast main line during the 1925 trials. The train consists of no less than 14 teak bogie vehicles. *(GWS/GWT)*

Centenary and the difficulties with the sanding gear on *Diamond Jubilee* were certainly unlucky rather than anything else, although the complications of the small range of grain size required of sand used in steam sanding gear cannot be ignored. The fact that No 4079 had a higher boiler pressure – 225psi (1.55Mpa) against the 180psi (1.24Mpa) of the A1 class at the time – meant that the steam had far more energy to use when it got to the cylinders. Coupled with the highly efficient long-travel valves and the Churchward design principles applied to her boiler, it meant that *Pendennis Castle* was making the very best output from every ounce of the energy released by the coal – even though it was an inferior grade to that which she was designed to burn, and which the wide firebox of the A1s was designed to use.

A lot has also been made about the debate between the weight distribution of the 4-6-0 wheel arrangement of the Castle against the 4-6-2 'Pacific' style of the A1s. It has been said that the advantage of the 4-6-0 was that there was never a time when the full available adhesive weight was not on the driving wheels. It is conceivable that there were situations when the carrying wheels at the rear of the A1s were taking adhesive weight off the driving wheels on some gradients and curves in the track. This is a hotly debated subject, but the superior pulling power of 4-6-0s when starting a train has been proven time and time again.

The agreement prior to the trials was that the results were supposed to remain secret, but the GWR publicity department got hold of them and published an article. This created much ill-feeling between the two railways and caused Sir Felix Pole, a director of the GWR who had been instrumental in setting up the trials, to distance himself from the whole affair. None of this was helped by No 4079 being sent to sit alongside No 4472 at the 1925 Empire Exhibition! There was a hearty discourse between the LNER and the GWR that was published in *The Times* newspaper, and the whole issue was only calmed down by a considerable amount of diplomacy. It has to be said that Gresley (who was never a supporter of the event) and the loco department at Doncaster learnt a great deal from the trials, such as long-travel valves and 225psi boilers, and applied those lessons to the A1s, then the A3s and then the A4s... It all started with No 4079.

After that No 4079 settled down to a fairly

BELOW The results of the 1925 Interchange Trials. *(Data from GWR Magazine 1925)*

Performance Table
EXCHANGE OF ENGINES – G.W.R. AND L.N.E.R.
Week ending May 2nd 1925
10.10 a.m. **KINGS CROSS** & Return 3.7pm **GRANTHAM**

Date	Engine	Actual Time of Arrival	Minutes		Load Tons T.C.	Station from	Miles	Coal Consumed lb. per mile	Weather
			Early	Late					
April 27th	GW 4079	G. 12.14 ½ KC. 5.06	- 1	3 ½ -	456.10 453.00		211	55.7	Fine
April 28th	LNER 2545	G. 12.27 ½ KC. 5.12 ½	 -	16 ½ 5 ¾	448.00 458.00	K. Cross Grantham	211	59.6	Showers & N. E. wind
April 29th	GW 4079	G. 12.10 KC. 5.06	1 1 ½	- -	455.00 457.00	K. Cross Grantham	211	55.9	Rain & side wind
April 30th	LNER 2545	G. 12.12 ¾ KC. 5.06	- 1	1 ¾ -	453.00 457.00	K. Cross Grantham	211	58.1	Showers
May 1st	GW 4079	G. 12.11 ½ KC. 5.03	- 4	½ -	455.00 456.00	K. Cross Grantham	211	59.4	Rain & N. W. wind
May 2nd	LNER 2545	G. 12.12 ½ KC. 5.12	- -	1 ¾ 5	453.00 476.00	K. Cross Grantham	211	59.2	Fine
1.30 **KINGS CROSS** to **DONCASTER.** Return 6.21 p.m. **DONCASTER** to **KINGS CROSS**									
April 27th and 28th These trips not included owing to failure of L.N.E.R. engine 4475									
April 29th	LNER 2545	D. 4.23 KC. 9.42 ½	1 -	- 17 ½	453.00 455.00	K. Cross Doncaster	312	54.1	Showers
April 30th	GW 4079	D. 4.22 KC. 9.24	2 1	- -	453.00 454.00	K. Cross Doncaster	312	48.8	Showers
May 1st	LNER 2545	D. 4.26 ¾ KC. 9.24 ¾	- ¼	2 ¾	451.00 442.00	K. Cross Doncaster	312	56.5	Showers
May 2nd	GW 4079	D. 4.22 ½ KC. 9.22 ½	1 ½ 2 ½	- -	420.00 462.00	K. Cross Doncaster	312	50.7	Fine & side wind
Final Total		GW **4079**	Early **14 ½**	Late **4**	Total Distance Travelled **1,257 miles**			Coal Consumption **53.4 lb per mile**	
		LNER **2545**	Early **2 ½**	Late **50 ½**	Total Distance Travelled **1,257 miles**			Coal Consumption **57.1 lb per mile**	
For comparison - the results of the trials on GWR (Paddington to Plymouth)		GW **4074**	Early **48 ½**	Late **-**	Total Distance Travelled **1,356**			Coal Consumption **41.9 lb per mile**	
		LNER **4474**	Early **4**	Late **-**	Total Distance Travelled **1,356**			Coal Consumption **47.9 lb per mile**	

LEFT No 4079 on shed in GWR days about a quarter of the way through her service life. She has had alterations to her sanding gear but still retains the tall chimney and forward-placed coupling rod joint. *(GWS/GWT)*

CENTRE *Pendennis Castle* in the early BR period. She is pulling an express train made up of the customary Western Region eclectic mix of vehicles, including what would have been the latest thing in the form of the straight-sided Hawksworth stock. *(GWS/GWT)*

mundane if slightly nomadic existence. She seems to have lived a fairly uneventful life, being given normal, run-of-the-mill duties but at the same time not being overworked. She called not only Old Oak Common but ten other sheds her home. Her record sheet shows a full 40 years of her career and in that time she received at least three sets of cylinders, 18 changes of boiler and ran with no less than 37 different tenders of four different designs. In that time she is recorded as achieving an official mileage of about 1¾ million miles (2,816,352km) – seven times the average distance between the earth and the moon; however, these figures are thought to be at least 15 to 20% short of the real total, so it is safe to say that if she had a car-style odometer it would be reading well over the two million mile (3,218,688km) mark by now.

By 14 March 1962 it looked like it was all over. One of the volunteers who helped rebuild her at Didcot remembers her in store at the back of the shed at Swindon not long after that date. Seeing her still, cold and with verdigris slowly claiming her name and number plates, he thought that he was witnessing her at her end (as the first thoroughbred Castle to be scrapped was No 4091 *Dudley Castle*, at Swindon, in March 1959, he had every reason

LEFT Towards the end of the steam era on the Western Region, *Pendennis Castle* became a popular performer on rail tours and specials. She was one of the locomotives adorned with buffer beam numbers as per GWR practice. Here she is seen on a tour organised by the Stephenson Locomotive Society. *(GWS/GWT)*

to suspect it), but his fears were thankfully premature, as she was reactivated in August of the same year. First allocated to Swindon shed and then to St Philip's Marsh in November of 1963, time by now was definitely running out for the legend. Like the vast majority of steam locomotives at that time she was past her best, in a woebegone and filthy condition. There was, however, one more act to be played out in BR service, which at first sight looked like a disaster but as soon became evident was her salvation.

It looked like 9 May 1964 was going to be a great day. It was the 60th anniversary of the achievement of No 3440 *City of Truro* reaching the 100mph mark on the Ocean Mail train. Despite the controversy surrounding this event, the Ian Allan publishing house was determined to mark the occasion with an enthusiasts' special. The train – named 'The Great Western' – would achieve two aims. Firstly, it would celebrate *City of Truro*'s run. Unfortunately the locomotive herself was, at that time, a static exhibit in the old railway museum at her birthplace, Swindon. All the Kings had been withdrawn, and therefore the honour of celebrating the run went to the Castles. Secondly, the train was to have one last 'fling' of GWR steam traction, and to this end the train was to hit the magic three digits, 100mph (160.934kph).

There would be three legs to the tour. The first would take the train from Paddington to Plymouth, the second would be from Plymouth to Bristol, and the final leg would be back home to Paddington. No 4079 was selected to take the pole position on the train between Paddington and Plymouth. The loco was polished to within an inch of its life and the boiler and tender were washed out. Unfortunately the tender had been full of sludge, and this had been sealing the leaks; as a result another tender had to be found to run with her.

On the day itself a great crowd had gathered at Paddington to see her off. *Pendennis Castle* stood gleaming in the light, with her driver,

RIGHT Ready for battle one last time… No 4079 has been polished to within an inch of her life, ordained with the paraphernalia associated with the run and is ready to go. Old Oak Common, 9 May 1964. *(Doug Godden)*

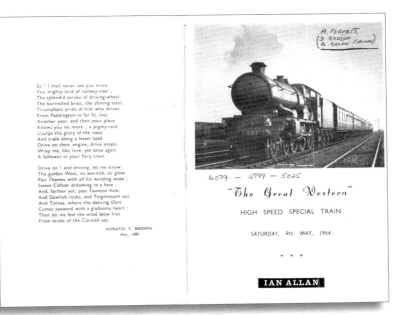

Alf Perfect (the WR Royal Train driver) at the regulator, two firemen (Doug Godden and Brian Green) and the chief inspector Mr Bill Andress. In the tender sat a full load of Ogilvie 1A steam coal, one of the highest calorific-value coals available. There had been much discussion about this back at Old Oak Common. Alf Perfect was of the opinion that the coal needed to have some slack coal mixed in with it or some old brick arch material scattered on the grate, as the heat would be too intense for the cast iron fire bars. He was overruled, however, and the loco went out as was. The press and rail fans alike swarmed all over the platforms and Alf and his crew were treated like celebrities, with autographs sought and photographs taken. The crew were determined

ABOVE This is the souvenir menu for the Great Western special of 9 May 1964. This particular copy belonged to No 4079's fireman on that day, Doug Godden. This explains the annotations on the front cover! *(Doug Godden)*

ABOVE AND RIGHT The crew on the day was (left to right) Bill Andress (inspector), Brian Green (fireman 1), Alf Perfect (driver), with Old Oak Common shed master Bill Coles. Taking the picture was second fireman Doug Godden, who is seen in the second picture when reunited with *Pendennis Castle* on 8 November 2008. *(Doug Godden/Frank Dumbleton)*

BELOW Disaster at Westbury. No 4079 comes to rest after the unluckiest lucky break ever to befall a steam locomotive... Smoke can be seen issuing from unnatural places by the rear driving wheel set. *(Peter Chatman)*

to make it a ride to remember and the sprightly start was matched by a faultless performance through to Reading. Speed limits were generously interpreted, and things were looking good for 'the ton'.

It was thought that the best chance for the 100mph barrier to be beaten was on Lavington bank and, as it approached, tension in the train was palpable. *Pendennis Castle* herself was flying – if this was to be the last cry of the Castles, then the crew were determined to make it a good one. The scene on the footplate was intense. The vibrations and rocking around in the cab were getting ever more evident. It is

important to remember that the locomotive and tender have different riding qualities, and Doug Godden, who was firing at the time, was really battling to do his job. He said afterwards that he had never seen a fire in a locomotive like it. The rushing air through the fire combined with the fuel was producing a fire so intense that he described the inside of the firebox as being "as white as a sheet of paper". Brian Green was keeping the boiler full and watching the road ahead and Alf Perfect had the locomotive just right. Both he and Bill Andress were calling out the speed as they went along. 94... 95... 96... And then it all went wrong. Just as they were about to hit their target the brakes were suddenly applied. They thought that in an act of sabotage or in error that someone had pulled the emergency cord in one of the coaches.

As they looked back down the train they saw the guard running towards them. When he got there he explained that he had seen a huge trail of sparks from under the locomotive and used his emergency brake. Upon closer inspection it was found that Alf's prediction had come true and the fire bars had collapsed in the inferno. This dumped the fire into the ash pan. Here it was right next to the axleboxes for the rear driving wheels, and the white metal bearings inside them had melted as a result. They limped their way to Westbury, where the problems could be dealt with.

The disappointment felt by the crew was intense, but their thoughts turned to what they were going to do to get the train moving again. When they got to Westbury they discovered that the only locomotive in the shed even vaguely capable of shifting the train at speed to Plymouth was tired-looking No 6999 *Capel Dewi Hall*. It had just done a day's work, its fire was run down and it had half a tender full of compressed coal dust ovoids. They made sure it was good enough to go and began transferring her to the head of the train. As the train restarted and headed off into the distance, the crew from No 6999 took *Pendennis Castle* to the shed, disposed of the fire as best they could and, with the last of the steam in her boiler, pulled her into the cripple siding. That was it. A slightly ignominious end to 40 years of almost faultless service. She wasn't badly damaged, but the kind of work required to put her back into service was an instant death sentence. Steam was being done away with at such a rate that a few days later her name was added to the withdrawals list. It looked as if the final fling had been her last and that a legend had ended.

But hope came from an unlikely source. Mike Higson was a bookseller. He had been a fireman on the London Midland Region but had come into money and set up Roundhouse Books. He had a large collection of railwayana, but there was one thing missing from the collection – a locomotive of his own. He originally made a request to the LM Region to buy a Black 5 Class engine. However, having had little success there he turned his eye to the Western Region, and his plan evolved into purchasing a late period Castle to contrast with No 4073 *Caerphilly Castle*, which had at this point taken up residence in the Science Museum in London. Again, he met with a negative response.

It has to be remembered that the authorities took a dim view of individuals purchasing steam locomotives in the early 1960s. The preserved line concept was something that was yet to make its mark, and they had little intention of letting these antiques run on their nice modern railway. However, there was

LEFT **This is possibly the last in-service photograph of No 4079 ever taken. It was snapped literally over Doug Godden's shoulder as he ran to take No 6999 to the train. In that fleeting moment, he captured the end of an era.**
(Doug Godden)

one group who bucked this trend. The Great Western Society (GWS) had been set up by four young gentlemen who had the express aim of preserving a 14XX class locomotive and its attendant auto trailer. Things got out of hand when the donations kept coming in. They had bought a number of items of rolling stock up to this point and were looking to buy more.

After aligning himself with the GWS Mike Higson had much more success with BR, and a sale was agreed in principle. The only problem was, which of the Castles still in service was to be saved? There wasn't a long list but he was still keen on seeking a late series machine. The GWS had other ideas, however, and managed to persuade him to take a look at a famous machine that had just come out of service. After inspecting her it was found that apart from the damage sustained during her high-speed run she was in fairly good condition, and following negotiations it was agreed that Swindon would repair *Pendennis Castle*. She was towed back to Swindon, where a comprehensive restoration was undertaken and the damage from the rail tour was fixed. However, the team at Swindon went much further. This was the last time a Castle would ever go through the works, and as such they were not going to let a mediocre job leave their care. Needless to say, what Mike Higson paid for and what he received as a finished product bore little relationship...

When the finished article was wheeled out of Swindon works in 1965, the effect was magnificent. Her paint was flawless and her brightwork shone. After Mr Hawksworth (by

the Great Western Society began to move into the main running shed at Didcot. Firstly they occupied just two roads in the shed, then when the site closed to BR diesels the whole site was turned over to the GWS.

It was Lord Gretton's desire to create a steam centre on his family land at Market Overton, and in the early 1970s *Pendennis Castle* said goodbye to Didcot for the first time and headed for its new home. There were big plans for Market Overton. *Pendennis Castle* was joined by another famous locomotive – No 4472 *Flying Scotsman*, which had been rescued by Sir William McAlpine when its former owner had gone bankrupt and marooned the engine in the USA. A number of other historic items of rolling stock, including Sir William's famous Great Eastern Railway observation coach GE1, also resided there. An engineering base for steam was set up under the Flying Scotsman Enterprises banner. One of the first jobs undertaken here was the sectioning and subsequent display preparation of BR Southern Region Merchant Navy Class No 35029 *Ellerman Lines* for display in the then new National Railway Museum at York.

The experiment at Market Overton was sadly short-lived, as there were problems with the relationship with BR, who were threatening to remove the main-line connection to the remaining stub of the High Dyke branch on which the centre relied. At the same time the economic situation in the UK was pretty poor too, which didn't help. There were many other contributing factors; all of them conspired to close the centre only a few years after it had opened.

As a result the ownership of No 4079

ABOVE *Pendennis Castle*, **safely installed in the lifting shop at Didcot locomotive shed in 1967. It was here she saw out the horrors of the main line steam ban and received her trademark red frames and exhibition lining that were impressive-looking but less than historically accurate.** *(Collection of Sir William McAlpine)*

RIGHT The Great Western Envoy at Didcot. The loco was by now wearing additions to her livery under the nameplates, and the GWR coat of arms on the tender in the form of the Hamersley Iron logo. The strength of feeling for the engine is clear from the number of people on hand to say farewell to her. *(GWS/ GWT)*

then the last surviving CME of the GWR) and the Mayor of Swindon amongst the other dignitaries had had their say, No 4079 was handed over to Mike Higson. The locomotive was initially based at Southall and ran a few rail tours, but Mike Higson found it too large a personal and financial strain and after a year resolved to sell the locomotive. Two new buyers appeared, in the shape of Sir William McAlpine and Lord John Gretton, and they were soon in possession of their new locomotive. They came to an arrangement with BR (WR) to base *Pendennis Castle* at Didcot in the now redundant lifting shop that was once used to repair steam locomotives. This gave her a few opportunities to run rail tours until the infamous BR steam ban came into effect in 1968. Didcot then became a safe home for the loco while this was in effect. During this time a few other locomotives and items of rolling stock from

became the exclusive province of Sir William McAlpine, and in an attempt to find a lasting home for Flying Scotsman Enterprises (and *Pendennis Castle*) he ended up lodging them at the steam centre at Carnforth locomotive shed. The move was great for the majority of the rolling stock, but not for No 4079. She was still at her full GWR height at this stage. As the Carnforth area was already electrified with overhead catenary, it was necessary for the power to be switched off to get her on and off the site. This complication saw her being used less and less, and slowly she came to be used only on site for open days. This was not a very auspicious fate for a machine of her stature. Fate, however, was about to make things a whole lot stranger.

During 1976 Sir Russell Madigan, an executive from the Rio Tinto mining company, visited the company's facility at Hamersley in North Western Australia. A Rio Tinto iron ore operation in the Pilbara had begun in 1966, being run under a subsidiary company called Hamersley Iron. During his tour of the facility he happened upon the Pilbara Railways Historical Society, which was an organisation concerned with the preservation of the history of the railways in the area. After being shown the collection of early diesels, the comment was made to Sir Russell that they had been on the lookout for a steam locomotive, but all the standard gauge ones in Australia were unavailable. 'Don't worry lads,' said Sir Russell, 'when I get home I'll buy you the *Flying Scotsman*!' Rather taken aback by this, they figured it was a bit of a joke. It wasn't to Sir Russell. On returning to the UK, he sought out Sir William and asked to buy No 4472. When Sir William discovered that Sir Russell wanted to take her to Australia he declined, but No 4079 was offered in its stead. This resulted in one of the greatest preservation telegrams ever written: 'Was not able to buy *Flying Scotsman*, will *Pendennis Castle* do instead?'

The arrangements having been made, No 4079's boiler was sent away to have an increased thickness tubeplate fitted to comply with Australian regulations. The locomotive was reassembled and one 'last' UK trip, known as the Great Western Envoy, was planned to take her from her home at Carnforth to Didcot, and

then out to Southampton docks for loading on board the MV *Mishref* for export. To all concerned, this was to be the last time that she would be on English soil, and there was a subdued atmosphere as thousands of GWR fans lined the route to say goodbye to this legendary machine. A route via the Suez Canal and across the Indian Ocean provided the exit from Europe. The engine's first landfall in its new home was Sydney, on 14 July 1977. To the most casual observer of geography it will be realised that this is entirely the wrong area of Australia to get to Hamersley. The plan was that she would wait in storage at Eveleigh Carriage Works for nine months and then be towed in light steam to Newcastle. She would then board a freighter together with a consignment of diesels and coal to undertake the final leg of her journey.

On 7 November 1978 there was an incongruous sight in the iron red hills of Western Australia. A Castle Class locomotive, built for the routes between Paddington and the west of England, was now in another hemisphere. One wonders what Mr Churchward and Mr Collett would have had to say about that. She had a number of initial trips with the PRHS, and eventually her operation in the winter months (it is far too hot to operate steam comfortably in this area in the summer) became quite an event.

There were a number of issues to overcome with the operation of a GWR express passenger loco in a desert. The first of these was the water supply. The water in the desert is laced with minerals that cause chronic 'furring up' as it is boiled. Thankfully HI already had a demineralisation plant in operation for all of its equipment, so this was easy. More of an issue

ABOVE **Aussie Castle. After a few years** *Pendennis Castle* **went increasingly 'native' and the results of the add-ons and modifications can be seen in this magnificent study. While the loss of No 4079 to the UK was a real blow, her value as an ambassador for our railway heritage cannot be disputed when you see an image like this.** *(John Lyas)*

ABOVE **The view from the cab as No 4079 crosses the causeway at Dampier in September 1983.** *(John Lyas)*

BELOW **A typical train formation for No 4079, with a preserved diesel inside the locomotive to assist with shunting and to cover failures. This is at the wonderfully named Pelican Junction in 1983.** *(John Lyas)*

was failing injectors. The heat, even in the winter, was causing the tender tank water to heat up, and GWR injectors do not like hot water. Obviously, not getting water into the boiler is a potentially very dangerous situation, and the solution eventually found was to replace the standard GWR injectors with Gresham & Craven units specifically designed for use in Australia. A further issue for the railway – having no watering facilities along its route – was resolved by the use of an ex 3ft 6in gauge tanker wagon fitted with standard gauge bogies. This wagon (known as a 'gin') also held the diesel-powered compressor for the brakes. Australia has an all air-brake railway system, so the vacuum brakes on No 4079 would be of little use. Westinghouse Australia came up with a neat proportional valve that enabled, with the simple addition of an air gauge and the requisite pipe work, the vacuum system on the engine to operate the air brakes on the train.

Coal was always an issue, as the supplies in the area were unsuitable for a machine such as *Pendennis Castle*. The supplies that came with her from Newcastle were obviously limited, and the import of further loads became so costly that one PRHS member quipped that it was 'too dear to burn'. Slowly, as the authorities and regulations caught up with her, she became more and more native-looking. Steps were added to her front buffer beam to allow easy access to her smokebox. A turbo generator was installed to power both the radio signalling system used on the HI system and a large smokebox-mounted electric headlight that was mandatory in Australia. This used one of the original steam feeds from the now removed injectors.

Crew issues also dogged her in the initial phase, as the drivers' unions began to get involved and all manner of complications ensued until an agreement was reached that the crews could undertake the trips on a voluntary basis. She ran well for a few years, being used on various tours, outings and excursions – a process that involved going into the bush for a distance, using some hot coals from the fire to light a barbecue, followed by dinner and a few drinks then home to her shed at Seven Mile. In the early 1980s, however, there were continuing niggling problems that began to plague *Pendennis Castle*, which culminated in a couple of very poor performances and then failures.

Her crew chief John Lyas and PRHS chairman Bob Vanselow decided that things had gone far enough, and that some mechanical work was required. She was taken out of service in 1984 and her boiler removed to aid access to a number of items. Whilst it wasn't a full overhaul, it did give her a new lease of life, and by 1987 she was ready to be reunited with her great rival No 4472 *Flying Scotsman*.

In 1988 *Flying Scotsman* visited Australia as part of the country's bicentennial celebrations. The tour of the Perth area was organised by Ian Willis, who was a builder of miniature steam engines. The tour required *Flying Scotsman* and *Pendennis Castle* to travel very long distances, including a distance record set by No 4472 and a low-loader trip from Hamersley to Perth for No 4079 and her gin. The tour was a big financial risk for Willis, who had to go to the expense of purchasing his own rake of coaches to make it happen. The moment when the two engines came face to face soon made all the trials and tribulations well worth it, and there were some magnificent performances out across the Nullabor Plains with runs organised with the engines double-headed, following each other or even running side by side. It must have been an incredible sight to see those two legendary machines charging through the beautiful Australian countryside. When all the excitement

ABOVE No 4079 at her home shed of Seven Mile. *(John Lyas)*

LEFT Didcot was pleased to welcome John Lyas himself to inspect progress on the restoration of his former charge on 18 April 2010. *(Frank Dumbleton)*

BELOW Peter Ward and his charge for the day at Wombat Junction (don't you just love the place names?). The special run here was to celebrate the locomotive's 70th birthday. *(Peter Ward)*

BELOW Rivals reunited. The bicentennial events of 1988 gave much opportunity for unique photography of No 4472 *Flying Scotsman*, but this is something really special. It was captured by Gary Merrin and brings to mind the trials of 1925. *(Kind permission of Gary Merrin)*

was over, *Pendennis Castle* returned to Hamersley to a more uncertain future.

By 1994 the situation for *Pendennis Castle* had become untenable. There were fewer and fewer crews available to run her. Her boiler was in desperate need of overhaul and she was very tired mechanically. The cost of all this was potentially huge and as a result she was retired from service. This left her thousands of miles from home without the kind of financial support needed to revive her. Withdrawn from service a second time, an uncertain future lay ahead of the locomotive for the first time since 9 May 1964.

The members of the preservation society and fans of this legendary locomotive were not about to let her lie idle. A suggestion that she should be stuffed and mounted on a plinth at the entrance to Hamersley Iron really made their minds up. Most vociferous amongst objectors was UK ex-pat and Hamersley Iron driver (and No 4079 driver as well!) Peter Ward. The preservation enthusiasts informed Rio Tinto that a new home was required where she could be restored to full working order, and several options in Australia were considered without success. In the end the final consensus was that No 4079 should be returned to the land of her birth. It was then that representatives from Rio Tinto contacted the editor of the UK's famous *Railway Magazine*, Nick Pigott, for his advice.

One Friday afternoon in 1998 Pigott put a call through to the then Great Western Society deputy chairman Richard Croucher, explaining the situation and enquiring whether Didcot would be interested in repatriating No 4079 and giving her a new home. Richard accepted the offer and after clearance from the GWS Council was obtained, formal negotiations began in secret. Under the supervision of Richard, Adrian Knowles began negotiations with Adrian Lumley-Smith, Rio Tinto's lawyer. The lengthy negotiations carried

on through 1999, and an agreement to donate 4079 to the GWS was finalised in early November 1999. There were two conditions to this offer, however. The first was that No 4079 was returned to traffic and kept alive so that she could be enjoyed by present and future generations. This was no problem to accept, as the Great Western Society has restored and operated two Castles in the past – both 5051 and 5029 had been restored from scrapyard condition at Didcot. The second condition, though, was a bit trickier. Once she left the gates at Hamersley in Western Australia, she not only belonged to the society but it was the society's responsibility to bring her home to the UK.

The return journey bit proved tricky. The company that took *Flying Scotsman* to Australia in 1988 said that they were able to help but their price was astronomical. The next avenue explored was to look at bringing her home on a container ship, but the problem here was that not only was the locomotive too big to fit in the footprint of a container, but she was also way too heavy, and would have to sit on the deck of the ship. This meant that rather than displacing the containers around her, she would also displace the space above her too. Richard worked out that this would result in the loss of about 60 containers from the ship. Consequently this was another far too expensive option. Thought was given to hiring a giant Russian Antonov transport aircraft to pick her up and fly her home. If Richard thought the bill for the ship was steep, the £300,000 required for this aerial operation was completely unattainable.

Just when Richard thought he wouldn't be able to return the icon home, he was contacted by a friend of a friend who was in the shipping business. Having heard the GWS' tale of woe, Steve Smith of Premier Forwarding said that the best thing was to leave it to him, and he would get back to them later to let them know what he had learned. After a couple of weeks he was back with a potential solution. The big problem had been getting a suitable container ship to call at Hamersley or Perth. At the time this wasn't easy, and if a stop was requested or the weather was bad the society would have been charged tens of thousands of pounds for each day's delay. Not a good gamble. There was, however, one other option. Steve came up with a proposal for a round the world roll-on/roll-off cargo ferry called the *Toba*, operated by Wilhelmsen Lines. This had another great advantage in that it cost just £41,000! Although it did not call at Hamersley Iron's port, it did at Perth. This gave her a way out of the country. It still meant that she had to get to the docks at Perth, though. The answer was to put *Pendennis Castle* on a pair of low loader trucks, one for the loco and one for the tender, and to start driving.

When she arrived, a number of the more collectible and all too easily 'liberated' components – such as nameplates, safety valve bonnet, cab fittings and so on – were taken off and packed on to a pallet to fly home separately in a secure manner. The official legal handover was then completed, ironically in an establishment known as the Great Northern Hotel, under a picture of none other than No 4472 *Flying Scotsman*! And so *Pendennis Castle* went home via the Panama Canal, the opposite direction to her outward journey. She left Perth on 25 April 2000, and the Society tracked her voyage round the world from Fremantle to Singapore, Hong Kong, Taiwan, China, South Korea, Japan, California, through the Panama Canal to Miami, New York and on to Halifax, Nova Scotia. The ship spent almost two weeks at Halifax, where she received her routine maintenance.

Pendennis Castle finally arrived at Portbury docks on 8 July 2000, and reached Didcot a few days later – only the second UK main-line steam locomotive to have circumnavigated the world, the first being her old rival No 4472. The final movement from Portbury to Didcot was carried out free of charge by Moveright International's Andrew Goodman.

Getting *Pendennis Castle* home was just the start of her restoration problems, though. The last heavy mechanical works carried out (aside from those done in Australia in the 1980s) were way back in the 1960s, and her last official overhaul was in 1959! As a result she was very tired and was in need of extensive works to bring her back to full health. Every last mechanical component was stripped from the engine, tyres were turned, new cab-end drag boxes were added on both the loco and tender, new valve and cylinder liners were fitted and, indeed, every single bearing surface (almost without exception) required refreshing or replacement. Her boiler was

ABOVE A Castle going places. *Pendennis Castle* arrives at the docks for loading. *(Peter Ward)*

LEFT The last few moves to get No 4079 ready for transport. Lifting such an important and heavy relic always sharpens the mind and focuses the attention… *(Adrian Knowles/GWS)*

thankfully in great shape, and despite needing new firebox stays in a few areas and a number of other relatively minor repairs, the pressure vessel was in great condition. This can be in no small part due to the time and attention lavished upon her by her Australian carers. This overhaul also necessitated the fitting of main-line electronic packages, something not dreamt of when she left these shores back in 1977. At the time of writing this is an ongoing process but one day the legend will be reborn and her fans, young and old alike, will once again marvel at the GWR's 'Wandering Warhorse' in steam.

BELOW No 4079 safe and sound on No 2 Turntable Road Didcot on 23 July 2000, still covered in red dust and sand after having been fumigated in case any of Australia's more poisonous residents had hitched a ride to Blighty. *(GWS)*

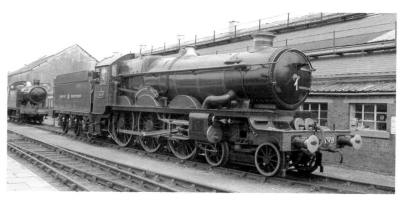

Chapter Three

The Castle Class

A spotter's guide

As you can imagine, with 171 Castles built or converted from other locomotive types, and a series of production runs between 1923 and 1950, there was tremendous variation within the fleet. The locomotives also had a number of modifications undertaken on them over the years, as a result of which the purity of their original build specifications was diluted still further.

OPPOSITE The pinnacle of Castle Class technical development embodied in preservation. No 5043 *Earl of Mount Edgcumbe* was completed in January 1936 and was originally named *Barbury Castle*, but was renamed in September 1937. She was rebuilt in 1958 and received a four-row superheater boiler, mechanical lubrication and a double chimney. This engine was a resident of Barry Scrapyard, and although she was bought from there as a source of spares she was rebuilt in her own right to steam again in 2008. *(Frank Dumbleton/GWS)*

This was not done wholesale either, as some engines had extensive modifications whilst others remained largely unaltered throughout their lives. The potential for model makers, historians and indeed restorers of these fine machines to make serious mistakes in their projects, without careful research and good photographic evidence, is consequently legion. As a result, presented here is a spotter's guide to the various incarnations and developments that were contained within the fleet, which should enable interested readers to obtain greater insight into the preserved machines and more accurate interpretation of photographs of their long-lost classmates.

Castle Mk 1

We will first consider the originals as built. These were, as mentioned in a previous chapter, simply enlarged Stars with a new boiler, larger cab and larger cylinders fitted. Indeed, the drawings used were simply those for the Stars, altered with a red pencil! Numbered from 4073 to 4092, they are immediately identifiable as early batch Castles in original condition as the frames at the front end are what is known as the joggled type. This 'S' bend in the front end of the main frames, when viewed from above, was introduced to ensure the front bogie wheels do not hit them as the locomotive travels through curves in the track. This shape meant that the inside cylinder block is of a narrow design, and the most visual part of this frame arrangement is the fluted steel cover used for the inside valves. In the early locomotives this was known by the workers

at Swindon as the 'Vauxhall' front. This was because the curves in a Vauxhall car of the period in some ways echoed that of the casing. The covers over the valve stems themselves were cylindrical with a hemispherical end, as per the Stars. They were also fitted with elegant tapered buffers.

The first few of these machines were also fitted with bogie brakes, it being a Churchward policy that all wheels on a locomotive should be braked. Tests carried out by Collett saw no appreciable benefit to their use, however, and indeed they involved a great deal more complication in the locomotives' design, build and maintenance. There is some evidence to suggest that these were actually doing damage to the Castles, as No 4079's records from Swindon indicate that she had her bogie wheels changed at Old Oak Common a number of times in her first few months of service. This is quite an unusual practice. Whatever the reason, study of the 1925 trials photographs indicate that they had been removed from her at least by then, and the remainder of the engines with bogie brakes followed suit.

The removal of the bogie brakes allowed a step to be fitted just behind the front wheel, although this was not fitted to all engines in a uniform manner and thus cannot be relied upon as an indicator of the period of a photograph.

Continuing our tour around the frames, the sanding gear had two boxes that were mounted so that they fitted under the running plate and fed the front two driving wheels. The coupling rods were split so that the knuckle that allowed movement between the two sections was between the front and middle driving wheels. The wheels themselves had small balance weights that went between four of the spokes. Finally on the frames, the ATC (automatic train control) shoe was mounted under the cab. This was a retrofit, as it did not become standard until No 5003 *Lulworth Castle* in May 1927.

Moving above the running plate, the boiler was the new standard No 8 unit with a two-row superheater. This was surmounted by a tall GWR chimney that gave the locomotive a total height of 13ft 5½in (4.1m). The lubrication at the front end was provided by a three-glass sight fed hydrostatic lubricator. This only had a few feed pipes running forward to the regulator,

LEFT Another Castle Mk 1 – this time No 4082 *Windsor Castle*. For many years this was the royal loco on the GWR (for obvious reasons!). This photograph was taken when the loco was on display in the 1925 Railway Centenary celebrations. Of note are the absence of bogie brakes, the porthole windows above the firebox, the Vauxhall-style front end with cylindrical valve stem covers and the unique brass plate recording the time the engine was driven by King George V on 28 April 1924. *(GWS/GWT)*

valves and pistons at the front end. As a result, only the driver's side had the small cowling to cover the pipe elbows as they curved up from the side of the boiler and into the smokebox. The top lamp bracket was also mounted on the smokebox top itself rather than on the smokebox door as in later machines. This was also a practice that was relatively short-lived, as the door position eventually became standard.

In the cab of these original Castles, in addition to the regular side and front cab windows of the Collett cab additional porthole-style windows were fitted to the spectacle plate above the top level of the firebox. These were a hangover from the Churchward-style cabs and were eventually removed from all those so fitted. There are two survivors of the 1923 to 1925 type, Prototype No 4073 *Caerphilly Castle*, which is part of the National Collection, and of course No 4079 *Pendennis Castle*, which lives with the Great Western Society at Didcot.

Castle Mk 2

Numbered between 4093 and 5012, the first redesign of Castles came in 1926 and gave Collett a chance to think about production techniques, which resulted in a few changes. The biggest at this stage was the new front-end design that did away with the joggle, which, when looking at the thickness and size of the steel plates involved, cannot have been easy to replicate. They were, of course, handed too, so this meant two different bending operations. The bogie clearances were now taken care of by a simple dished pressing in the frames where the front wheel set swung underneath it, thereby eliminating the complexity of the original design. Another change was to the inside cylinder casting, as this was altered to a wide design to accommodate the increased distance between the frames. On the front of the running plate the inside valve cover changed from the original 'Vauxhall' style to a wider yet still fluted

LEFT Another view of No 4082 at the 1925 celebrations. This time she is in charge of the GWR royal train, with a bowler-hatted inspector leaning out of the cab to monitor proceedings. Note the rather impressive-looking lamps. *(GWS/GWT)*

LEFT No 5003 *Lulworth Castle* is in fine early condition. A proud crew shows off their machine to the photographer, which enables us to appreciate the revised front end arrangement of the Mk 2 machines. She is in regal company, with an early King parked behind her. No 5003 was completed in May 1927 and served until August 1962, having changed little in the intervening 35 years. *(GWS/GWT)*

CENTRE As if to prove the point, here we see No 5003 in the second incarnation of BR livery, with the Lion & Wheel insignia, post-overhaul at Swindon. The sanding arrangements have changed and she sports a five-glass lubricator and 4,000-gallon Collett tender but still retains the essence of her original form. *(GWS/GWT)*

design. They retained the original cylindrical valve stem covers. Unfortunately there are no surviving examples of the 1926 to 1927 type of Castle.

Castle Mk 3

The next type of Castle were the engines built with numbers from 5013 to 5082 and (for reasons that will become clear later) 5093 to 5097. These continued with the straight frames that remained standard from here on, and with altered front casing from the fluted type to a box type with a rounded front edge. This was undoubtedly another of Collett's time and money saving moves. The valve stem covers were changed from the cylindrical design to a simple pressing that went straight down to the running plate. This was the same design as fitted to the last batch of King Class locomotives that were built in 1930.

From No 5013 there was a fire iron tunnel

LEFT No 5017 is in the G (crest) W livery applied from 1942 onwards. *St Donats Castle* was part of the first batch of Mk 3 Castles and was completed in July 1932. She is sporting the later type of driving wheels here, with the larger balance weights. She was renamed *The Gloucester Regiment 28th, 61st* in April 1954 and was withdrawn in September 1962. *(GWS/GWT)*

provided on the fireman's side running plate. With a couple of exceptions all Castles were retrofitted with this. The locomotives that were retrofitted can be easily identified, as they lost the upright brass trim strip on the front edge of the cab. Also retrofitted to most, if not all, the earlier machines was the five-glass lubricator that provided better lubrication to the front end. This increased the number of pipes running forward, which were split between the driver's and fireman's sides of the boiler, and covers for the pipe elbows appeared accordingly. The wheel balance weights were modified at this time to larger weights that were spread over seven spokes. Wheels were exchanged between locomotives at overhaul so both types were soon to be seen on any Castle.

With the construction of No 5044 in 1936, a new style of chimney was introduced that was 3in shorter. Eventually all Castles ended up with this unit. The ATC shoe was moved from under the cab to under the front bogie on No 5023. This necessitated the inclusion of an electrical conduit from the bogie to the battery and controls in the cab. This ran along the lower edge of the driver's side running plate. The cab windows on Nos 5013–5062 were slightly larger than other Castles, but the reason for this is unclear.

Up to this point the knuckle joints on the coupling rods between the front and rear pairs of driving wheels were ahead of the centre set. After No 5013 the joint was put aft of the centre wheels. This was due to the fact that the rear axleboxes were more prone to damage due to their proximity to the firebox and ash pan.

By this time the locomotive sanding arrangements had changed to being a box in front of the leading driving wheel set and a hidden box that fed on to the rear of the trailing set. To enable easier filling, from No 5058 onwards the rear sandboxes were lowered to be visible under the cab sides. As far as it is possible to

ABOVE Preservation favourite No 5051 seen at some point between completion in May 1936 and August 1937. The date can be surmised because she is carrying her original name of *Drysllwyn Castle* here rather than her later name of *Earl Bathurst*. The conduit for the ATC wiring is just visible at the bottom edge of the hanging bar under the running plate. *(GWS/GWT)*

ascertain, all Castles ended up with the second or third arrangement, but some with the third in the end went via the second set-up. The majority of machines in preservation today are of this type built between 1932 and 1939. No 5029 *Nunney Castle* is privately preserved (although it was originally restored by and once part-owned by the GWS); No 5043 *Earl of Mount Edgcumbe* (ex-*Barbury Castle*) is part of the fleet at Tyseley in Birmingham; No 5051 *Earl Bathurst* (ex-*Dryslwyn Castle*) keeps No 4079 and No 6023 company

RIGHT One of the most evocative names ever applied to a Castle was given to No 5069 *Isambard Kingdom Brunel*. Here we see the locomotive in the famous shirt-button livery used from 1934 until 1942. This puts the date of this image sometime after her completion in June 1938, and we can see all of the modifications alluded to in the text in wonderful clarity. *(GWS/GWT)*

ABOVE The last of the many. No 7037 *Swindon* is shown at Swindon shed in the early 1950s. There are several features of note, of which the Hawksworth tender of later years is the most obvious. The three-row superheater boiler is easily identified by the long, square pipe union cover on the smokebox, the single chimney and the mechanical lubricator on the running plate behind the steam pipe. The lubricator is mounted in front of the steam pipe on some machines. *(GWS/GWT)*

BELOW No 7000 *Viscount Portal* storms through Southall with a fast milk train consisting of a multitude of six-wheel tankers and a full brake coach for guards' accommodation. *(GWS/GWT)*

at Didcot as part of the GWS express passenger fleet; finally, No 5080 *Defiant* (ex-*Ogmore Castle*) is also a part of the Tyseley collection.

Castle Mk 4

The last batch of 'proper' Castles were those built in the post-war period between 1946 and 1950. Two engines that were originally supposed to have been built but were stopped by the need to concentrate on war work in 1939 were No 5098 *Clifford Castle* and No 5099 *Compton Castle*. The remainder were in the 70XX series, as the Kings occupied the 60XX series. They were numbered 7000 to 7037.

Undoubtedly the biggest step forward in the Castle design to date was the fitting of three-row superheated boilers. The reason for this was because the quality of coal available to the GWR and then BR was beginning to deteriorate and as a consequence the Castles, with their narrow firebox, could in certain situations lose their edge on performance. The three-row superheater took the Castle boiler to a new level of performance and allowed them to enter new realms of efficiency. Although Nos 5098 and 5099 were fitted with the by then standard five-row lubricator, the new superheater arrangements meant that higher degrees of superheat were attained. The margins for error with the sight-fed lubricators became very small, so a mechanical lubricator was fitted to increase oil flow. This was continued for all subsequent builds as well as a number of earlier machines – Nos 4087, 4088, 5084 and 7013 (ex-4082). Another minor but easily spotted feature of the post-war locomotives was the handrail under the cab window that was extended forwards to curve up and around the window frame.

The ever-changing inside valve casing changed again to a square front edge design, and the earlier locos with 5013-type covers also gained this type as time and overhauls progressed post-nationalisation. This was a safety modification, as it was considered that a crewman working on the smokebox or fitting lamps on the top of the boiler could easily slip if the curved edge was made greasy by oil and/or water. The later parallel-sided buffers had become standard by this time and were disseminated throughout the entire class. There are two survivors from the forty 1946–50 series of machines: No 7027 is privately owned and at the time of writing is the only unrestored Castle from Barry Scrapyard. It is hoped that one day it will live again. No 7029 *Clun Castle* is the last of the Castle trio cared for by Tyseley.

The rebuilds

Between 1924 and 1929 another six machines joined the ranks of the Castle Class. Four of these engines were Star Class machines. No 4009 *Shooting Star* was so treated in April 1925 and was eventually renamed and numbered No 100 A1 *Lloyds* in 1936. It became the only GWR locomotive with two number plates, the top one reading 100 and the bottom reading A1. No 4016 *Knight of the Golden Fleece* – rebuilt in October 1925 – eventually became known as *The Somerset Light Infantry (Prince Albert's)* in January 1938 (becoming the only Castle with brackets on its nameplate). No 4032 *Queen Alexandra* was rebuilt in April 1926, and finally No 4037 *Queen Philippa* became a Castle in June 1926 and was renamed *The South Wales Borderers* in March 1937. The two other imports to the ranks of the Castles have been mentioned before and were No 111 *Viscount Churchill* (which was originally the GWR Pacific *The Great Bear*) and, finally, the great granddaddy of all GWR four-cylinder express locomotives, No 4000 *North Star*. No 4000 was easily recognised as it had a higher running plate than all other Castles and never got the fire iron tool tunnel (this was also not fitted to No 100 A1). They retained their cylindrical valve stem covers and 'Vauxhall' fronts.

The reason for the odd gap previously mentioned, comprising numbers 5083–5092, was that these engines were all rebuilds of the last batch of Star Class engines built at Swindon between May 1922 and February 1923, numbered 4063 to 4072. They were known as the 'Abbeys', all being named after famous such buildings in the UK. They all kept the names they were carrying at the time of their rebuild between 1937 and 1940. Despite clearly having the joggled Star frames that Swindon reused, they were officially written off and classified as new machines

ABOVE No 4000 as a Castle. *North Star* was one of the few of the class, rebuilt or otherwise, that never received the fire iron tool tunnel on the fireman's side of the running plate. It also had a running plate that was 2½in (63.5mm) higher than standard. This picture shows the Great (crest) Western livery to wonderful effect. *(GWS/GWT)*

by the GWR accounts department. They were recognisable by their narrow version of the 5013 round-edged inside valve cover, which was similarly altered to a square-edged narrow type by BR, and the late King-style valve stem covers.

Unfortunately no rebuilt Castle has survived into preservation, but the boiler carried by No 4079 in preservation (No 6672HD) was built in 1937 to be fitted to No 5086 *Viscount Horne* (ex-Star No 4066 *Malvern Abbey/Sir Robert Horne/Viscount Horne*), so it could be argued that at least one major component survives.

RIGHT Here we see one of the 1937–40 rebuilds, No 5087 (formerly No 4067) *Tintern Abbey*. The locomotive is freshly overhauled outside Swindon works in the BR period and awaits uniting with a tender before being run-in on local services from Swindon shed. The 'unique to the Abbeys' inside valve cover can easily be seen here, as can the speedometer on the rear driving wheel. *(GWS/GWT)*

Post-construction modifications

Lubrication

A number of Castles became the recipients of a later type of Davies & Metcalfe mechanical lubricator. This was a special valveless design that required a reservoir to be fitted to the driver's side of the smokebox barrel just below the centreline. The idea behind this fitting was that it extended the refilling interval and was of a mechanically more simple valveless design. The engines receiving this modification – carried out between 1956 and 1957 – were Nos 4087, 4088, 5084, 4082/7013 and 7014.

Steam pipes

As built the Castles had steam pipes leading from the smokebox to the outside cylinders, which had a 90° bend towards the cab, and then a straight section before a second 90° bend to mate up with the cylinder. The problem with this design was that the pipes were prone to fracture in service. The solution to this problem was found in 1954, when BR started to fit steam pipes that eliminated the tight bends by getting rid of the straight section in the middle.

Oil burning

Oil burning was a method of firing that had been used a great deal by other countries, particularly towards the end of the steam era. It usually entailed the use of heavy fuel oil (sometimes referred to as 'Bunker C') to provide the heat, and came about because of the poor quality of coal from 1944 onwards. The finest coal had been earmarked for export only, and locos in the UK generally – and the GWR in particular (used to being fed the best South Wales steam coal) – were struggling to maintain performance. As a result the railways started to look to other sources of fuel, and oil-firing seemed a logical alternative. Initial experiments centred on the 28XX class 2-8-0 heavy freight locos but were soon rolled out to include Hall and Castle class machines.

The most notable modifications on the locomotive were in the firebox and cab. The firebox had a new firebrick arrangement in the ash pan and a set of injectors and burners for the oil. The cab had a new semi-permanently sealed firebox door (only opened during maintenance) with just a peephole for the crew to inspect the flame as and when required. There was also a set of controls for the burners and a steam heating system for the oil, as under normal temperatures it was too thick to flow.

The locomotives, when operated effectively, worked extremely well, but the programme to re-equip sheds and locomotives that was being enthusiastically pursued by the railways was curtailed by the fact that the government had insufficient foreign exchange in the post-war

BELOW In a two-for-one deal, this picture illustrates two post-manufacture modifications. Firstly, No 4087 *Cardigan Castle* was fitted with both a Davis & Metcalfe lubricator and a new-style inside cylinder cover in the 1950s. She is wearing the BR totem livery known to railwaymen as the 'ferret and dartboard'! *(GWS/GWT)*

austerity period to pay for the fuel. The railways were nationalised by then, and the millions of pounds spent on the programme was quietly forgotten. The most visual reminders of the experiment are the two concrete buildings opposite the lifting shop at Didcot. These were built as pump rooms for the oil tanks, but the programme was curtailed before the tanks and heating gear could be installed. Many generations of Didcot volunteer have good reason to be thankful for this fact, as one is now used as a mess room, and many a freezing-cold GWS member has been warmed inside them!

Speedometers

Remarkably, something that modern railwaymen would expect as essential equipment was only fitted to Castles from the mid-1930s onwards. Fewer lineside indicators had led to some impressive performances and a Star was clocked at the 60mph restriction through Banbury at 80mph. This, coupled with the advent of the very heavy King Class, could have led to some serious accidents. Therefore tests with Castles Nos 5003 and 5008 soon resulted in speedometers being fitted throughout the fleet from 1934.

Streamlining

One obvious 'sore thumb' that sticks out amongst the Castles is the GWR streamlining disaster to which an unsuspecting and undeserving No 5005 *Manorbier Castle* (and No 6014 *King Henry VII* for that matter) was subjected. It was as a result of the publicity department getting involved in the engineering of engines again in 1935. It had worked with their first interference in 1927, when their demand for an engine to beat the SR Lord Nelson Class had resulted in the introduction of the Kings, but this time it was an unmitigated disaster. Steam locos in the US and Germany had been streamlined and semi-streamlined against air resistance, and the LNER was getting in on the act with its P2 class as well. It was in response to this that the Board, spurred on, no doubt, not only by its PR department but also by the need to be seen as forward-thinking, and by the white heat of technological progress at the time, asked Collett to streamline a King and a Castle.

In the time-honoured fashion of people who really don't want to do what they have just been asked to do, Collett obviously decided to make such a complete hash of the job that he would never be asked to do it again. The legend goes that a subordinate was sent to a Swindon toyshop for a stick of Plasticine. When he returned, the CME had great fun smearing it all over the King model on his desk. He then sent that down to the works in lieu of drawings! The resultant look was not well received either

ABOVE An unidentified Castle with oil-burning equipment. The oil tank in the tender and the roof vents can plainly be seen. *(GWS/GWT)*

BELOW Quite what No 5005 *Manorbier Castle* did to deserve this is quite unclear but it can only have been monstrous – which is convenient, as that is the effect of the whole ensemble! The only things this did were to make a beautiful locomotive hideous and to make maintenance (not the easiest thing on a Castle in any case) next to impossible. *(GWS/GWT)*

by the GWR or the public at large. One wit on BBC radio likened the hemispherical blob on the smokebox door to having 'Teddy Brown [a leading and rather portly comedian of the day] welded on the front!'

The exercise succeeded in only two things. The first is that it probably inspired the look of the one-piece splashers on Hawksworth's 10XX County Class engines designed about ten years later; and the second was to make the motion of the engines almost impossible to service and maintain. Needless to say, the casings were slowly removed in a piecemeal fashion, and bit by bit the locos returned to their original configuration. There have been many who have described this as something of a lost opportunity. Swindon *could* do streamlining well – their cooperation with AEC had produced the beautiful early diesel railcars (nicknamed the 'Flying Bananas' by enthusiasts), which simply

ooze style, and the even more austere wartime 'razor-edged' versions have a certain something about them; but alas it was not to be.

'Fake' Castles

In 1952 BR (W) was presented with something of an issue. Whilst the death of King George VI was not a total shock, as he had not been in the best of health for some time, it still came as a bit of a surprise. The request went out for the engine bearing the name of the family seat, *Windsor Castle*, to be made available to pull the great man's funeral train. BR were keen to oblige, as this was the wartime king who had led his people through one of the most tumultuous times in the nation's history. The big problem was that No 4082 was inside Swindon works in the middle of being overhauled and was therefore not available. The Western Region, in their wisdom, decided that no one would notice if they put the name and number plates from No 4082 on another engine. Had they been cleverer or had access to this book (!) and selected the *right* engine – *ie* another member of the original batch numbered between 4073 and 4092 – they might have just got away with it. Unfortunately, they took the first Castle they could lay their hands on, and it happened to be No 7013 *Bristol Castle*.

As my now educated readers will realise, this was a big mistake – especially considering the number of train spotters around at the time. The story goes that the subterfuge was actually discovered by a young lad who quite rightly, and probably quite loudly (knowing how young lads can sometimes announce their discoveries), pronounced No 4082 *Windsor Castle* to be a fake! It has to be said that there was some explaining and embarrassment over the affair at Paddington. In a move seeming to confirm the air of corporate denial, the locos never regained their original identities and went to the scrapyard still lying through their number plates. This means that what is written in this chapter thus far and in photographs taken after 22 February 1952 will seem to be a complete lie with regard to these two engines – compounded by the fact that No 7013 (the ex-No 4082, that is) was also the recipient of a later-style inside valve cover!

BELOW Spot the mistake... The Nos 4082/7013 that the BR (WR) would have you believe! The differences are hugely obvious now that you look at it, and hopefully the book you hold will help you become a discerning Castle enthusiast and enable you to tell the difference. *(GWS/GWT)*

Tender allocations

There were a wide variety of tenders used with the Castles over the 40-plus years they were in service. The first was the 3,500-gallon Churchward-style tender with a coal capacity of 6 tons. This had become a standard for the large GWR tender locomotives in the latter years of that CME's reign. This situation continued during Collett's incumbency, and there was a version of this tender, known as the 'Collett intermediate', with similar capacity to the Churchward unit but with longer top fenders and higher sides. Not many of these were built and they were infrequently used on the Castles. This could have been down to the fact that they only had a coal capacity of 5½ tons, which made operation of a larger locomotive more challenging.

In 1926 Collett introduced the 4,000-gallon unit that became the standard for most of the GWR period. This was used on engines from the Castle, King and Hall classes and was retrofitted to engines in the Star and 47XX classes. This tender also had the higher sides and the long top fenders of the intermediate design, and had a coal capacity of 6 tons, although an astute fireman could have a good go at getting closer to 6½ tons aboard. It became far more likely to see a 4,000-gallon Collett tender behind a Castle by the mid-1930s than any other version, and the Castles all pulled one of these at some point in their careers, as it was a very successful design. Needless to say, even though this was the case, experimentation on this design was still carried out. There was a version built in 1931 with eight wheels instead of the more normal six, in an attempt to spread the load a little more. Even though this was successful, it was not deemed enough of an advantage to proceed beyond the prototype. Even as late as 1949 a new version of this tender was produced with an experimental alloy tank, but again the advantages over the standard unit were not deemed sufficient to continue down this path.

With the advent of a change at the top in the form of Fredrick Hawksworth, and then the Second World War, the production of tenders was streamlined further by the introduction of Hawksworth's own version of the 4,000-gallon tender with a welded instead of riveted tank.

These are readily identified by their flat, smooth sides, as opposed to the curvaceous lines of the earlier tenders. Construction of these began during the Second World War but became standard with new Castles built after 1948. After WW2 the Castles were all running with 4,000-gallon tenders of one sort or another with one or two minor exceptions.

During the oil-burning experiments of 1946 a number of converted Collett 4,000-gallon and one converted 3,500-gallon (fitted to No 5091 only) tenders that had oil tanks in place of the coal space were used on the specially converted locomotives. The locos and tenders reverted back to their original design at the end of the experiment.

There were all sorts of other types that were seen on Castles, including the Dean 4,000-gallon and the later Collett version of the Churchward 3,500-gallon, and during experimentation and recording the two GWR/BR (W) self-weighing tenders could be seen behind Castles. The thing to remember here is that locomotives that were taken into the works would have been separated from their tenders, and would have been united with the next suitable finished unit when they were released back to traffic, so it was possible to see later Castles with 4,000-gallon Collett tenders just as much as it was to see early ones with Hawksworth variants.

ABOVE Most of the tender types hauled by Castles have been illustrated elsewhere in this book, but this picture of one of the self-weighing tenders behind No 5086 *Viscount Horne* will be of interest to the reader. It carries the first BR logo, known to some as the 'unicycling lion'. *(GWS/GWT)*

ABOVE If you were looking for a logical and obvious example of locomotive naming and numbering, you won't find it here. Originally built as Star No 4009 in May 1907, *Shooting Star* was converted to a Castle in April 1925. She was then renumbered first to A1 and later to 100A1, and renamed to *Lloyds* in February 1936. She is seen here in GWR shirt-button livery sometime after renaming. *(GWS/GWT)*

Names

There was a profusion of names used on the Castle Class locomotives, and surprisingly they were not all something-or-other Castle! The original intention was to use only names of castles in England, and preferably within the GWR's operational area. The batches can be traced (with one or two exceptions) to the list of castle names as they tended to be allocated alphabetically within a batch. For example, the first batch was No 4073 *Caerphilly Castle* to No 4082 *Windsor Castle*, with No 4079 *Pendennis Castle* somewhere in the middle. This held true until the GWR board wanted to name some of them after peers. This resulted in locomotives Nos 5043 to 5063 being renamed after earls, the two most famous examples being No 5051, which went from being called *Drysllwyn Castle* to *Earl Bathurst*, and No 5043 going from *Barbury Castle* to *Earl of Mount Edgcumbe*.

Both locomotives are now preserved. The next batch of renaming concerned locomotives Nos 5071–5082 in 1941, when they were renamed after Allied aircraft that took part in the Battle of Britain – no doubt as part patriotic gesture and part publicity move. The Star rebuilds, often referred to by enthusiasts as the Abbeys (locomotives Nos 5083–5092) have already been mentioned. All Castles with a non-castle name had a supplementary smaller plate fixed below the main one on the steel mounting plate (except the Earls, for some unknown reason), that read 'Castle Class', as if to confirm their membership of that exclusive club.

Being frugal (and in a move that causes confusion with GWR historians to this day), the GWR and later the Western Region simply reused discarded names on later machines. Certain names became particularly nomadic. For example, when built No 5056 was named *Ogmore Castle*. It was then renamed *Earl of Powis* in 1937, which was then used on No 5080 built in 1939. No 5080 (now preserved) was subsequently renamed after the WW2 *Defiant* fighter bomber in 1941. The name was then reused on No 7007 in 1946, which later became *Great Western* in 1948, and *Ogmore Castle* was then built in 1950! This time it stuck... The other name used four times was *Denbigh Castle*, being used on Nos 5049 (which became *Earl of Plymouth*), 5074 (*Hampden*), 7001 (*Sir James Milne*) and finally 7023.

There were a number of other oddities in the Castle naming policy – some have already been mentioned, but others included GWR celebrities such as *Isambard Kingdom Brunel*, *Sir Daniel Gooch*, *Sir Felix Pole* and *G.J. Churchward*.

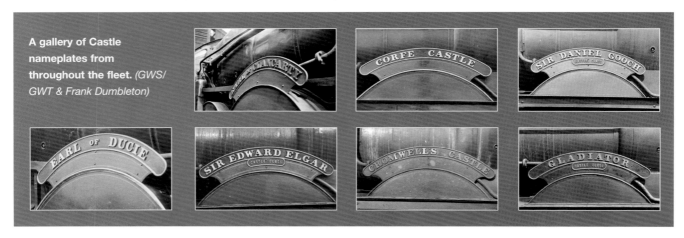

A gallery of Castle nameplates from throughout the fleet. *(GWS/ GWT & Frank Dumbleton)*

There were regiments too (such as ex-Star No 4037 *The South Wales Borderers*), and composers (No 7005 *Sir Edward Elgar*). The original No 4000 *North Star* retained its name throughout its life as a Castle, as did No 4032 *Queen Alexandra*, although these did carry a supplementary 'Castle Class' plate beneath the original. And finally the last Castle, No 7037, was named after the town of its birth, *Swindon*.

Liveries

The basic GWR livery was largely unchanged from 1906 to 1947 in all but relatively minor details. Since the earliest days GWR engines had been painted green, and would continue to be for the majority of the company's existence. In 1881 Middle Chrome Green was introduced at Swindon, remaining the standard paint used until the 1940s, although slight changes to the formula meant that its shade was successively lightened, first in 1906 and then again in 1928. Black-painted frames had been introduced in 1906 in place of the Indian Red of the Victorian era; between the frames Venetian Red remained standard for all plate work and the eccentric rods, with the remainder of the motion being left bright steel. Buffer beams were China Red, with the engine number in yellow, shaded black. Express locos (except in times of austerity) all had copper-capped chimneys and polished brass safety valve bonnets that were synonymous with the GWR's corporate identity.

This was the livery the Castles found themselves in for the entire GWR period. The big differences came with the lining and company crests used. The Collett livery was

perhaps the most ornate, with orange/green/black/green/orange lining on the locomotive boiler bands, splashers, cab sides and various panels on the tender, together with orange and black lining around the cab fronts and buffer beams. In addition there was a great deal of orange lining on the hanging bar under the running plate, the steps, tender frames, and cylinder cladding etc. Finally, the route restriction was painted above the number plates, with the power class inside, whilst the code for the engine's home depot was painted inside the cab, above the driver's head. By mid-1942 the austerity brought about by the Second World War meant that niceties such as lining were dispensed with. The instructions went out that all locomotives were to be repainted black, although Kings and Castles were allowed to remain green. There were, of course, exceptions and Nos 5001 and 5018 were both recorded as being in wartime black.

In addition, the depot allocation was moved from inside the cab on to the hanging bar, just behind the buffer beam. From 1945 there was a slow return to lining, now in a slightly more reddish shade of orange, but restricted to solely above the footplate, whilst the fronts of the cabs were also left plain. Middle Chrome Green was also dispensed with, in favour of the slightly darker Engine Green.

Tender logos during the GWR period were indicative of the period. The early Castles from 1923 featured the company name 'GREAT WESTERN' (Egyptian Serif font, gold letters, shaded with black and red) with the elaborate 'garter'-style crest central between the two

ABOVE No 5035 *Coity Castle* **displays the intermediate BR livery.** *(GWS/GWT)*

BELOW An unusual picture of a Castle with the Gill Sans BRITISH RAILWAYS logo on its tender. It is likely to be in the apple green livery. This example is sported by No 7013 *Bristol Castle.* *(GWS/GWT)*

words. Then, from 1928, the more simple 'heraldic'-style crest was substituted for the garter version. In 1934 the words and crest disappeared in favour of the famous GWR roundel logo, in gold edged with black. This lasted until 1942, when the heraldic crest returned on larger engines, although this time simply flanked by the initials GW, in straw shaded with black and red. After nationalisation in 1948 the Great Western insignia slowly disappeared as engines were repainted following overhaul. Initially sporting 'BRITISH RAILWAYS' in the GWR-style Egyptian Serif, during 1949 this was replaced by the lion and wheel emblem (known to some railwaymen as 'the unicycling lion').

There was also a series of experiments in 1948 that lead to Castles Nos 7010–7013 (from new) and Nos 4089, 4091, 5010, 5021 and 5023 being painted in Apple Green with red, cream and grey lining and 'BRITISH RAILWAYS' written in Gill Sans typeface on the tender. Thankfully, this hideous apparition – which never really suited any of the locomotives to which BR applied it (which included ex-LMS Black 5s and Jubilees) – was not inflicted on any other Castles. Fortunately the basic colour was standardised as Deep Bronze Green (BS381C–1980 Tint No 224), which only the most informed of spectators could distinguish from GWR green.

Because of their cast brass number plates, ex-GWR locomotives retained their old company numbers. However, a number of Castles had a regional 'W' painted under the cab side plate. It was soon realised that this was superfluous and it was only put on Nos 111, 4084, 4087, 5001, 5010, 5018, 5019, 5022, 5035, 5041, 5048, 5065, 5077, 5088, 5097, 5099 and 7001. From mid-1948 the numbers at the front were changed from being painted on the buffer beam to a cast iron plate on the smokebox door. In addition, from early 1949 depot allocations were carried on a small oval plate at the bottom of the smokebox door. This causes further problems for historians, as the GWR/Western Region had a habit of putting train reporting numbers on the front of the smokebox, often making a loco unidentifiable when viewed from the front. Lining returned to the cylinders, albeit only running vertically, and was omitted from the firebox bands and the rear of the tender, whilst only the lower half of the cab sides was now lined. In addition the hanging bar on both engine and tender was now painted green.

The final livery change for the Castles occurred in 1956, when the lion and wheel was exchanged for the later BR totem (colloquially known as the 'ferret and dartboard'), which remained standard until the last Castle was withdrawn in 1965.

Double chimneys and four-row superheaters

The most significant Castle class modernisation programme was initiated in 1956, when a series of experiments was carried out under the supervision of Swindon engineer Sam Ell. The aim was to make the locomotives more efficient and to improve the running on the now slightly inferior grades of coal that was sometimes supplied. Ell took the most unpopular of the lot to work his magic on. The worst Castle at that time was thought to be No 7018 *Dryslwyn Castle*. She steamed poorly and was not a favourite of the crews that had to drive and fire her. A number of experiments had led Ell to the conclusion that the problems lay at the front end. If the draughting of the engine could be improved the performance of the locomotive would be greatly improved. A fabricated double chimney unit was made and fitted and this transformed No 7018 from an unreliable engine that steamed poorly into a very capable machine.

This experiment was so successful that No 5043 *Earl of Mount Edgcumbe* was also treated to a double chimney. Then things really got going, and No 4090 *Dorchester Castle* was rebuilt not only with a cast double chimney but with a four-row superheater as well. This then gave Ell the chance to bring in his original guinea pig, No 7018, and fit not only the four-row superheater but also improve the lubrication to give her about 50% more oil. This turned a capable machine into an absolute flyer. After this a total of 64 Castles were eventually modified. The resultant machines can be thought of as Castle GTIs! There are two locomotives preserved in this modified state, Tyseley residents No 5043 *Earl of Mount Edgcumbe* and No 7029 *Clun Castle*.

The last engine modified was No 5078 *Beaufort* in December 1961, but by that time progress in the form of diesel traction had caught up with the Castles. When you consider that the first true Castle (No 4091 *Dudley Castle*) was scrapped in January 1961 and that No 5078 herself only lasted until November 1962, any more development effort here would have only been wasted.

BELOW Another magnificent preservation era study of No 5043 *Earl of Mount Edgcumbe*. As the double chimney represents the twilight of Castle development, a more apt image for the end of this chapter would be difficult to find. *(Frank Dumbleton)*

Chapter Four

Anatomy of the Castles

The inside story

While the way any steam locomotive works can be described and explained in such a way as to make it easily understood by the majority of people, express passenger locomotives such as the Castle class machines are highly complex, and draw from many fields of science and engineering.

OPPOSITE Preservation splendour – No 4079 *Pendennis Castle* in exhibition condition not long before she left on her Australian odyssey. *(Collection of Sir William McAlpine)*

Basic principles

A conventional steam locomotive is essentially a very large kettle that, through the use of a combustible fuel, generates steam. This steam is then used in the cylinders via valves and valve gear to drive the machine. There are a number of ancillary systems that are also required, including a method of replenishing the water in the boiler, braking, train heating and so on. The principles of the machine derive from the pioneering work of such luminaries as Trevithick and Stephenson in the first quarter of the 19th century, and indeed they would have had no trouble at all in recognising their work in the Castles, first built nearly a century later. There had, however, been a great deal of refinement in the intervening time that took the steam locomotive from those pioneering iron horses to the mighty machines that powered British railway transport until the late 1960s.

The Castles, along with their fellow Swindon sisters, are reckoned to be some of the finest steam locomotive engineering ever produced and were, as we have seen, developed through Churchward's extensive experimentation in the first decades of the 20th century. This gave them a technological edge that meant they were second to none for a long time, and even when they had been surpassed in terms of modernity, they were still useful and relevant enough to ensure that their construction continued into the 1950s.

In order to simplify this section, the

locomotive referred to will be No 4079 *Pendennis Castle* as she was when preserved in 1965, which has a two-row superheated boiler and a 4,000-gallon Collett-style tender. When referring to the sides of the locomotive, the right-hand side (if you were stood in the cab, facing towards the front of the locomotive) is known as the driver's side, and the left is known as the fireman's side. When dealing with multiples of the same part, such as the driving wheel sets, those in front are referred to as the leading set, the middle ones are the centre set and those at the rear are the trailing set. The locomotive weighs 79 tons 17 cwt (81.13 tonnes) in operating order, is 65ft 2in (19.86m) long over the buffers, 8ft 11in (2.72m) wide and 13ft 4½in (4.08m) tall. The Collett 4,000-gallon tender weighs 47 tons 6 cwt (48.05 tonnes) full, is 24ft 5in (7.44m) long, 8ft 8in (2.64m) wide and 11ft 0½in (3.36m) tall at the side flares. The tender wheelbase is 15ft (4.57m).

Steam generation

The boiler on a Castle Class locomotive is known as the GWR Standard No 8, which is pressed to 225psi (1.55MPa). As with the vast majority of locomotive boilers from this time, it is of riveted construction. It has a 14ft 10in (4,520mm) long conical section in the boiler barrel starting at 5ft 2in (1,570mm) at the front and rising to 5ft 9in (1,750mm) at the point where it attaches to the firebox. It is constructed from rolled-form special boiler plate steel to the BR standard 110 (BS Spec No 1501 151-400A). The conical shape was found by Churchward to offer better water circulation and provide greater capacity closer to the fire, where it is hotter, thus getting the best from the burning fuel.

Mounted on top is the safety valve. This is the primary safety device for the boiler and is actually composed of two separate valves that are held shut against boiler pressure by a spring acting on the valve spindle. This is known as a direct loaded safety valve system. As the boiler pressure rises past the working pressure of 225psi that is 'set' into the valves at overhaul, the valve lifts and allows steam to escape. When the pressure reduces back to below 225psi, the valve reseats itself and the flow of steam is stopped. It was favoured by the GWR over other more modern types (such as the Ross 'pop' valve) as they claimed it lost less steam between opening and closing, whereas the more modern types were open for longer on operation and therefore caused the fireman more work and required the burning of extra fuel. Indeed, it was common to see a locomotive working hard with just a wisp of steam being 'feathered' from the safety valve. Without looking at the pressure gauge the fireman could tell that the locomotive was bang on the mark!

The 10ft-long (3,050mm) firebox is a twin-walled hollow structure with an outer wall also made of boiler plate steel pressed into a form known as the Belpaire style. This was invented in the 1860s by Belgian locomotive engineer Alfred Belpaire, and virtually became standard across the vast majority of 20th-century GWR classes after the reign of Churchward. It has a square top section with rounded corners and edges and flat sides down to the level of the frames. On GWR locomotives, the bottom section of the firebox is pinched in to fit between the locomotive frames. This shape offers a larger heating surface at the top of the flames, which is the hottest part of the fire. The inner wall of the firebox has a heating surface of 163.76ft^2 (15.214m^2) and is made of arsenical copper (the arsenic being added to increase its strength at high temperature), chosen for its superior heat transfer capability, to BR Standard 301 (BS 2870 C107 CA3). The bottom of the structure is formed by a thick steel shape known as the foundation ring.

Mounted on the inside of the firebox are a number of carriers that hold up the cast iron grate. The grate has a total area of 29.36ft^2 (2.72m^2) and is semi-sloping: it has a flat section at the rear that leads to a sloped section at the front. This mirrors the shape of the bottom edge of the firebox. Bolted to the foundation ring via a series of studs, in threaded holes, is the ash pan. This is in two sections to enable it to straddle the axle of the rear driving wheels. Each of these sections has its own damper door to control airflow into the firebox.

At the top of the inner firebox there are two fusible plugs. These are threaded, made of a bronze-type alloy and have a square head to

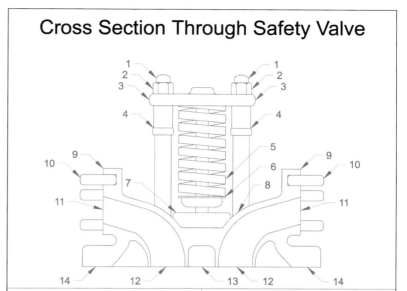

Cross Section Through Safety Valve

1.	Pillars	9. Clack Valve Mounting
2.	Setting Nuts	Flange
3.	Strongback	10. Clack Valve Mounting
4.	Setting Collar	Stud
5.	Spring	11. Water Inlet
6.	Spring Retaining Cup	12. To Boiler
7.	Valve & Seat	13. Steam Outlet
8.	Safety Valve Body	14. Safety Valve To Boiler
	Casting	Mounting Flange

ABOVE Drawing of a GWR safety valve. There are two sprung valves and the body casting incorporates the mounts for the clack valves that allow fresh water into the boiler. *(Author's Drawing)*

BELOW The inner firebox of 6672HD. The nuts on the ends of the stays are there to protect them from the ravages of the heat in the firebox. Ahead is the copper tubeplate, and the difference in size between the smaller smoke tubes and the larger flue tubes that carry the superheater elements can be clearly seen. *(Author)*

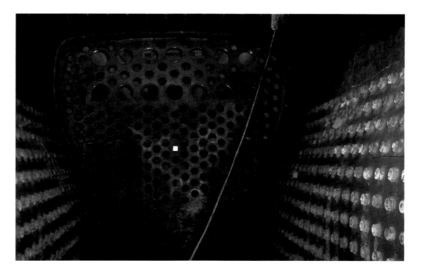

RIGHT The inside of No 4079's ash pan as removed at overhaul in the early 2000s. This shows the complex shapes required to get over the rear driving axle, and, indeed, why she had so much trouble when the fire ended up here on 9 May 1964. *(Russ Heyluer)*

ABOVE No 4073 *Caerphilly Castle* at Swindon's STEAM museum. You can see the two sections of the ash pan, and one of the damper doors is conveniently in the open position. *(Author)*

BELOW The front tubeplate of 6672HD, while de-tubed for overhaul. The longitudinal stays are visible through the tube holes, and the single hole at the top is for the main steam pipe. The regulator is bolted in front of this. *(Author)*

drive them into the firebox roof or crown sheet. They have a hole drilled through them that is filled with lead. In the event of the water level getting too low the lack of water covering the lead will cause it to melt and allow steam to escape from the plug. This gives the fireman the warning he needs to deaden the fire immediately and to fill the boiler with water to prevent a disaster.

The inner firebox also has a number of different controls built into it for directing airflow and heat, both passive and controllable. The brick arch is carried on studs and is made from specially shaped interlocking heat-resistant bricks. The purpose of the brick arch is to deflect the hot gasses back towards the rear of the firebox. Without this, the hot gasses would be sucked straight into the boiler tubes, wasting heat and resulting in unequal heating of the metal of the firebox, which could cause it to leak. At the back end of the firebox is the firehole where the fireman shovels the coal on to the grate. There is a pair of cast iron doors on a pair of runners top and bottom. They are opened using a long lever and a linkage that causes them to open at the same time. The fireman is also provided with a lift-up flap to effectively plug the hole while he is putting a large amount of coal on to the fire, to prevent cold air entering the firebox during the process. In addition there is a deflector plate on the top inside edge of the firehole that directs any secondary air taken in via the door to the heart of the fire. This makes the combustion of the fuel more complete.

The rearmost plate on the boiler is known as the backhead and it is here that the various steam-related cab controls and feeds for such things as injectors, vacuum brakes etc are attached via precisely machined plates that ensure a good seal between the body of the control castings (usually in an LG4 bronze-type alloy or steel) and the mounting pad on the boiler. The sheets on the sides are known as the side sheets (!), and the sheet where the barrel joins the firebox is known as the throat plate. There are corresponding plates on the copper side too, with the copper throat plate incorporating the inner tubeplate as well.

Within the boiler it is a game of keeping the pressure in and the heat flowing. Firstly, there are a great many bar-like round-section pieces of metal that hold the plate work in place. These are called stays, and there are several types within the boiler. The firebox walls are held apart by stays and they can be made of either steel or copper depending upon their size and position, different diameters and materials having different expansion rates. These stays are effectively a sort of double-ended bolt screwed in from one side then caulked with a pneumatic hammer and specially shaped chisel to make them steam-tight. There are longer stays in the water and steam space at the top of the firebox called crown stays. There are a number of more specialist types too; the firebox has a number of stays around the inside of the boiler barrel attaching it to the firebox, known as palm stays. There are also cross stays, which go from one side of the water space above the inner firebox. The final type of stay is known as a longitudinal stay, and these run the full length of the barrel from the front to the rear tubeplate. There are only a few of these in the top steam space of the boiler; the remaining stress is held in check by the tubes themselves.

Inside the barrel section there is a nest of 197 2in (50.8mm) small and 14 5in (130.17mm) large flue tubes, giving a total heating surface area of 1,854.31ft^2 (172.27m^2). The small tubes simply take the hot gasses from the fire and allow them to pass through the boiler barrel to heat the water. They are expanded in place with a special tool, and the ends are beaded over to prevent them burning or corroding away. The flue tubes are of a larger diameter to carry the superheater elements, more of which later. These larger tubes are arranged in two rows in the upper half of the boiler's circular cross-section. They have a special threaded end known as a bottle end (so called because of its shape) that is screwed into the copper tubeplate. The outer end is expanded into the steel front tubeplate as per the small tubes. There is one other large tube that takes the steam collected at the top of the boiler and delivers it to the regulator valve fixed to the front tubeplate inside the smokebox. The casting for the safety valve sits on top of the boiler in a roughly central position. This also incorporates the mountings for the clack valves that let fresh water into the boiler. Underneath this, inside

the boiler, is a series of trays that form a table that helps to dilute the feed water within the boiler to cause it to heat and dissipate, reducing the quantity of bubbles created and therefore excess hydraulic action on the barrel.

Once the steam has been generated by the heat of the fire, it goes from the main steam pipe into the regulator valve. This is a sliding-type valve that is controlled from a lever in the cab via a long operating rod that stretches the entire length of the boiler. This has a small operating cam-type device on the end that slides the valve back and forth over the ports. There are two valves, one within the other, which are known as the smaller pilot valve, for slower speed and less power, and the larger main valve that supplies more steam, which is used when the engine is required to work harder. The regulator is mounted in the smokebox to increase the controllability and sensitivity of acceleration of the engine. This is achieved by having less pipes work and therefore less steam in those pipes between the regulator valve and the cylinders. In a more traditionally dome-mounted regulator (halfway down the boiler barrel) there is a great deal more steam between the valve and the cylinders, and that has to be used up even after the valve is shut.

Once the regulator valve is opened and the steam passes through, it then moves on to the superheater. This consists of a large cast manifold called the header. This distributes the steam into a series of smaller tubes or elements that are routed down and then back up the inside of the large boiler flue tubes. This gives the steam a second pass at the hot gasses coming from the fire by providing a superheater area of 295ft^2 (27.41m^2). This method of superheating was one given great consideration by Churchward in the early 20th century, and the system he developed was immensely simple in its construction. The versions he looked at to start with (the Cole and Schmidt types) gave him a starting point from which to develop the Swindon system, but their complexity and the fact that they were subject to patents caused him to think again. Churchward's design is a work of genius in that it takes the best elements of those designs but gives them a method of attaching the elements that involves

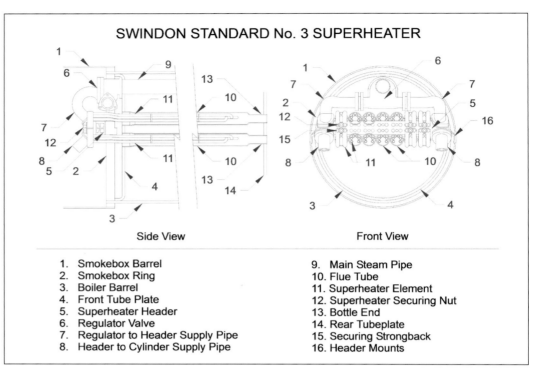

SWINDON STANDARD No. 3 SUPERHEATER

Side View   Front View

1. Smokebox Barrel
2. Smokebox Ring
3. Boiler Barrel
4. Front Tube Plate
5. Superheater Header
6. Regulator Valve
7. Regulator to Header Supply Pipe
8. Header to Cylinder Supply Pipe

9. Main Steam Pipe
10. Flue Tube
11. Superheater Element
12. Superheater Securing Nut
13. Bottle End
14. Rear Tubeplate
15. Securing Strongback
16. Header Mounts

a strong back with a single nut to attach the triple element clusters. This makes his design relatively easy to maintain and enables replacement of elements that are damaged or life-expired, and as a result reduced maintenance costs as well as improving the efficiency of the locomotives.

Superheating is quite simple in theory but benefits from a little explanation. Firstly you have to get your head around the concept of wet and dry steam. Wet or saturated steam is that which you see when you boil your kettle. At atmospheric pressure the water boils when the temperature reaches 212°F (100°C). Raising the water pressure increases the amount of energy required to boil it, and therefore you need to increase to a higher temperature in order to do that. Therefore water at 85psi requires the temperature needed to make steam to be 327°F (163.9°C), and at the 225psi working pressure of the Castle's boiler 397°F (202.8°C). This saturated steam is perfectly useable, of course, but there is a way to get more energy into the steam to make it even more efficient: if you put more energy into the boiler you could create hotter steam, but you will also make more of it, and this in turn raises the boiler pressure further. This can be a problem if your boiler is designed to work at 225psi – either the

safety valves will lift and you will lose the steam, or if the safety valves don't work and there is a horrendous bang as the boiler explodes...

This is where superheating comes in. Because the steam is now in the superheater elements, and has therefore been removed from the main boiler and the water from which it was generated, we can increase the amount of heat within it without increasing the pressure in the boiler. In its journey through the superheater system, the temperature has been raised from 397°F to a little over 600°F (315.6°C). What has happened is that any excess water that was still being carried by the steam has been converted, thereby increasing its volume by about 30%. This is why superheated steam is also known as dry steam. Not that you would want it escaping, but if it did it would be to all intents and purposes invisible, as all the moisture has gone and it has now become a gas.

The advantages of the use of dry steam are that firstly it retains its energy in the cylinders a lot longer, resulting in the offset of condensation and the better use of that energy. The extra volume produces extra steam, and this in turn reduces the amount of fuel burnt (you have had to burn it anyway to get to the saturated stage, so passing it back through the heat is just good economics, reduces the water

LEFT The smokebox on 6672HD. The crinolines for carrying the outer cladding can be seen on the boiler barrel to the right. The attachment point where the smokebox is bolted to the saddle is at the bottom.
(Author)

consumption and reduces the demands upon the boiler – and fireman – to produce large volumes of steam all the time). It was estimated by Churchward that the 625 superheated locomotives that were in service in 1913 had saved the company about 60,000 tons (approx 70,000 tonnes) of coal!

The outside of the pressure vessel is not what you see when the gleaming Castle streaks past you. The boiler is lagged with insulation. This would have been the highly dangerous white asbestos used at the time, which was applied wet with a plasterer's trowel to give a thick layer all over the boiler. Although the mixing process wasn't good, the wet process wasn't the greatest problem – the dry process of chipping it all off was where the major issues started. As a result, a great many of the inhabitants of Swindon suffered from what was known then colloquially as 'Swindon disease' but we now know it as asbestosis or mesothelioma. Needless to say, this asbestos has long since been replaced on the preserved locomotives by a ceramic wool or glass fibre equivalent. On top of that goes a layer of thin sheet steel cladding, formed to the various shapes and curves and then clamped in place by screws and boiler bands. It is this outer layer that carries the paint and lining out. As a result

of the loss of the underlying form provided by the asbestos 'plaster', the modern survivors have steel bands that form a structure for the boiler cladding to form up against. These are known as crinolines – the word, of course, has the same derivation as the structure in historical female attire.

The boiler is somewhat remarkable as it is only fixed to the rest of the locomotive at the smokebox end. The smokebox is a drum type and is 5ft 6½in (1,689mm) long and 6ft 2½in (1,892mm) in diameter. It is attached to the front of the boiler barrel by a strip of plate work that extends beyond the front tubeplate. This section is known as the dry extension, as it is not part of the pressure vessel. There is a rolled steel ring between the dry extension that is shaped to accommodate the difference between the diameter of the boiler barrel and the rolled steel tube that forms the smokebox barrel. The front has a 6in (152.3mm) wide circular ring-shaped pressing with a large hole in the front of it where the smokebox door is attached. The smokebox requires internal access so that it can be emptied of ash and char and to allow easy maintenance of the components within. It does, however, need to be airtight, as the smokebox is a very important part of the efficient working of the boiler.

When the steam has been used in the cylinders, it is sent through the exhaust pipe work up to a device known as the blast pipe. This directs the blast of steam (which still contains considerable energy) up through the chimney. The blast, as it is directed from the blast pipe through the chimney by the petticoat (a sort of funnel attachment on the bottom of the chimney casting), causes a partial vacuum in the smokebox. This has the effect of drawing the hot gasses from the firebox through the boiler. The secondary effect of this is that more air is pulled through the fire, and that causes it to burn hotter. Therefore the harder the locomotive is worked, the hotter the fire burns and the quicker the water boils.

The blast pipe also has what is known as a jumper top fixed to it. This clever device pops open to provide more space for the exhaust to clear the cylinders when the engine is working hard, and thereby eliminates excessive back pressure inside them. This also prevents the huge blast that roars up the chimney from sucking large amounts of air through the grate and tearing holes in the fire bed. When the pressures are normalised again the device closes and the blast pipe works as normal.

The smokebox door has two handles in the centre to lock it. The rear one is attached to a spade-shaped lock that engages in the appropriately named locking bar that stretches horizontally across the entrance to the smokebox. This is turned through 90° to lock it, and the outer one is on a screw thread and this pulls it tight to seal the door.

Also within the smokebox is the pipe work leading away from the regulator/superheater header that distributes the live steam to the cylinders. This splits at each end of the header and then splits again to the outside and inside cylinders on each side. Another device within the smokebox is a twin ring annular casting with a series of holes on the top of the blast pipe that can send a jet of steam up the chimney. This is known as the blower. It is used to either assist with raising steam by drawing air through the fire, or to prevent air rushing down the chimney when the locomotive enters a tunnel or goes under a bridge when the regulator is shut. This can cause what is known as a blowback, which can be very dangerous, as it can cause fire to shoot from the firehole door into the cab. Another interesting feature of the smokebox is the small tap on the driver's side of the front ring. This is known as the lance cock. This was connected by the cleaners and boilersmiths, via a flexible hose, to a steam lance that delivered boiler-pressure steam that was used

BELOW Smokebox arrangements with two-row superheater and jumper top. *(Author's Drawing)*

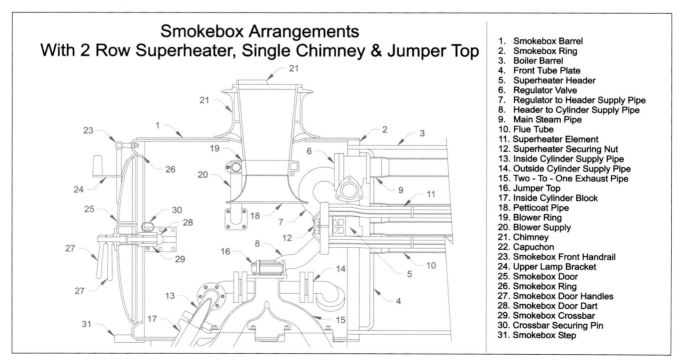

Smokebox Arrangements
With 2 Row Superheater, Single Chimney & Jumper Top

1. Smokebox Barrel
2. Smokebox Ring
3. Boiler Barrel
4. Front Tube Plate
5. Superheater Header
6. Regulator Valve
7. Regulator to Header Supply Pipe
8. Header to Cylinder Supply Pipe
9. Main Steam Pipe
10. Flue Tube
11. Superheater Element
12. Superheater Securing Nut
13. Inside Cylinder Supply Pipe
14. Outside Cylinder Supply Pipe
15. Two - To - One Exhaust Pipe
16. Jumper Top
17. Inside Cylinder Block
18. Petticoat Pipe
19. Blower Ring
20. Blower Supply
21. Chimney
22. Capuchon
23. Smokebox Front Handrail
24. Upper Lamp Bracket
25. Smokebox Door
26. Smokebox Ring
27. Smokebox Door Handles
28. Smokebox Door Dart
29. Smokebox Crossbar
30. Crossbar Securing Pin
31. Smokebox Step

to blast the boiler tubes clear of soot when the locomotive was in the sheds being serviced.

At the rear the boiler is held to the frames on a sliding bracket arrangement. There are two long twin-section sliding brackets that are bolted via steam-tight studs that pass all the way through the outer firebox. These, when mounted to the locomotive, rest on the top of the frames, just in front of the cab. They are clamped to the frames by the appropriately named holding-down brackets. These are steel plates with a hook-type section along one edge that interfaces with the firebox brackets and keeps them clamped to the top of the frames but still allows them to slide back and forth. This is, of course, very necessary, as the boiler expands and contracts as it heats up and cools down. There can be as much as an inch (25.4mm) or so difference between the length at each end of the thermal cycle, and as a result the controls actually extend further into the cab when the engine is at working temperature. These brackets are by no means infallible and even with good lubrication can sometimes stick. The result can be an earthquake-type situation where eventually something has to give, and when the boiler does finally overcome the jam the resultant loud bang as the tension is released has caused many a member of shed staff over the years to jump out of their skin.

Injectors

A steam locomotive has a fundamental problem when it comes to replenishing the water level in the boiler. This is twofold. Firstly, as the boiler is a sealed pressure vessel it will be necessary to maintain the boiler pressure whilst feeding in water. This is relatively easy to overcome by the use of a non-return valve. On a GWR locomotive, non-return clack valves are mounted either side of the safety valve casting on the top of the boiler. They are simple one-way valves that are held shut by boiler pressure and opened by the injection of feed water. They have earned their name by the noise they make when they slam shut, thereby making an audible 'clack' noise.

The second, larger problem is how to overcome the pressure in the boiler in order to get feed water in. In the early days of the

railways, this was achieved by the simple expedient of connecting a mechanical pump to the locomotive that was driven as it went along. This was clearly unsuitable as it made it necessary to detach the engine from the train, when the locomotive was waiting for its next duty or at a station, and run it up and down to get water into the boiler. Steam-powered pumps were also tried, but these were inefficient as well as being a maintenance headache. Frenchman Henri Giffard came to our rescue in 1858 when he invented the steam injector. This was patented in the United Kingdom by Messrs Sharp Stewart & Co of Glasgow.

Unlike a pump, an injector effectively has no moving parts. It consists of a series of cones. The first one facing into the injector is the steam

LEFT A message from the past… John Lyas was here! The welcome graffiti is on the spring plate to return the boiler to its original position on cooling. Above are the grate carrier brackets, being used as boilersmith carrying brackets with a temporary wooden floor in the firebox. *(Author)*

BELOW A schematic drawing of the GWR-type live steam injector. *(Author's Drawing)*

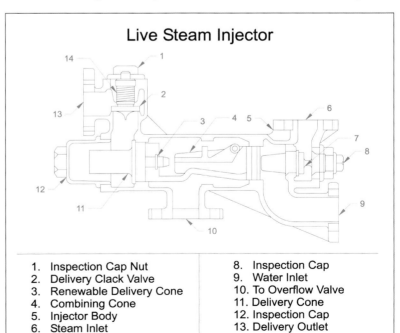

Live Steam Injector

1. Inspection Cap Nut
2. Delivery Clack Valve
3. Renewable Delivery Cone
4. Combining Cone
5. Injector Body
6. Steam Inlet
7. Steam Cone
8. Inspection Cap
9. Water Inlet
10. To Overflow Valve
11. Delivery Cone
12. Inspection Cap
13. Delivery Outlet
14. Valve Spring

cone. In our case this is steam at boiler pressure, and this narrowing of the pipe essentially creates a Venturi effect. A Venturi effect is where a fluid or gas flowing through a conical constriction in a pipe experiences both a drop in pressure and a rise in velocity. At the end of this cone the drop in pressure sucks in the water, which mixes with the steam in what is known as the combining cone. During this process the steam condenses and transfers all of its energy to the water in the form of velocity. This results in a very powerful jet that is now capable of overcoming the pressure in the boiler that is holding the clack valves shut. A small gap known as the overflow allows excess steam and water to flow out of the injector when the device is started.

The combining cone is very carefully aligned with a third cone known as the delivery cone, this time facing in the opposite direction. As the steam and water mix passes through the delivery cone its special shape allows the steam's velocity energy to convert back to pressure. The feed water will now have the required pressure to open the clack valves and enter the boiler. The combining cone of a GWR injector also has a hinged flap portion that in normal operation is held shut by the forces of operation, but if there is a problem – through vibration or small variances in operation that cause the flow of water to be upset – the resultant overpressure forces the hinged flap open. This releases the pressure into the overflow, the hinged section snaps shut again and the injector automatically resumes operation.

There are two types of injector on a Castle Class locomotive. The first is of the live steam type which, as its name implies, uses steam direct from the boiler as the motive fluid and operates pretty much as described above. These are relatively small units; however, the other type of injector on this engine is definitely not. The exhaust injector, as its name suggests, makes use of exhaust steam to assist with the injection of water into the boiler. Its name is also something of a misnomer, as it also supplements the exhaust steam with live steam for its operation. It is nevertheless a more efficient way of achieving the same outcome, making use of heat energy that would otherwise be lost. It is, however, only of use where an engine is in motion for long periods of time to sustain its operation. This means it can work on both a mix of exhaust/live or live steam only. As the exhaust steam supply is variable, the changeover is automatic, via a pressure-sensitive valve in the body of the injector. Unlike more modern exhaust injectors, however, this changeover is one-way, and if the exhaust steam supply is lost the injector will stop working. The fireman, therefore, must be aware of the layout of the railway on which he is travelling and what the driver is doing in order to keep it running. This type of injector has not only a live steam but also an exhaust steam motive fluid cone prior to the combining cone. It can be best described as a sort of steam combining cone.

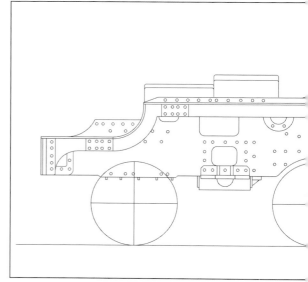

Exhaust steam also comes with its own issues, not least of which is the fact that not only is a long pipe run required to get it from the smokebox to the injector, but it is also carrying the lubricants used in the valves and cylinders. A grease separator is therefore required to prevent this material entering the boiler.

Both types of injector are made from large LG4 bronze castings that are machined for the purpose, and both have removable cap nuts to facilitate the withdrawal of the inner workings of the injector and the steam cones – which are renewable, as they are subject to the most wear. The injectors are mounted under the cab on brackets fabricated from steel plate. This makes the pipe runs from the steam and water supply valves relatively short and allows the fireman to observe the function of the overflow when starting the injectors. To ensure the water is flowing, it is good practice to turn the water valve on, look over the side to ensure that it is flowing and then introduce the steam. The overflow pipes are mounted so that they eject to the rear of the cab steps, and the pipe is directed to empty towards the outside of the track.

Frames and structures

The frames of Castle Class locomotives are made from 1¼in thick (31.8mm) steel plate. These were cut out using oxygen/coal gas torches (Swindon had its own plant for producing coal gas). They were then shaped

ABOVE The other side of No 4073 shows the live steam arrangements. The pipe in the top is the live steam supply and the hose connection to the rear is the water feed. Underneath at the far left is the overflow valve. On the right is the ATC shoe – of which more later. *(Author)*

using a purpose-made slotting machine. Next the holes were drilled using a special extra-long, multihead drilling machine. This was undertaken with the frames in a stack, enabling the frames for more than one locomotive to be prepared at the same time. They were also pressed to form the front end 'joggle' (this became the dish on later variants) to clear the bogie wheels. The two plate frames were held apart by a variety of different types of stretchers. At the front end the massive cast iron inside cylinder block

BELOW This is based upon the original drawings for the 5013-type Castles but it ably illustrates the way the frames are arranged in a Castle Class locomotive. *(Author's Drawing)*

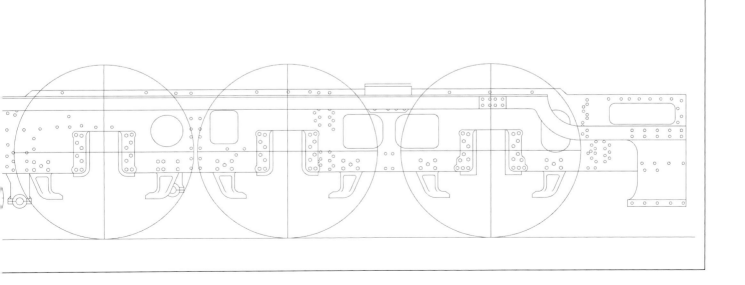

RIGHT What that all looks like in real life: the frames of *Pendennis Castle* while under overhaul at Didcot. The cylinder blocks are at the bottom of the picture. In between the outside cylinders can be seen some of the cast stretchers that are pierced to allow the various motion components to move about. The two linkages reaching back from here are for the reverser, and the connection between them and the reverser pedestal in the cab is seen resting on the top of the frames. Further back we can see the brake cylinder and then the horizontal vacuum reservoir. The next large gap, where the final driving axle can be seen, is the space for the firebox, and the space at the far end is where the rear drag box would normally be located, but is being replaced due to wastage.
(Chris Handby)

performs this function. It has all of the steam passages and ports along with the valve and cylinder apertures precast into it so that only the bores and any faces that interface with other components required machining to finish. It also contains the saddle in which the smokebox rests. This is in two sections, the front half being integral with the inside cylinder casting while the second half incorporates the exhaust pipe work from the outside cylinders to the two-to-one adaptor to which the blast pipe fits.

As we go further back the next major structure is the bogie pivot. This has a large machined central pin to locate the bogie, and there are two hemispherical side supports bolted to the outside of the frames. The outside cylinders are next, and there are a number of cast stretchers between the frames to resist the massive stresses imparted by the pistons, but these are all carefully perforated with a number of slots, holes and mounting points to accommodate the valve gear. A little further back there are plate stretchers, and between these the vacuum brake cylinder is mounted on a pair of trunnions. Next is the space where the firebox and ash pan sit.

Finally comes the cab. This is a fabricated structure. It provides a firm base for the locomotive with swept-down cab sides that are so characteristic of later GWR practice. Also contained within this structure is the rear drag box. This is the area where the couplings for the tender are attached, and when you realise that all the forces exerted on the train by the locomotive go through this structure

you will understand why it is constructed in a correspondingly strong manner. There are two horizontal steel plates riveted to the rear of the main frames via a number of angle iron brackets and specially shaped sections. The connector itself is a massive forged eye bolt with a simple drop pin that secures the special tender bar coupling in place. There are two smaller versions of these either side of the main one in case the primary coupling should fail. The eye bolts are fixed to the frames via a steel cup-type structure and a series of sheets of rubber in order to lessen the 'structural shock' should either the train or the locomotive suddenly snatch as it is in motion.

The front-end coupling arrangements are somewhat different for two reasons. Firstly, it is a simple screw link-type coupling used on many types of rolling stock throughout the British Isles. Secondly, it has to be capable of being removed to allow for inspection and repair of the inside cylinders. To facilitate this, unlike the majority of GWR locos – which have riveted front plates, known as buffer beams – it is bolted to the frames of the locomotive via two cast brackets. It is also bolted at its outer edges to the hanging bar (the bottom of the running plate). The plate on its own would not be sufficient to support the weight of a train or a pilot locomotive on the front buffer beam, as there is no support for the plate over quite a distance between the frames. The solution to this is a V-shaped bracket that bolts around the coupling hook aperture at the front and leads back to the main frames just ahead of

BELOW Two views of No 4079's rear drag box. This area had become heavily corroded and required almost complete replacement when the overhaul started. On the left we see the job about 50% completed, showing a rare view inside the structure. On the right we see the finished job. The two heavy sections are the buffing plates that absorb the forces from the tender buffers. The smaller, lower slot is where the three couplings link to the tender and the new injectors are in the process of being fitted. *(Peter Chatman & Frank Dumbleton respectively)*

RIGHT The cab area with the steps and the hanging bar is visible, as is the tiny ledge arrangement around the cab side sheet with its tiny step to enable the crew to get to the running plate above – not the most generous walkway ever provided! To assist the crew a handrail is also provided under the cab window. *(Collection of Sir William McAlpine)*

the cylinders. The coupling hook then passes through the buffer beam and is secured as at the rear, via the steel cup, rubber layers and a large diameter nut with a split pin.

Around the edge of the frames is the running plate. This is the 'walkway' that allows shed staff and crews to access the upper parts of the locomotive for maintenance. This is reinforced around its edge by the hanging bar referred to above. Holes to allow the wheels to penetrate the running plate are cut into it and the wheel tops are covered by sheet steel covers called splashers. There are three of these per side. The rearmost pair continue into the cab and therefore do not form the whole circular sector shape, and the middle pair are wider to allow the rods attached to the wheels below to clear whilst in motion. The running plate is reduced to a thin strip around the cab sides with a step and a handrail. This is the only way to access the upper parts of the locomotive as there are no steps at the front end – something a modern Health and Safety risk assessment would never countenance!

Bogie

The bogie is the four-wheeled carrying truck at the front of the locomotive, which serves a number of purposes. Firstly and most obviously it helps to carry a small proportion of the load of the cylinder block and smokebox

BELOW The Swindon/De Glehn bogie is a masterstroke of engineering. It has a compact springing system, is very strong and is beautiful to look at as well. In this preservation view, we can see the pads on the side that contain the hemispherical bearings; the large inverted leaf springs used for the suspension of the wheels can be seen at the top of the equalising beam. The guard irons at the front of the bar frame prevent any objects left on the track from going under the wheels. *(Collection of Sir William McAlpine)*

end of the engine. It also helps to guide the fixed wheelbase of the coupled driving wheels into curves. This not only improves the ride of the engine but also reduces wear and tear on the track. The design of the Swindon bar-framed four-wheel locomotive bogie is based on one pioneered by Alfred De Glehn, the noted English-born French locomotive engineer. The inspiration undoubtedly came from the French compound locomotives bought by Churchward to evaluate in the early 20th century. As with all things imported to Swindon, there has been just enough change to both improve it and escape copyright payments... The first locomotive to receive the Swindon–De Glehn bogie was Star No 4011 *Knight of the Garter* in March 1908, and as other 4-6-0 machines entered the works for overhaul they had the same type of unit fitted. They were fitted to all Castles from the first engine.

The bogie itself has a series of bar frames that make up the basic structure of the truck, and a set of slides at each corner to accept the bogie wheel bearings. It has a wheelbase of 7ft (2,133.6mm) and the wheels themselves are 3ft 2in (965.2mm) in diameter. The springing is achieved by a pair of large leaf springs mounted inverted, one each side, and located behind the wheels. These are fitted between a pair of equalising beams that have a horn-type shape at their ends. The outer ends of the springs are attached to the equalising beams and the centre is attached to the bogie pivot casting and thus to the frame of the bogie. The horns press down on the top of the axleboxes, thus providing springing. This provides the vertical springing but the lateral springing is dealt with in the pivot casting.

The actual pivot itself that engages with the bogie pin on the frames is mounted on a cross slide that is controlled by a pair of coil springs, one in front of the pivot and one behind it. This is the part of the mechanism that guides the front of the engine into curves. As the bogie negotiates around a curve, the springs around the pivot transmit energy to the bogie pin. This then has the effect of pulling the front of the locomotive into the curve. This does mean a slight increase in tyre wear on the bogie wheels but lessens the wear on the leading coupled driving wheels, which are not

ABOVE Rightly pleased with his day's work, volunteer Dudley Alleway stands next to No 4079's bogie frame. The simple and almost delicate-looking structure belies its immense strength. You can also see the guard irons and the guides for the axleboxes. The pivot casting is in the centre and the lateral springing gear is underneath this component. *(Dudley Alleway)*

BELOW No 4073 again. The bogie centre pin with its retaining collar can be seen here under the bogie. The two lateral control springs that help guide the front of the locomotive into curves in the track are fore and aft of the pin. Also of interest are the train pipe for the vacuum system attached to the bottom of the bogie, and the canvas-covered flexible rubber sections at either end. *(Author)*

ABOVE The first of the major castings at the front end of No 4079. The narrow cylinder casting is unique to her, 4073 and 4003 in preservation. The valves are over the top of the cylinders, and the two 'rectangular tube'-like structures are the exhaust passages that connect to the blast pipe. The hole in the centre between the valves and the cylinder is the mounting point for the snifting or anti-vacuum valve that assists when the locomotive is coasting with no steam supplied to the pistons. *(Russ Heyluer)*

BELOW An interesting view of the inside cylinder block of the Castle. The second section, comprising the exhaust pipes from the outside cylinders and the rear of the saddle for the smokebox, had to be removed to repair a crack. You can see the mating faces in the unpainted sections of the frames. Also visible are the slide bars (covered in anti-corrosion oil-soaked paper) connected to the rear covers of the inside cylinders. Inboard of the slide bar brackets are the two mounting points for the pressure relief valves. Above are the valve bores for the rear of the cylinder block. *(Author)*

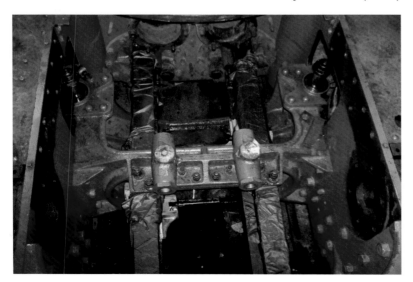

only larger and therefore more expensive to replace but also far more difficult to replace, as the whole of the engine's motion has to be removed before the wheel set can be dropped out. This arrangement also helps to control the forces of the pistons as they impart lateral forces to the track. The weight of the front end of the locomotive is transmitted through the two hemispherical bearers that are bolted to either side of the locomotive's frame just forward of the outside cylinders and in line with the bogie pin casting. These sit in bronze cups that rest on flat, machined bronze surfaces on the bogie that allow movement in a variety of different planes.

Cylinders

There are four main castings that go to make up the cylinder block of a Castle Class locomotive. The largest and heaviest is the inside cylinder block. From the bottom upwards, there are two 16in (406.4mm) diameter cylinder bores with a stroke of 26in (660.4mm). The cylinders have a cover at each end that is fixed in place with 16¾in (19.05mm) diameter studs, washers and nuts around its end circumference. Both have a large brass pressure relief valve mounted in their lower half to help if an over-pressure situation is brought on by water in the cylinders (known as a 'hydraulic').

The rear covers also incorporate the front mounts for the slide bars in which the crossheads run and the mounts for the packing gland that makes a steam-tight joint between the piston rod and the cylinder cover. Along their internal length the cylinder bores have a number of holes in them. The first are at the bottom and are the all-important cylinder drains. Mounted on the outside of the cylinder casting on the other end of these holes are the cylinder drain cocks. These are valves that are operated via a fairly complex linkage system leading to a single lever in the cab. They are opened when the locomotive is in steam and at rest. When the locomotive sets off they are left open for the first few cycles of the valve gear. This way, they allow the water that forms from the condensation of steam while the engine is stationary to be ejected. If this water is not expelled, and builds up to an extreme level whereby the pressure relief valves mounted on the front and rear cylinder covers cannot cope, this will cause hydraulic pressure to build (due to the incompressibility of fluids) to such an extent that the front and/or rear covers can be blown off or, in extreme cases, the cylinder block could rupture. There are two ports in the top of the cylinder's circumference at each end. These are the live steam and exhaust ports.

Above and slightly inboard of the cylinder bores are the valve bores. It is perhaps a little misleading to talk about them in terms of being two cylindrical tubes, as the surfaces on which the valves run are only at the front and back of the casting. There is a central live steam 'void', which is why this area is more often known as the steam chest. The steam chest is linked to the top of the casting by an internal passageway that terminates in a flange to which is coupled the live steam supply from the boiler. At the other end, the steam chest leads to an inboard annular ring of steam ports that supply the steam to the valve. There is a further ring of larger ports to the outboard of the live steam ports and these lead off to the exhaust pipe work and up to the blast pipe. These ports have to be larger than the live ones, as by the time the energy of the steam has been used in the cylinders it has expanded in volume, and the greater size allows it to exit the cylinder and avoid any back pressure on the piston as it is pushed by the live steam at the other end.

These internal passageways come up and over the top of the steam chest and join together at the back of the cylinder block before exiting up through a single flanged square-section tube. The valve bores have a cover with a bearing in it at each end. The front ones have a cylindrical casting with a hemispherical end bolted to the centre to allow the valve stem to move within it. The rear ones have a more complex arrangement to house the steam-tight gland that allows the valve rod to pass through and connect to the valve gear. These covers are fixed in place with a circle of six studs, nuts and washers. To reduce the weight but maintain the strength of the component, the outside has a number of strengthening ribs where the full thickness of metal is not required for functional purposes.

The vertical sides of the cylinder block are machined flat, and this is where it is connected

ABOVE When No 4079 returned to Didcot, one of the things missing was the GWR-style cylinder drain cocks and all the control linkages. The originals were removed at some time in preservation and lost, so this whole mechanism had to be remanufactured from scratch. Here we see (left to right) Angus Pottinger, Mike Bodsworth (4079's pressure vessel manager and GWS council member) and Clive Sparling ensuring a good fit of the new linkage under the driver's side cylinder. On the ground can be seen one of the valves. *(Frank Dumbleton)*

to the frames with a series of fitted bolts. Also mounted on the block and connected to the cylinders are a number of anti-vacuum/back pressure or snifting valves. These are valves that open up automatically when the locomotive is coasting or moving without the

LEFT The missing component from the previous photograph above the frames. Back from its repair, it is seen here upside down, awaiting refitting. The crack was in the mating flange between the block and the two-to-one exhaust pipe. This is the only part of the four main front-end castings that has no moving components in it. Despite the locomotive being well over 80 years old it still took two full days to remove it properly, and a further two to replace it. After all that time the fit is still *that* good. *(Author)*

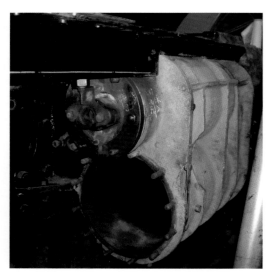

regulator being open and the cut-off is in certain positions. When this happens, the pistons, rather than being the motive power of the engine, can begin to act like pumps, causing a vacuum in the cylinders. This not only causes loss of momentum but also leads to exhaust steam, and possibly ash and char, being drawn into the cylinders, which causes unnecessary wear. For a variety of reasons it can also cause lubrication problems. Despite the valves, it was always considered good practice to keep the regulator open just a crack to allow a wisp of steam to flow when the engine was coasting with the valve gear at certain settings.

As well as bearing the steam supply and exhaust pipe flanges, the top of the inside cylinder block is formed into an inverted saddle shape into which the front of the smokebox is bolted. A separate casting, mentioned previously, sits behind the main inside cylinder block and incorporates the exhaust pipes for the outside cylinders, the square flange to which the exhaust pipe joins up, and the rear

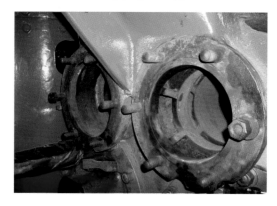

half of the smokebox saddle. The two other large iron castings are the outside cylinders, a mirrored pair of castings which contain a steam chest and a cylinder each. They share a broadly similar layout to those found in the inside cylinder block but with a few alterations. Firstly, the steam chest is directly above the cylinder so as to reduce the width of the casting as far as possible and keep the locomotive within the loading gauge. It too has strengthening ribs where the full thickness is not required. The exhaust steam passages exit via the front of the casting and through a hole in the frame, the other side of which is a flange and exhaust pipe for the rear saddle casting. The vertical side that bolts up to the frames is machined flat and incorporates a cut-out to enable the bogie wheel to move past it when the locomotive is cornering.

The live steam supply is brought into the steam chest via a flange on the top of the casting that passes through the running plate. These are connected to the live steam supply in the smokebox with a 3½in (88.9mm) diameter pipe that bends through 90° towards the front of the locomotive and then another 90° into the smokebox. This pipe is lagged to prevent heat loss and then covered in sheet steel cladding. There is a snifting valve mounted on the front of each outside cylinder casting, just inside the cylinder and valve bores. The valve cover, with a gland packing in it, is on the front of the casting to meet with the rocking arm that drives it. The valve tail cover casting is therefore on the rear cover.

Naturally, as time goes by the valve and cylinder bores wear. To accommodate this there were a number of standard sizes they were machined out to on works visits. They went from A1 to A3 and then from B1 to B3; B3 was considered to be the cylinder block's final size. There were then two options open to the engineers at Swindon, the more straightforward being to replace the cylinder block. No 4079, according to its records, is on her third set of cylinders. However, replacing them was a costly process requiring much labour and materials.

The second solution, developed later on in the life of the GWR, was simply to bore out the diameter one last time and fit a new cast iron liner in place of the original running surface. These liners had to be of an interference fit, and the method of fitting them was somewhat extreme. The cylinder block itself had a fire lit in it 24–48 hours before the fitting was to commence. The fire was constantly attended to during that time, and the heating caused the cylinder block to slowly expand. At the end of the heating period the new liners were put into vats of dry ice (frozen carbon dioxide), which caused them to shrink. The fire was then raked out of the block and, hopefully (!), the difference between the heated block and the frozen liner was enough to allow the latter to slide into place.

When the temperatures had returned to normal four holes were drilled into the four cylinder liners. The two outermost were for the cylinder drain cocks and the two inner ones were threaded to receive bronze securing bolts to further retain the cylinder liners. The eight valve liners are retained by a combination of the interference fit and the protection provided by the end covers themselves.

When fitting liners in preservation we avoid heating the cylinder and they are fitted with the simple expedient of liquid nitrogen, which freezes at −210°C (−346°F) and can therefore get the liners far colder and means that only the liners have to be chilled. With dry ice atmospheric pressure sublimation/deposition occurs at a mere −78.5°C (−109.3°F).

Valves

Steam locomotive valves have a number of functions that require explanation. Firstly, they act as a kind of switch to supply live steam to one side of the piston and then to the other. Whilst they do this, they also have to allow the exhaust steam out. The valves in a Castle are of the piston type and look like long, extended dumbbells. In the valve bores there are two sets of ports: the inner port is the live steam 'supply' and the outer is the exhaust. As the piston moves backwards and forwards, the heads cover and uncover these ports in the correct sequence to power the piston. The dimensions and position of the heads is critical to the efficient running of the locomotive.

The period of valve events must be carefully

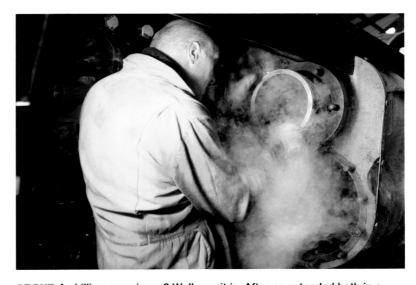

ABOVE A chilling experience? Well, yes it is. After an extended bath in a tank of liquid nitrogen, a replacement valve liner is refitted to the bore. All of the moving surfaces on No 4079's cylinders have been replaced, meaning eight valve liners and four cylinder liners have been cast, machined, fitted and bored out to suit. *(Frank Dumbleton)*

calculated so as not to create too much compression on the side of the piston that is exhausting steam, otherwise this would rob the engine of power and it would essentially be fighting itself, which is very inefficient. Conversely, when a locomotive is running quickly the piston valve is moving very fast and the wheels can be doing several revolutions a second. This means that the amount of time available to allow the steam into the cylinder can easily be less than a tenth of a second. The valve therefore opens just before the piston reaches the end of its exhaust stroke. This is known as the lead. It is the fine balance between the lead and the lap that makes or breaks the design of a valve, and it is this that Churchward spent so much time perfecting in the early 20th century. The design he developed came from an American idea and is known as the semi-plug type.

Castle valves comprise a valve head on each end of a central shaft that is fixed in position by a large diameter brass nut. The nut is prevented from coming off by a taper pin that goes through the nut and the shaft. The pin is split at the end and is opened out to prevent it falling out during operation. There is a shorter section of shaft that protrudes beyond the

valve heads. One end is plain, sits in the closed end of the valve chest and runs in a bronze bearing which is lubricated internally. The other end is different, dependent upon whether it is an internal or external valve assembly. The external valves have a simple taper that is fixed in place with a cotter pin to the external valve adjuster. The internal valves have a thread on the end that forms the internal valve adjuster with two nuts and a locking clip that bolts into place. These ends likewise run in bronze bushes but also incorporate the parts and springing required to produce a steam-tight gland packing.

The valve heads themselves are a work of art in their own right – a very simple but very clever design. They consist of two cylindrical castings, each forming half of the valve head. The inner part of the head has a series of holes that forms a steam passage between the steam chest and the inside of the valve. Between the two main castings there are a series of rings that work in concert to provide a seal against the valve bore. The two outer rings, or snap rings, are the ones that run against the wall of the valve bore. These have a split in them arranged so that the end of one slides inside the other, thereby maintaining a steam-tight seal. They also have a groove in the inner edge into which slots the spacer or

wide ring that holds the two snap rings against the inside edges of the valve head. This has a series of grooves around it and has a straight expansion split in it. Inside this assembly are a series of wedge rings. There are two outer rings that are square on the outer edges and bevelled on the inside. The inner ring is bevelled on both the outer and inner edges. As steam is applied the centre ring is forced up against the two other bevel rings, which forces the two snap rings up against the valve bore, thus making it steam-tight – but only when steam is present. When the steam is off and the locomotive is coasting, the valve head is free to float inside the bore. This reduces both wear and friction.

Because both valve heads are supplied with steam from their inside faces (known as inside admission), this means that the forces are balanced and require no more pressure to move them fore and aft with the regulator open or closed. They were a significant challenge to manufacture in the early days of their adoption, but in time the amount of hand-finishing required was reduced considerably, and by the time the Castles were introduced they had been perfected.

Pistons, crossheads, connecting and coupling rods

These are the components that take the power of the generated steam and convert it into mechanical power to drive the locomotive. The pistons are 16in (406.4mm) in diameter and have a stroke of 26in (660.4mm). It is a calculation derived from these figures, combined with the wheel diameter and boiler pressure, that gives the often quoted tractive effort figure used for rail vehicles: this is a measure of the pulling or pushing force that can be exerted by a railway locomotive on other vehicles. The calculation for two-cylinder machines is as follows:

$$t = \frac{c \times P \times d \text{ squared} \times s}{D}$$

– where:

t is tractive effort

c is a constant representing losses in pressure and friction (normally 0.85 is used in UK main-line railway practice)

P is the boiler pressure

d is the piston diameter (bore)

s is the piston stroke

D is the driving wheel diameter

The result should then be multiplied by 1½ for a three-cylinder locomotive and by 2 for a four-cylinder locomotive.

The result of the above maths gives the standard Castle a tractive effort of around 31,625lb, and given that 1lb tractive effort = 0.004kn, this converts to 126.5kn.

The piston head itself is a hollow disc-shaped steel casting that is machined about its circumference to the diameter to fit into the cylinder. It also has two grooves cut to receive cast iron piston rings. These rings are cast and machined slightly larger than required and then split by taking a measured section out. They are then shaped to become springy by tapping the inside circumference with a hammer. Needless to say, it is a highly skilled job to get the correct amount of springing around the entire circumference and not to break or damage the ring. Fitting them to the piston also takes nerves of steel, as they have to be stretched open to fit over the outer edge of the piston head and slid across to click into the groove. Open it too far and it will snap! The piston rod is screwed to the head and is attached at the other end to the crosshead via a taper and cotter pin.

The crosshead provides support for the tail end of the piston rod and creates the connection between the piston and the coupling rod. This is a large steel casting with a cylindrical section protruding from the front that contains the connection for the taper that is on the end of the piston rod and the hole for the cotter pin. Top and bottom are U-shaped channels. These contain white metal bearing

ABOVE This is the driver's side arrangement. The tail of the piston rod has a taper on it, which locates in the hole visible in the front of the crosshead. Also visible is the taper pin hole to secure the piston. The upper and lower slide bars are much more massive on the outside due to the lack of support structures here. The little end is fixed in place with a complex multi-fixing gudgeon pin to ensure it doesn't come loose. The connecting rod stretches back to the centre driving wheel set. *(Author)*

surfaces that run on the slide bars. The slide bars themselves are the guiding surfaces that constrain the movement of the crosshead. They are large, flat, forged and machined bars that are suspended between brackets cast into the rear cylinder covers and a special bracket on the outside of one of the frame stretchers on the inside. They are aligned by the use of brass packing pieces that are machined to provide the required correction. The crossheads are hollow and open at the rear with a hole through the middle where the gudgeon pin for the little end is located.

ABOVE This is the pair of inside connecting rods looking from the cylinder block towards the leading driving axle. The two massive combined cranks and counterbalance weights can be seen, along with the two eccentrics to drive the valve gear. In the top left is the vacuum pump for the brake system. The brake linkage is in the lower area of the picture, as are the two suspension springs for the driving wheel. All the connecting rods are the same length, hence the forward position of the centre cylinders. *(Author)*

BELOW This is the left trailing (LT) coupling rod retaining nut on No 4079. 'LT' is clearly stamped on it, as are the numbers of locomotives to which it used to belong. Components big and small were swapped at overhaul and the previous owners can sometimes be traced. Crossed out and slightly faded is a 50XX series machine, but more interesting is No 4074 *Caldicot Castle*, No 4079's fellow 1925 trials machine. It is nice to know that a few small parts of this engine are still extant today, and in a most appropriate place! The taper pin is actually threaded over a short distance at the hexagon end and is locked in place by a split pin at the other. Belt *and* braces... *(Author)*

The connecting rods are used to convert the reciprocating motion of the pistons into the rotary motion required to drive the wheels of the locomotive. They are large and immensely strong steel forgings, as befits their purpose. They were formed in a forge where the steel was heated until it was above their re-crystallisation temperature. They were then shaped via the use of a drop hammer. This was not a job for the faint-hearted – the extreme temperatures and the sheer weight of the parts being manufactured made Swindon's F shop (blacksmiths' shop) potentially hazardous in almost every conceivable way, and that is without considering the noise generated by the enormous automatic hammer itself. The hot metal was manoeuvred using a combination of trolleys and cranes and was held and guided by a team of men with specialist tongs. One slip could result in a man falling on to a red hot piece of metal or into a hammer that exerted hundreds of tons of force and was capable of dozens of blows per minute. The purpose of all this activity was to shape a part in such a way that the grain in the metal is continuous and follows the shape of the part. This means that the part has a much higher strength than a similar part that has been cast or cut from a sheet of the same metal.

The rods themselves are of the fluted type, which means that if you were to cut across one the resultant cross-section would be of an 'I' shape. This has the effect of reducing the weight of the component whilst maintaining much of its strength when compared to a square rod of the same section. There is a bearing in each end of the rod. The end that connects with the crosshead (known as the little end) has a bronze bearing made a few thousandths of an inch larger than the hole in the rod. This is then pressed into place using several tons of force. It is possible to have a smaller bearing in this end due to the fact that the joint only undergoes a limited range of movement. This is unlike the bearing at the other end (the big end), which has to undergo full rotations at high speed.

There are two different types of big end bearing. The first is a single tubular type that slips over the pin of the centre set of driving wheels. This is formed from a brass top-hat-

shaped machining that, like the bronze bush in the other end, is an interference fit in the rod. Before it is fitted, however, its internal circumference and the outer 'brim' of the top hat shape (which forms the thrust face that rubs up against the coupling rod bearing) is covered in white metal and machined to suit. One side of the big end of the coupling rod also has a layer of white metal applied to form the other thrust face of the rod bearing. This is then fixed to the pin on the centre driving wheel with a large nut and conically sprung washer. This in turn is fixed in place with a taper pin that has a threaded section at the top. The bottom of this pin then has a split pin through the end. This may seem like overkill, but a connecting rod coming off a steam locomotive at speed had been the cause of several accidents during the steam age, some of which resulted in fatalities. Each of the bearing housings has an oil pot on top of it to lubricate the joint.

This type of bearing is fine for the outside rods but is of no use where the inside connecting rods are concerned. The problem is that the cranks on the inside are on the axle of the front driving wheel set, and each bearing journal is bordered by a massive crank web. What is required here is a split-type bearing where there are two separate bearing half-shells that can be clamped around the crank journal, much like the arrangement in a car engine. The principle may be the same as an internal combustion engine but the practice is very different. This is another of Churchward's innovations brought in from elsewhere and improved to his specification. The design is based on the type found on the De Glehn Atlantic locomotives, and was sometimes known as the 'French' type. The end of the inside rods is formed into a tuning-fork shape with the customary oil pot on the top fork. Into this, the

first bearing half-shell is slid and the rod is then offered up to the crank journal. The second half-shell then slides into the fork. A bearing backing piece, with a hole top and bottom to accept the two forks, is then slid up to the rear of the second bearing shell. This is then fixed in place with a 10½in (266.7mm) long cotter pin with a taper along one edge to wedge the two bearing shells together and closed. The cotter pin then has two retainers bolted in place either side that fit between the top and bottom forks. These bolts have castellated nuts and a split pin to prevent them working loose. In the unlikely event that this little lot was to come off, a secondary failsafe in the form of a cotter pin through the end of the main cotter pin, that is also fixed in place with a split pin, is also provided.

The coupling rods are the rods that link the three sets of driving wheels together. There is a set on either side of the locomotive. The centre bearing shares the pin on the driving wheel with the connecting rod bearing, the coupling rod being inboard and the connecting rod big end outboard. They are in two pieces, the original set-up being to join the rear two together and then have the front wheel set's rods joined up to it via a bronze bush in a knuckle joint. It was later realised that it was far better to join the front two wheel sets together with one rod and have the knuckle joint to the rear wheel set. This was because the connecting rods drive the front two wheel sets and it is far better to have these with a solid connection. Also, the slide bars, crossheads and so on for the outside cylinders are in front of the leading wheel set. This means that it can be a real fiddle to get the pin for the knuckle joint in place. The wheels have to be in the right position, and this means jacking the engine up to allow the wheels to turn. The rear position knuckle is open no matter what the position of the wheels and therefore makes maintenance that little bit easier. The rear wheel bearings, due to their proximity to the firebox and ash pan – as No 4079 found out – were the most likely to suffer from problems, so the connecting rods did not have to be removed.

The bearings that connect the rods to the wheels are of the same type as the outer big end bearing, and the main difference between the designs of the connecting and coupling rods is that the connecting rod cross-section is square. This is due to the early trials with No 40 (later No 4000 *North Star*) at the beginning of the 20th century. Whilst out on test, the locomotive had a nasty habit of bending its I-section coupling rods. The logical step for Churchward was to use heavier square-section rods and this modification was retained for all of the GWR four-cylinder designs until the last one was built in 1950.

Valve gear

The valve gear is the mechanism on a steam locomotive that is responsible for the distribution of live steam and the opening of the exhaust ports in the correct sequence to drive the pistons back and forth in the correct order to move the locomotive forwards or backwards. The amount of steam put into the valves is controlled by the regulator (think of it like the accelerator pedal in a car), but the way that steam is used is controlled by the valve gear. Taking the car analogy further, if the regulator is the accelerator then the gearbox is the valve gear and the gear stick is the reverser. This is where the similarity ends, however. The reverser in GWR four-cylinder engines is of the screw type, as opposed to the equally common lever type. This consists of a four-start screw thread with a double-ended winding handle on one end, and the reverser reach rod connecting to the valve gear at the other.

There is a scale on the top of the frame in which the screw thread is mounted. The neutral or mid-gear position is in the middle of the scale. Going forwards or backwards are graduations up to 75. These indicate the percentage of cut-off to which the valve gear is set, the cut-off being the amount of distance of the piston's travel from one end of the cylinder to the other. So, to start a heavy train the indicator would be wound fully forward to the 75% mark. This means that for every stroke fore or aft of the piston steam is being admitted for

RIGHT Volunteer Leigh Drew tightens one of the coupling rod nuts with one of the many specialist (and very heavy) tools required to keep a machine like *Pendennis Castle* running. Also of interest here is the fact that this is the trailing driver's side nut, and this one has the speedometer drive crank incorporated into it. *(Frank Dumbleton)*

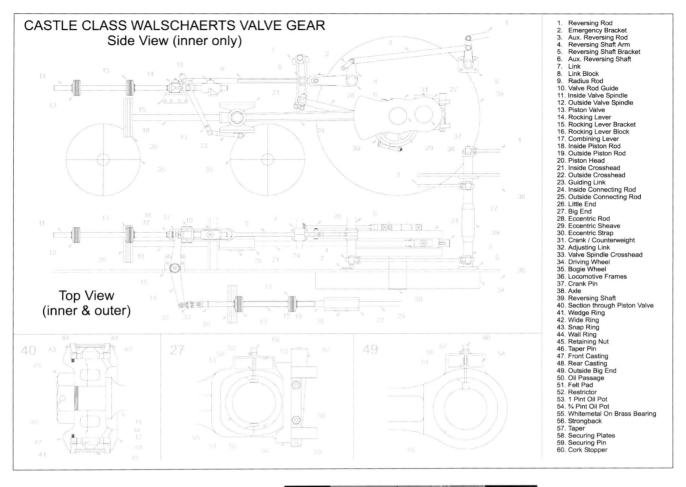

CASTLE CLASS WALSCHAERTS VALVE GEAR
Side View (inner only)

Top View
(inner & outer)

1. Reversing Rod
2. Emergency Bracket
3. Aux. Reversing Rod
4. Reversing Shaft Arm
5. Reversing Shaft Bracket
6. Aux. Reversing Shaft
7. Link
8. Link Block
9. Radius Rod
10. Valve Rod Guide
11. Inside Valve Spindle
12. Outside Valve Spindle
13. Piston Valve
14. Rocking Lever
15. Rocking Lever Bracket
16. Rocking Lever Block
17. Combining Lever
18. Inside Piston Rod
19. Outside Piston Rod
20. Piston Head
21. Inside Crosshead
22. Outside Crosshead
23. Guiding Link
24. Inside Connecting Rod
25. Outside Connecting Rod
26. Little End
27. Big End
28. Eccentric Rod
29. Eccentric Sheave
30. Eccentric Strap
31. Crank / Counterweight
32. Adjusting Link
33. Valve Spindle Crosshead
34. Driving Wheel
35. Bogie Wheel
36. Locomotive Frames
37. Crank Pin
38. Axle
39. Reversing Shaft
40. Section through Piston Valve
41. Wedge Ring
42. Wide Ring
43. Snap Ring
44. Wall Ring
45. Retaining Nut
46. Taper Pin
47. Front Casting
48. Rear Casting
49. Outside Big End
50. Oil Passage
51. Felt Pad
52. Restrictor
53. 1 Pint Oil Pot
54. ¾ Pint Oil Pot
55. Whitemetal On Brass Bearing
56. Strongback
57. Taper
58. Securing Plates
59. Securing Pin
60. Cork Stopper

75% of that movement. This delivers maximum power in the forward direction. This is great for starting a heavy train or when the going gets difficult. If you were to leave it in this position, though, you would soon get beyond the boiler's and fireman's ability to make steam to keep the cylinders supplied.

Without considering the influence of rising or falling gradients, as inertia is overcome and

RIGHT This is a usually unobtainable view of the reverser pedestal and its mechanism, which is usually hidden under cladding and obscured by the boiler. You can see the indicator and scale on the top; the handle is in the vertical position, with the locking handle at the top. The four-start thread and the travelling 'nut' that pulls and pushes on the reverser reach rod is in the mid position, and the guide to hold it steady is on the bottom. The brake pipe is not in its correct position, I hasten to add... *(Author)*

ABOVE Castle Class Walschaerts valve gear. *(Author's Drawing)*

RIGHT Volunteer Doug Middleton shows off his handiwork with a trial-fitting of a new bearing and thrust washers for one of No 4079's combining levers that connects the radius rod (shown in place), the valve rod and adjusters, and the inside crosshead. The lower connection for the valve rod shows the bearing arrangement with three bronze components, the bush itself, which is pressed into the combining lever, and the two outside thrust washers. The flow of oil between the top reservoir and the two bearings is being tested here. Readers will be pleased to know that it passed first time.
(Frank Dumbleton)

speed builds up the amount of energy needed to maintain the momentum is far lower than to attain it in the first place. As a result the reverser can be wound back to a lower cut-off to make more economic use of the available steam. When cruising along at 70 to 80mph (112.65 to 128.74kph) – going through the relatively flat terrain between Paddington and Slough, for example – the cut-off could be wound back to around just 20%. To move the locomotive in reverse, the indicator was simply wound from the mid-gear position backward towards the rear of the locomotive. There is the same range of cut-off in reverse as there is going forward, making the steam locomotive unusual in being able to work as well backwards as forwards. The only limitation for tender locomotives like the Castles is the tender itself. As a relatively small six-wheeled vehicle, its riding qualities as the lead vehicle are not as good as they are as a trailing vehicle. As a result, running at above 45mph (72.42kph) in reverse was avoided.

The valve gear used on the vast majority of GWR steam locomotives was of the Stephenson type. This is fine if you have two cylinders, either inside or outside the frames, but once you start putting four large cylinders on your locomotive you start to get into the problem of space between the frames. This is

due to the fact that Stephenson motion relies on four eccentrics, two for forward and two for reverse motion. This takes up a lot of room, and the fitting of Stephenson gear, big cylinders, connecting rods and so on in the same place becomes difficult.

The valve gear that was eventually chosen for the Stars, Castles and Kings was a Swindon-derived version of the arrangements first developed by Belgian engineer Egide Walschaerts in 1844. Its first known use in Britain was in 1878, when the Swindon Marlborough & Andover Railway's 0-4-4T Single Fairlie entered service. This was a one-off, however, and the gear did not resurface on another British machine until the 1890s. Even when Churchward and his valve gear expert W.H. Pearce were developing their version in the following decade it was still very unusual, but it later became very popular in the United Kingdom, with the vast majority of the more modern outside-cylinder tender locomotives having the outside version of this gear.

However, outside gear did not suit Churchward or the GWR. Apart from the aesthetic considerations, Churchward also objected to the fact that you had to remove a great deal of the valve gear before being able to effect repairs on the big end or the coupling rods. This is because in the outside version, the motion to drive the gear comes from a return crank that is usually mounted on top of the pin to which the big end is connected. To overcome this a pair of eccentrics was used to provide the motion. These were attached inboard of the two cranks on the leading driving wheel axle. This makes for a very compact set of valve gear. The downside, however, is that there is a lot of machinery in a very small space, which makes any maintenance and even daily filling of lubrication pots quite tricky. The possibly apocryphal story is that when confronted with the question as to why day-to-day maintenance was potentially so difficult on his engines, Churchward simply uttered words to the effect that 'My engines don't go wrong'.

The control of the Walschaerts valve gear is centred on the expansion link. This is a curved open frame with a pair of bronze bushes called die or link blocks that can move up and down inside it. It pivots on a centre pair of trunnions that are connected to its eccentric via a strap and rod to drive it fore and aft. The link blocks themselves connect to the radius rod that has a tuning fork shape at the front end, and at the other a slide that is shaped not unlike the eye of a giant needle. There is another link block contained within it, and the end of the radius rod is connected to the reverser reach rod via a linkage. The reverser is therefore capable of lifting and lowering the far end of the radius rod. The angle at which the reverser puts the radius rod is what changes the valve events.

Lifting it to its highest point puts the locomotive in 75% cut-off in reverse, and lowering it to its furthest point puts it in full forward gear. The front end of the radius rod is connected to the top of the combining lever that, as its name suggests, combines the motion of the eccentric and the motion of the crosshead to which it is attached at the bottom via the union link. Just below where the radius rod connects is the connection for the valve itself, which is made a little more complex for two reasons. Firstly, the whole system has to be adjusted to make it work efficiently and to time the valve events in the correct sequence. Secondly, as there is only one set of valve gear per side, the drive has to be divided at this point to power both the inner and outer valves.

ABOVE Another view of No 4073. This time we can see the two expansion links in situ. The drive from the eccentrics is at the inside bottom of each link. The reverser has the effect of lifting or lowering the radius rods (seen going through the expansion links), and the resultant change in geometry changes the valve events. The connection to the reverser is above the bearings, and the cross-member they are attached to is in the middle of the picture. *(Author)*

LEFT Left to right, Jim Secchi, Keith Gilbert, Clive Sparling, Angus Pottinger and Mike Edwards, with your author chaining up in the pit, prepare to lift the leading driving wheels. Of interest here are the cranks and the eccentrics without the straps in position and the two bronze axleboxes. *(Dudley Alleway)*

RIGHT In a period
shot of No 4079 we
see the rocking lever
responsible for the
transfer of the valve
motion from the inside
to the outside valves.
The adjustment for the
motion is on the link
between the valve rod
and the rocking lever.
It takes a great deal of
skill to correctly set up
all four valves into the
correct sequence and
get them in time with
each other. (Collection
of Sir William McAlpine)

The division of drive is taken care of via a rocking lever that pivots on a pin mounted in a hole cut into the frames at the level of the motion. As the valves of the inside cylinder move in one direction, the valves in the outside cylinder move in the other. The rocking shaft itself is slightly cranked to allow for the corrections in the valve gear geometry made on the inside valves. There is a special adjuster on each valve rod. These are in the form of two large-diameter nuts with a series of indentations on the outside that can be wound up and down to lengthen or shorten the valve rod and therefore adjust the timing of the valves. They are locked in position by the use of a locking plate that engages in the indentations in the perimeter of the nuts. The adjusters on the inside are integral with the valve rod and on the outside are part of the knuckle joint that attaches the valve rod to the rocking shaft.

Gland packing

It is most important that all of the various parts of the pistons and valves remain steam-tight. Lost steam is lost energy, and therefore means extra work for the crews and lost profit for the railway company. Sealing static parts, such as the end covers and pipe unions, was simple enough, by means of an asbestos jointing sheet material – replaced today, of course, by a non-asbestos equivalent. The problem, however, comes when moving parts such as the valve and piston rods require sealing. High-pressure steam creates a very hostile environment, and the elastomers of the period when steam was king were simply not up to withstanding it. As a result a different approach was called for. The

solution uses an asbestos-type rope wound in a very specific way around the shaft and then sandwiched between two bronze turnings. The pressure is kept on the turnings via a spring and then the whole lot is bolted down under a cap. The cap is pulled on via the studs on the cylinder or valve end cover, and as the nuts are tightened down the tension increases until the cap seats against the end cover and a steam-tight joint is created. Similar systems, known as glands, are used on the vacuum pump, vacuum cylinder and a few other similar applications on both the locomotive and tender.

Wheels, axles and suspension

The wheels on the locomotive are of three separate designs. There are two axles in the bogie that have 3ft 2in (965.2mm) diameter wheels and inside bearing journals. There are six main driving wheels of 6ft 8½in (2,044.7mm) diameter and inside bearing journals, and there are six tender wheel sets with 4ft 1½in (1,257.3mm) diameter wheels with outside bearing journals. The wheel sets are made up of a forged axle, a pair of spoked wheel centres and a pair of steel outer tyres. The wheel centres are made of cast EN3 steel and are carefully machined to be a very tight interference fit on the axle.

The press required to fit a wheel on to an axle needs to exert a force in excess of 100 tons (101.6 tonnes)! The wheel is also prevented from turning on the axle by the insertion of a cotter. This too is driven in under pressure, although this time it is done with a special pneumatic hammer device. The wheel outer edges are then turned, as are the insides of the tyres. Again, this is done using an interference fit to prevent them slipping in service. Instead of being pressed on, however, they are placed in a circular set of gas burners and then heated in order to expand the internal circumference. The wheel and axle assembly is then lowered into the red hot tyre and allowed to cool. This traps the tyre on the wheel in a very similar way that cart wheels have received their iron tyres for centuries. The tyre is then locked in place using a special securing strip that is locked in the rear face of the wheel. This is known as a Gibson ring, and a special rotary machine is used for locking them in place.

The outside of the tyre is then turned to make it completely concentric to the wheel and to attain the correct tyre profile. The profile of cross-section of the tyre is essential to the riding qualities and safe running of the locomotive. The outer flange must be of sufficient depth to allow the locomotive to stay on the track throughout its speed and power range, and the running surface of the wheel must be tapered. This taper, reducing in diameter outwards from the flange, is why railway vehicles do not need differentials. When a vehicle with four or more wheels goes around a corner, the outside wheel travels a further distance than the inside wheel. In a car this is dealt with by the use of a differential – a set of gears to allow the driving wheels to turn at different speeds. In a rail vehicle this is clearly impractical, as solid axles must be used. The taper on the tyre allows the wheel to ride up one side to the section that has a larger diameter and on the inside to the section that has a smaller diameter. The difference in diameter obviates the need for a differential.

The flanges all have a specific pattern to conform to. The GWR had two types of profile for steam locomotives, the thick and the thin. The thick profile was used on the vast majority

of locomotive wheels, including the bogie and tender wheels as well as the front and rear driving sets. The centre wheel set on a 4-6-0 design, however, was set to the thin profile, and this was to allow the locomotive to transition through curves more easily and reduce the amount of wear on the flanges and, indeed, the track. The driving wheels also require pins to be inserted into the cranks to secure the connecting and coupling rods. Swindon practice was to press the crank pin into the wheel centre and either rivet it over or, in later years, to weld it to the inside of the wheel centre. The crank pin was an interference fit in the wheel centre, and typically an allowance of +0.001in to +0.002in per inch (0.0254–0.0508mm per 25.4mm) of crank pin diameter was added to the nominal diameter.

The wheels are then balanced. This is a complex process as far as the driving wheels are concerned, as the rotational forces that the rods exert upon the wheels have to be taken into account. Large counterweights are fitted opposite the cranks and these have to be very carefully sized and positioned. The only complication to the basic wheel-set design is in the leading driving wheels. Production of the axle on these is made more difficult by the need to include the cranks for the inside

LEFT The locomotive wheels and axles after having been tested with both ultrasonic and magnetic particle impregnation methods to ensure that they are mechanically sound. They have also had their tyres turned to restore the flange to the correct profile. They are not in the correct order here, as the middle driving wheel in the picture is actually in front of the set with the crank axle. The easy way to tell them apart is that the front crank pins are short so they clear the crosshead and slide bars, the centre ones are long to accommodate the coupling and the connecting rods, and the rear set have medium-sized pins as they have to just accept the connecting rod. *(Russ Heyluer)*

cylinders and the eccentrics for the valve gear. The eccentrics are actually fairly simple inasmuch as they are a pair of castings that are clamped together with bolts over the plain centre section of the axle. This is essentially the same basic design as is to be found in the two-cylinder GWR engines. The complex crank axle is another matter entirely. This is made from a number of very heavy forgings that go together to make up the combined crank webs and counterweights, the crank journals and the axle and axle journals proper. Not only does it have to be assembled straight and true but also in the correct orientation to ensure the correct offset of cranks and crank pins on the driving wheels. This is known as quartering. This

alignment is critical, as it determines the way in which the wheels are powered by the cranks.

Suspension is provided through the use of leaf springs in a variety of different arrangements. All wheel sets are arranged in axleboxes that are arranged to slide up and down between two machined vertical surfaces in the frames that engage in corresponding slots in the sides of the axleboxes. The method of springing the bogie has already been described; however, the systems used elsewhere benefit from explanation. In the tender, the frames are set wide enough apart to allow the bearings to sit outboard of the wheels, and the journals that the axleboxes run on are essentially extensions of the axles themselves. The spring is mounted above the box and has a dish on the top that engages with a short post on the bottom of the spring shackle. The spring is retained on each of its outer ends by a pin that is part of a shackle that terminates in a long bolt that marries up with a bracket attached to the frame. These bolts provide the adjustment for the spring. There are two nuts on the end of the bolt; one is tightened or loosened to pull the spring up or release it down, the other is used to lock it in position. There is a split pin arrangement to ensure that it does not come adrift in service.

The axle and its attendant bearings are pushed up into the guides and a keeper plate is fixed across the bottom to ensure that if the tender is lifted the axleboxes and wheels do not fall out. The springs are then tensioned and adjusted after fitting to ensure that the weight is correctly distributed across all wheels. The method for springing for the driving wheels is best described as the same as the tender system but with the whole thing mounted upside down under the wheel as opposed to on top. Here the bearing is inserted first and then a swivelling shackle is connected to the bottom of the axlebox. The spring is then manhandled into position and the adjuster bolts fitted, again in inverse order to that previously explained. The spring is necessarily larger than those in the tender to cope with the increased weight and forces of the locomotive itself.

Bearings

In simple engineering terms a plain bearing is one where a moving part meets the surface against which it moves. In a GWR steam locomotive such surfaces usually comprise a hardened steel surface or journal and a surface made of a softer bearing material. The idea behind this arrangement is twofold. Firstly, the bearing material is carefully selected to reduce friction in the joint. Secondly, rather than the complex and expensive parts (such as the journals on a wheel set, for example) wearing out, the much more easily replaced bearing is the component that suffers the wear. The vast majority of bearing surfaces on the Castle can be grouped into two main categories. Firstly there are plain metal bearings. These are usually made of a leaded bronze material and are simply machined to a running fit clearance of a few thousandths of an inch per inch of diameter. These are to be found throughout the motion, for example, and come in a range of different sizes.

The second variety is the white metal type of bearing that is usually held in a brass shell, into which the white metal is poured and then machined. There are lots of different types of white metal bearing on a Castle, the most obvious being the axle bearings and motion bearings. The inside axle bearings are among the most complex to do and require several surfaces to be coated in metal. There is the main horseshoe or saddle-shaped bearing that

sits on the axle. This has not only the surface that rests on the axle but also a thrust face that allows the inside face of the wheel to run in contact with the bearing when lateral forces are experienced. It also has a U-shaped bearing on the two remaining vertical faces that run in the horns. These are the special faces that line the edges of the frames where the bearings are mounted. These allow the bearing to slide up and down as part of the suspension system. The difficulty in producing these complex shapes is that it not only requires complex jigs to pour them, but the axleboxes also require three separate pours of white metal in order to complete all the necessary surfaces. Given that you also have to heat the bearing to enable the white metal to effectively 'stick' to the brass, the possibility of too much heat and a previously metalled surface beginning to melt becomes a fine line down which engineers have to walk very carefully.

Some white metal bearings are made as two half-shells, such as the big ends on the inner connecting rods. These are cast as half-shells and then dressed to fit together. The machining is done with a jig employed to hold the half-shells together. There are the more simple 'top hat'-shaped coupling rod bearings which have a tapered steel form cast into their centre that is simply pressed out afterwards. Another type of bearing is the U-shaped channel present on the sides of the axleboxes and the top and bottom surfaces of

ABOVE Volunteer Russ Heyluer touches up a few missed paint patches while they are visible prior to re-wheeling *Pendennis Castle*. The bearings are in position on the journals and the springs suspended ready to fit into the loco. The rear axlebox keeps have an eye cast into them, as can be seen. These tie the two sides of the frame together in this area, as the firebox and ash pan fill the void and mean that normal stretchers cannot be used. *(Dudley Alleway)*

RIGHT A typical white metal bearing. This is the left outside connecting rod. The join between the bearing proper and the white metal face fixed to the rod itself can just be seen. The lubrication pot is on the top, with the cork hole visible. The keen-eyed reader will spot that this was once a possession of No 5083 *Bath Abbey*, a 1937 rebuild of Star No 4063. *(Author)*

the crossheads. These can be either filled up completely and then machined back or can have a smaller-than-finished size block cast into them which, again, is pressed out prior to machining.

Lubrication

Lubrication is the introduction of a film of oil between bearing surfaces to reduce friction and wear. Oil has the capacity to cling to and form a very thin film over a metallic surface. This film can be as thin as 1/100,000in (0.0000254mm), but a properly designed bearing will maintain this film and the bearing will actually ride on the surface of the oil and not the metal. Steam locomotive lubrication is of the 'total loss' type, which means that prior to every day's work that the Castle has to undertake all of its 100-plus lubrication pots have to be checked and filled. Missing just one can cause a major mechanical failure. There are also two different types of oil used. A very methodical approach is required to ensure that all the pots are filled and the correct oil is used.

There are three main types of motion in a steam locomotive, all of which require slightly different approaches to the problem of lubrication. These are rotational (as per the axle in the axleboxes), sliding (as found in the crossheads or piston and valve rods), and rocking (as in the little ends of the connecting rods of many parts of the engine's motion). The key to good lubrication is to maintain an oil film over the moving parts.

Of all of these motions, the simplest to lubricate is the rotary as this has the advantage of constantly picking up and distributing oil over the bearing surfaces. The other two require a

little more innovative design to achieve constant lubrication of their moving parts. Also added to the lubrication conundrum is the fact that some surfaces within the locomotive – the valves, pistons and regulator – are exposed to high pressure and high temperature steam. This brings with it a whole new set of problems, not only in the delivery of oil in the first instance but the fact that regular oils have their lubricating qualities destroyed under these conditions. In order to conquer these challenges, Swindon employed six different solutions.

Hand lubrication is where oil is simply poured on to a surface to provide smooth operation. Mechanisms that are treated this way include the slides and linkage for the firehole door, handbrake gear and the screw section of the locomotive's couplings. This will have been simply poured on using a feeder (the name railwaymen give to oil cans) at the start of a day's work and repeated as required.

Siphon lubrication is where the moving part has either an oil pot as part of the component or as an external oil pot that is connected to the bearing via a copper pipe. The pot consists of an internal space where the oil is stored and has a filling hole at the top with a very coarse thread machined into it. The hole is plugged with a cork that is tapered towards the bottom and has a hole drilled down the middle that has a cane dowel inserted into it. This dowel allows air to enter the oil pot as the oil empties. If it wasn't there the oil leaving the pot would create a vacuum, and this would prevent further oil leaving and thereby starve the bearing surface of oil.

On the inside of the pot a pipe leads from the bearing surface to about 1in–¾in (25.4–19.05mm) below the bottom of the cork. The oil sits around this pipe and is drawn up from the reservoir by a worsted trimming. Worsted is a type of yarn, the name of which derives from Worstead, a village in the English county of Norfolk. It is made from the long-staple pasture wool from breeds of sheep such as Teeswaters, Old Leicester Longwool and Romney Marsh. It is the same material as might be used in the making of tailored clothing, such as suits. Here it is used in a series of strands that form a wick that draws the oil up from the reservoir, down the pipe and on to the bearing surface. These wicks are known as trimmings and are made to a number of standard forms that usually incorporate a twisted loop of wire that not only keeps the strands of worsted together but also enables the trimming to be pulled out at the end of a shift to stop the siphoning action and preserve the remaining oil in the pot for the next duty. The manufacture of these trimmings was one of the first things that a young boy who had dreams of becoming a driver would learn. These lubricators are most common amongst the myriad of motion bearings but occur elsewhere too.

Worsted pad lubrication not unsurprisingly involves the use of a pad made of strands of worsted that have tails that lead into a sump of oil which sits below the bearing. This is typically used on axle bearings, where the worsted pad is attached to a metal frame that uses springs to keep the pad in contact with the axle journal as it spins. The oil bath is a separate brass casting that is machined to slide in under the open side of the axlebox. The oil filler is a pipe that sticks out from the main body of the component and is cast integrally with this. It again has a cork stopper in the end to prevent the ingress of dirt and grit.

Felt pad lubrication is another form of siphon lubrication and can be found in the crossheads of the Castle. Like the worsted trimmings, these have a U-shaped felt pad that absorbs and delivers oil either from above or below. Its U shape means that it can lubricate both sides and flat running surfaces of the slide bars at the same time.

Restrictor plug lubrication is most commonly used on the rod bearings, and the oil pot and reservoir design is identical in concept to that for the siphon system. Where it differs is that the restriction plug version does away with the worsted trimming. Instead it uses a restrictor that looks somewhat like a tap used for cutting screw threads. This is screwed into the delivery pipe of the oil pot. The motion of the rods shakes the oil in both the horizontal and vertical axis. This causes the oil to 'slosh around' in the pot, and the small holes left by the restrictor allow a small amount of lubricant to enter the bearing. By careful calculation of the size of the oil pot and the size of the restrictor it is possible to provide a measured amount of lubricant flow to the bearing. The bearing itself has a felt pad in the inner circumference located at the end of the oil delivery pipe, and this distributes the oil across

the width of the bearing and thence across the whole journal. These can be seen in figures Nos 27 and 49 on the valve gear diagram on page 87.

Sight-fed hydrostatic lubrication is a type used on GWR locomotives where the lubricant has to cope with the high heat and pressures in a live steam environment. This not only requires a different supply mechanism but also a different type of oil. Cylinder oil is far more viscous than regular lubricating oil and is also differentiated by its green colour (as opposed to the golden syrup colour of lubricating oil). A number of additives enable the cylinder oil to remain viscous at high temperature, to separate from the steam when introduced to the cylinders but resist the washing action of the moisture and prevent it from carbonising and forming deposits or evaporating too rapidly. It was always the last lubrication task on a Castle, as the procedure was to leave the cylinder oil can on the shelf above the firehole door to warm up whilst all the other work was completed. By the time this was done the

temperature made the oil less viscous and easier to pour. Crews will tell you, however, that this shelf is also there to keep their tea warm.

To the uninitiated the hydrostatic displacement lubricator looks like the work of a mad plumber, but in operation it is quite simple. It relies on the fact that oil floats on water, hence the name. The main body of the lubricator is situated in the cab and looks like a large brass box that is in fact the main steam oil reservoir. Inside there is a quantity of oil floating on a quantity of water. The water enters the reservoir via a saturated steam supply from the main boiler. The steam that exits the valve is then condensed in a coil of small-diameter copper pipe that is located above the head of the driver in the cab roof. Visitors to the footplate of GWR locomotives often ask what the 'heater' is for in the roof, but in fact its use is quite the opposite. Whilst the steam has been condensed it still retains the full boiler pressure behind it, and this pressure forces it to the bottom of the oil reservoir. This in turn forces the oil to the top of the reservoir where it enters the internal oil feed pipe work of the lubricator known as the gallery. The gallery feeds five separate oil control valves. There is one for each valve and cylinder and one for the regulator valve itself. Just above each oil control valve is a small glass tube that allows the driver to see the oil drip upwards under pressure on its way to the front of the locomotive. The rate of oil flow could therefore be very finely controlled by the driver. The oil is then mixed with fresh steam to propel it forward on the long journey in the pipe work concealed under the boiler cladding to its delivery point in the steam supply pipe work at the front end.

There are two main factors when operating a locomotive with this system. Firstly the reservoir can only be filled when the steam supply is shut off and the water is drained down, so it is something that has to be done before the locomotive sets off for its duties. Secondly, because the lubricator only operates when the regulator is open, when the locomotive is coasting the regulator handle is closed and then immediately lifted open a fraction to enable the jockey valve to operate and oil to continue to flow to the front end. It also has the advantage of letting a very small amount of steam into the cylinders, providing a cushioning 'bounce' as they get to the end of each stroke.

Brakes

At its most basic level a brake is a device used to dissipate energy – in the case of a locomotive that energy is its momentum. Energy is dissipated through the use of friction, ie a brake block being pressed against a wheel, which turns the stored energy of the train's momentum into heat energy. After a number of accidents, in 1889 an Act of Parliament decreed that all passenger trains must be fitted with a continuous brake system. This means there have to be brakes on every vehicle in a train, that these brakes can be applied together and instantaneously by either the driver or the guard, and in the event of a coupling failing and the train becoming divided the brakes should automatically be applied and stop the train.

Throughout the 20th-century era of steam in the UK the vast majority of trains were braked using a vacuum-based system. The pressure of atmospheric air is around 15psi (103.4kpa) and a perfect vacuum is 0psi. The scale used by the railway to measure braking was inches of mercury, 0in corresponding to atmospheric pressure and 30in being a perfect vacuum, although weather conditions can vary this to between 28in and 31in. The Great Western system was designed to work on 25in, which was unusual for the UK as all other railways settled on 21in as a standard. This gave benefits in terms of having more brake force available but also caused other technical challenges that had to be overcome. The early systems had a steam brake on the loco and vacuum systems on the train, the advantage of the steam brake being that it is quick to blow off again, which is why it was retained on shunting locos to the end of the steam age. Large locomotives, however, later became vacuum-fitted like their trains.

The vacuum on a Castle is created by the ejector. This is the large piece of plumbing situated just outside the driver's forward cab window. An ejector works by passing steam through a steam delivery cone situated within a larger air cone. The rushing action of the steam causes a kind of 'friction' with the air in the outer cone and is known as entraining. The action of the air being drawn along the pipe leaves a vacuum behind it and thus creates the motive

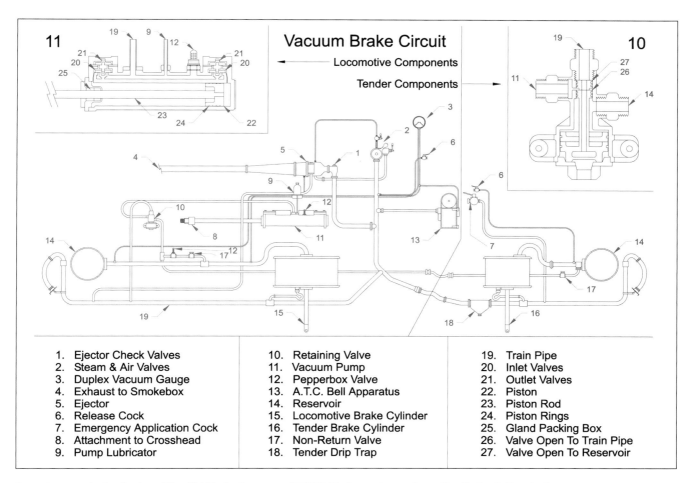

Vacuum Brake Circuit

← Locomotive Components

Tender Components →

1. Ejector Check Valves	10. Retaining Valve	19. Train Pipe
2. Steam & Air Valves	11. Vacuum Pump	20. Inlet Valves
3. Duplex Vacuum Gauge	12. Pepperbox Valve	21. Outlet Valves
4. Exhaust to Smokebox	13. A.T.C. Bell Apparatus	22. Piston
5. Ejector	14. Reservoir	23. Piston Rod
6. Release Cock	15. Locomotive Brake Cylinder	24. Piston Rings
7. Emergency Application Cock	16. Tender Brake Cylinder	25. Gland Packing Box
8. Attachment to Crosshead	17. Non-Return Valve	26. Valve Open To Train Pipe
9. Pump Lubricator	18. Tender Drip Trap	27. Valve Open To Reservoir

ABOVE Brake system schematic. *(Author's Drawing)*

BELOW **The vacuum ejector in front of the cab of No 4079. The actual cones are contained within the casting that has the handrail lands mounted on it. The one-way valve that maintains the vacuum when the ejector is not running is to the rear of the unit, with the pipe twisting away behind the reverser reach rod and under the cladding.** *(Collection of Sir William McAlpine)*

force to operate the brakes. The GWR ejector is what is known as a multi-cone type. There is a series of four cones within the body of the injector. Three are linked together to produce the large ejector. These are used to provide the vacuum as the train is about to move off. This is fine for occasional use, but if it were to be used constantly it would become an undesirable drain on the steam supply from the boiler. As a result, there is a fourth cone that is operated separately and is regarded as the small injector. This is used to maintain the vacuum and keep it topped up. The exhaust steam and air is routed along the large pipe on the driver's side of the boiler and then via a large elbow into the smokebox and out via the chimney.

The problem with this is that the GWR's decision to use 25in instead of 21in means that the potential for leaks – not only in the systems on the locomotive but also in the rest of the train – is far higher, and a minor leak with the vacuum will quickly cause a problem. This, of course, has the potential to bring the train to a

ABOVE Although this is the vacuum cylinder from Churchward Mogul No 5322, it is of the same design as that in No 4079. We can see the top and bottom cover, the piston itself and, underneath it, the rubber band and a broken (hence its removal) cast iron piston ring. The various parts of the airtight gland are also on the trolley. *(Author)*

ABOVE This is a tender vacuum cylinder from the tender of No 2999 *Lady of Legend*, and although it is from a Churchward 3,500-gallon tender it is broadly similar to the one carried by No 4079. This picture shows a counterpoint to the disassembled unit in the previous picture. *(Author)*

BELOW On No 4073 we can see that the locomotive vacuum cylinder is in the centre of this picture. There is a single linkage from the cylinder out to the beam at the top of the photograph, behind the bogie cross-member. Attached to this are the two adjusters leading back towards the first set of equalising links and leading driving wheel cross-beams. A pair of linkages (one of which is rather bent) lead back to the centre drivers, then another set go back again to the trailing set. *(Author)*

halt. To overcome this without resorting to the use of more ejectors, Swindon devised an air pump that was driven by the crosshead of the locomotive. This has the ability to keep up with the inevitable minor leaks without draining the steam resources in the boiler. On a Castle the pump is between the frames and is driven by the driver's side inside crosshead. This pump gives the distinctive 'tick-tick' sound to a GWR locomotive when it is coasting along with the regulator closed.

From the source of its generation the vacuum is piped to the vacuum retaining valve. This sits under the driver's side footplate at the very front of the locomotive. It is essentially a big switch-type valve that, when the brake is applied, switches the pump's action from the train pipe to the reservoir to prevent its action from becoming counterproductive to the brake application. It is connected to both the reservoir and train pipe to ensure a constant pressure is maintained throughout the system. The reservoir is a tank that is used to store a 'charge' of vacuum, and in a Castle this is situated between the frames in front of the firebox with the brake cylinder. The brake cylinder itself has two connections – one above that is connected to the brake reservoir and one below that connects to the train pipe.

The train pipe connects all the other vehicles in the train and is also connected to both the driver's brake handle and a brake 'setter' or guard's brake device in the coach and the emergency cords in the coaches. The theory is that all the time there is an equal vacuum on each side of the brake piston in the cylinder the piston remains still. When the driver operates his brake valve, air is allowed into the train pipe; all the brake cylinders in the train experience a disparity in pressure and this higher pressure on the bottom side of the cylinder forces the piston up and thereby operates the vehicle brakes via a linkage system connected to the piston. When the vacuum is restored to the train pipe the state of equilibrium in the cylinder allows the piston to fall back under gravity, thus releasing the brakes.

The linkage provides brake force to the six main driving wheels via a pair of adjusters that can be lengthened or shortened in order to

either compensate for wear in the cast iron brake blocks or be let out when new blocks are fitted. The cylinder itself is a domed-top design and the piston is sealed against its wall by a sliding rubber band. The only problem with this system is that if the pressure gets too low it is possible that the brakes could be applied whilst pulling a train, and it would not be possible to get them off again. Worse still, however, is the situation where during light engine manoeuvres around a shed at the end of a shift the lack of pressure might mean that the vacuum could not be created though the loco might have enough steam to at least start moving. A runaway loco is no joke at all, and it did occasionally happen, with machines ending up in turntable pits and demolishing the walls or doors of their shed. The tender handbrake could, however, be used in these situations.

Sanding

In order to assist in conditions where the rails are greasy, slippery or icy the locomotive is equipped with a sanding system. This comprises four steel boxes with tapered bottoms that each have a pipe leading down to the head of the rail. The application of sand is controlled by a rotary valve that allows it to flow only when required. The boxes are arranged so that there are two feeding the leading pair of coupled wheels and two feeding the trailing pair of coupled wheels, so there can be sanding in either direction of travel. The valves are connected to the cab via a linkage to a simple lever mounted in the cab floor adjacent to the reverser pedestal. The one point to make is that in order for the sanders to work efficiently the sand must be absolutely dry.

Speedometer

The speedometer is essentially a voltmeter with its gauge recalibrated so that the markings on the dial register different voltages as the speed in miles per hour. The driver's side trailing coupled wheel crank nut has a special extension to the crank pin nut. There is a brass slider that fits into a steel frame and

ABOVE This picture of the driver's side sander affords us a view of several points of interest. The linkage for the sand valve is just on top of the sandbox. The filler cap is also visible and is attached to the loco with an internal chain to prevent its loss. The sand delivery pipe can be seen leading down to the rear of the trailing driving wheel. The live steam injector and its delivery and overflow pipe can be seen as well as the brake hanger and block and the suspension spring and its adjustment bolt. *(Collection of Sir William McAlpine)*

the rotary motion is transferred to a gearbox. The drive is then transmitted via a bevel gear arrangement to a small alternating current generator. The more voltage generated, the higher the reading on the voltmeter and thereby the higher the registered speed. Simple yet effective, but not always accurate; consequently a clever driver would always check his speed alongside a calculation based upon counting the time between mile posts.

BELOW The speedometer and drive crank on the rear driver's side of the locomotive. The lubrication point can be seen as can the electrical wire leading to the speedometer itself. *(Collection of Sir William McAlpine)*

ABOVE A composite
photograph of the cab
of No 5051 *Drysllwyn
Castle* rather than the
cab of under-overhaul
No 4079, but due to
the standardisation of
the GWR footplate the
view is substantially
the same. *(Author)*

Cab and controls

By the time No 4079 was built the cab and
controls on GWR-designed locomotives
were to a greater degree standardised, but there
were a few late developments, notably in the
previously discussed hydrostatic displacement
lubricators and speedometers (not added until
later). The driver's controls were set around
his seat, which is on the right-hand side of the
cab. On the floor are the levers for opening and
closing the cylinder drain cocks and sanders.
Moving up, the reverser sits at waist height on
a special pedestal clad in steel sheet that just
reveals the handle and gauge on the top of
the unit. Just to one side of the reverser is the
speedometer in its own special binnacle.

The next major feature is the lubricator with
its various control taps, sight glasses and filling
points. Moving up the boiler back head there
is the control valve for the blower, the brake
handle and the ejector controls. The ATC box
(of which more later) is on the cab side-wall
opposite. The large regulator handle with its
counterweight and connection to the jockey
valve is mounted in the centre of the back
head, with the handle stretching within easy
reach of the driver. The next major feature is the

duplex vacuum gauge. This has two needles
that display the vacuum in the train pipe on
the left and the reservoir on the right. Each is
graduated from 0–30in of mercury.

The last major controls are the chains hanging
above the driver's head. They are used to operate
two whistles. The first, higher pitch one is the
regular signalling whistle, used while manoeuvring
and shunting. The second is lower pitched and
was originally used by the crew in broad gauge
days for sending braking instructions. This was
before the advent of continuous brakes but was
retained for emergency use. The chain for the
running whistle stretches across the whole cab
so that the fireman can use it if required. Also
above the driver's head on the inside of the cab
roof is the condensation coil for the hydrostatic
displacement lubricator and a small document
holder for any defect report cards and other
notes made by the crew.

The fireman's controls are more spread
around the cab. I will deal with the remainder of
the controls on the back head first. Along the
top is a major casting known as the fountain
or steam manifold, and this is where a great
deal of the steam used in the cab originates.
The main feature is the three spherical-shaped
'global valves'. These are used to control the

steam supply to the injectors. To the left and slightly lower is the Mason steam reducing valve. This is used to control the very low-pressure supply to the steam heating in the coaches. Its attendant gauge is below the pressure gauge and shows graduations in numbers of coaches. To the left of the Mason valve is the all-important boiler pressure gauge. This has a 0–320psi range, and when fitted to a Castle the red line for maximum operating pressure is, of course, marked in at 225psi.

Adjacent to the carriage-heating gauge is the boiler water gauge frame. This is a fairly complex unit in itself and bears closer inspection. The GWR, unlike all the other 'big four' railway companies, only used a single gauge glass. It was enshrined in law that any steam pressure vessel should have at least two methods of determining how full of water the boiler was. To get around this, GWR engineers provided a pair of try cocks as part of the frame. To use these was a simple process of opening the cock. If steam came out the water level was below that point, and if water came out the water level was above that point. The outlet for the cocks is small and is located below the main tap so as not to run the risk of causing clouds of scalding steam to fill the cab.

In front of the try cocks is the gauge glass itself. There are three valves in this set-up. There is a valve top and bottom of the gauge glass itself. These are linked together so that should a glass break, the frame can be isolated in the minimum time to limit the amount of escaping steam. There is a hole in the top valve that is normally sealed with a nut. This allows the glass to be replaced. The seal between the glass and the valves is achieved by rubbers that are pulled up tight by a ring that has a bevel edge inside a nut. The bottom of the glass assembly also has a hole in it to accept a final valve that is used to drain the contents of the glass once the main valves are shut.

The valve empties through a pipe that leads to the track bed. There is also a lamp bracket on the gauge glass, and remarkably it was the only part of the cab to be lit at night, so the weak oil lamp illuminated the glass. A protective metal shroud is placed around the vulnerable gauge glass to protect it from accidental damage and to protect the crews in the event of the glass rupturing. This consists of a three-sided front section with thick glass panes and a solid metal rear section. The rear section is painted in a black and white chevron pattern. This clever expedient means that, because of the refractive

ABOVE The view behind the photographer in the previous shot, and again a composite shot. This is actually No 4078, the Hawksworth 4,000-gallon variant fitted to No 5051 for much of its preservation career, shown here as a counterpoint to the illustrations in the next section. The two water fillers at the top of the picture with modern fire hose attachments are modern fittings for main-line running. *(Author)*

qualities of the water in the glass, the chevrons are reversed when viewed from the front, giving an easy visual check to the fireman.

At the bottom of the back head is the firehole with its two doors, an open and shut linkage and the firehole flap. To the left and sticking up through the floor is a rack of four levers that lift up and down. They control the damper doors on the two sections of the ash pan fore and aft of the trailing driving wheel axle. Above the firehole door is the shelf for warming the thick steam oil. In her later rebuilt form, No 4079 has a fire iron rack on the fireman's side running plate, and this is an enclosure within the open end in the cab. Above this is the oil pot for lubricating the rear axleboxes.

Moving round to the inside of the fireman's cab side, there is a hook for single line working staff or token. The fireman's seat is opposite the driver's, and nearby is the pep pipe valve. This is a hot water take-off that comes from the boiler and can be used to wash down the footplate to clean it, or slake the coal to prevent the dust becoming troublesome for the crew.

Tender

The Collett 4,000-gallon (18,184-litre) capacity tender is a fairly simple three-axle vehicle that became the standard design of tender for most large GWR locomotives. Although theoretically replaced by the Hawksworth type during and after the Second World War, the number of them in service meant that by the end of steam on the Western Region of BR in the mid-1960s they were still the most common type. The tender preserved with No 4079 is No 2913, which was built in 1943 and first saw use with Hall Class machine No 6954 *Lotherton Hall*. They are outside-framed vehicles with a second inner frame known as the ladder located between the outer frames with outriggers and the front and rear buffer beams and drag boxes attached to it. The drag box at the rear has a standard screw link coupling and standard buffers. The locomotive to tender connection end is somewhat different. It has small buffers on the tender only. The drag box on the locomotive has just buffing plates.

There are three couplings that join the locomotive to the tender. They are forgings that have an elongated loop at each end. The drag boxes have pins that drop down into the loops to attach them to the vehicles at either end. There is a heavy main coupling in the centre and two smaller couplings that are capable of taking the strain should the main coupling link fail. The necessity for this was ably demonstrated by a BR Britannia Class machine that once parted company with its tender whilst on the road...

The coal capacity of the tender is six tons (96.281kg) and is held in a sloping coal space in the centre of the tender. The slope assists slightly in bringing the coal forward as it is used, and there is a slightly raised shovelling plate, but that is about the limit for concessions to ergonomics! The coal was usually soft Welsh steam coal and was loaded from tubs via a coaling stage.

RIGHT No 2913 – the tender that survived with *Pendennis Castle* in preservation. Although she was built with a 3,500-gallon tender, No 4079 spent most of her working life attached to a tender of this type.
(Collection of Sir William McAlpine)

There is also a pair of half doors that look similar to Wild West saloon doors (!) with a very heavy securing latch on them that is used to retain the coal load when it is very full but still allow the fireman access to the coal at the bottom. When the coal has been removed from below the level of the doors they can be opened, allowing further access to the fuel. On either side of the coal space there are two toolboxes that would contain tools and spares for the engine (such as replacement gauge glasses and the attendant special spanner), lubrication and feeders, as well as the crew's personal effects and food.

The water tank takes up the majority of the rest of the tender. It is C-shaped along both sides of and around the back of the coal space. The filler for the water is at the rear of the tender on a flat plate behind the coal space. In order to prevent the water surging with the movement of the locomotive, the tank is fitted with a number of baffles that take the form of flat plates with a number of holes of varying shapes cut into them. There are two water valves with simple L-shaped handles on them situated at the front of the tender. They each feed one of the injectors. The pipe work for each is separate. This ensures that if there is a problem with one the other will continue to provide feed water to the injectors.

Whilst the six-ton coal capacity was usually more than sufficient to complete the journeys that the GWR required of the engine, 4,000 gallons of water simply wasn't enough. This would mean that a non-stop express would need to stop to replenish water, and that simply wouldn't do. It would be possible to make a bigger tender but there were limitations both on the axle weight permissible on the GWR and the length of their turntables, so another solution was needed.

The answer to this was the water scoop. This was a large casting situated underneath the tank between the second and third axles. This is in two parts. There is a large pipe with a hinge bolted to a flange that itself forms part of a pipe that leads to the top of the tender water space under a large pressed dome structure. The second casting is a hinged section attached to a linkage that is operated via a winding handle on a pedestal located on the driver's side of the tender. This casting is

ABOVE The front of tender No 2913 while under overhaul, showing the water scoop and handbrake columns and the two water valve handles with their attendant control rods diving under the drag box to the valves themselves. The two small buffers can be seen, as can the three slots for the coupling links. The main coupling link can be seen sat above the slots. The doors to the coal space are open, with the locking bar on the left and the two toolboxes on top. The water gauge is to the top left and the additional sanding chute is on the top right. The valve for the emergency brake is usually mounted on the right alongside the handbrake column, and the 'ghost' of its pipe is present in the paintwork. *(Author)*

BELOW The coal space of No 2913 with its two air vents or 'mushrooms', one behind each toolbox. The fire irons have been removed from their rack so that it can be painted, and are piled on the back of the tender at the bottom left of the picture. *(Author)*

ABOVE Tender No 2210, the 3,500-gallon unit preserved with No 4073 at Swindon, shows off its water scoop apparatus to great effect. *(Author)*

scoop-shaped. In addition it has a thin gauge steel extension fitted to the mouth of the scoop. It is this extension that makes contact with the water stored in troughs between the track that were built at strategic points on the network. The lowered scoop could take on water whilst on the move. It could pick up three-quarters of a tank in one go, but this required the displacement of a large volume of air. To accommodate this, the tender is provided with two vents situated about halfway along either side of the coal space. In recognition of their shape, these are known as mushrooms. Also located on the fireman's side of the coal space is a tool rack for fire irons. These are used for tending the fire, raking it through, manipulating it and disposing of it at the end of a shift.

The brake system on the tender follows

the same arrangement as the locomotive (if a slightly different size) with a similar cylinder, reservoir cylinder and equalising linkage. In addition the tender brake system carries the emergency application valve on the front of the tender that allows air immediately into the train pipe. All six wheels are braked with a set of adjusters. The biggest difference between the two systems, however, is that the tender has the locomotive handbrake on it, and to this end a handle is provided, not unlike the one on the water scoop on the driver's side. The end has a threaded linkage mechanism that manually pulls the brakes on. The pipe work to the reservoir contains a drip valve to expel excess moisture from the system. There are brake reservoir release cocks on both the tender and the locomotive. There are several loco-to-tender connections: two water feed pipes to the locomotive's injectors, the steam heating pipe going back to the train including a drip valve, the vacuum reservoir pipe and the train vacuum pipe. It is somewhat simpler at the outer end of the tender as there are only connections for the train pipe and the steam heating. The steam heating connection also includes a shut-off cock.

ATC

In terms of safety, the Great Western was one of the most forward-thinking railways in the country, and the foremost of its safety measures was the ATC, or Automatic Train Control system. In modern terms it would be considered an AWS (automatic warning system), but it was sufficiently advanced and worked so well that after its introduction on the Fairford branch in 1906 it was trialled on the GWR main line between Reading and Slough in 1908. It eventually went system-wide and remained in active service until the 1970s, when it was superseded by the BR version of the same system.

The idea of the ATC system was to give drivers an audible indication of the state of a signal they were about to pass and allow them to apply the brakes in time if a home signal was going to be passed at danger. This equipment requires the integration of the system between the signals, the signal box and the locomotive, so we shall examine the lineside equipment first.

Each distant signal on the GWR main line had

RIGHT The rear view of No 2913 showing off the essential details, including the works plate, steps, handrails and lamp irons. The vacuum hose and the steam heat hose with its valve can be seen on the buffer beam. The two chains hanging down are a safety precaution present on all of the brake cross-beams on both locomotive and tender. *(Collection of Sir William McAlpine)*

a steel ramp associated with it. This was 40ft (12,192mm) long and was 3½in (88.9mm) higher than the running rails, with a slope at each end. It had two states, firstly de-energised and secondly electrically live. A telegraph wire led from the ramp to a switch on the relevant lever in the local signal box. When the distant signal was in the safe or precede normally position, the ramp was electrically live. If the signal was set at caution the ramp was electrically dead. This is important, because being dead at danger means that if there is a failure within any of the equipment it fails to be safe, and therefore the locomotive is stopped. This is the most important feature of any safety system.

The equipment on the locomotive consisted of a box with a shoe on a sprung plunger located under the engine that makes contact with the ramp. For the majority of Castles this was positioned on the bogie, but on the early machines like No 4079 and the Kings it was positioned under the cab. When the plunger was depressed and the shoe made contact with a live ramp (signal at the off position) the ATC box in the cab caused a bell to ring. If, however, the ramp was not energised and the shoe depressed the plunger this sounded a horn in the cab, and if the driver did nothing to cancel it by operating a handle and applying the brakes himself, then a full application of the brakes would result. The distant signal and ramp was set at such a distance (usually 440 yards or 402.34m, although this did change with certain local signalling circumstances) that the train would be brought to a halt before it went through the home signal set at danger.

The system was trusted and very well respected by the crews, and they would trust their lives to it. ATC allowed the drivers to operate to schedule in adverse weather conditions and especially in poor visibility during blackouts in WW2. There were recorded occasions where loco crews from another company, whilst being piloted by a GWR machine on GWR lines in thick fog, had been so frightened to see the GWR driver flying along at speed without being able to see the signals that they stopped the train. They would storm round to the cab of the GWR machine, cursing the driver and all his kin, only to receive a somewhat rural description of the finer points of the operation of the ATC box

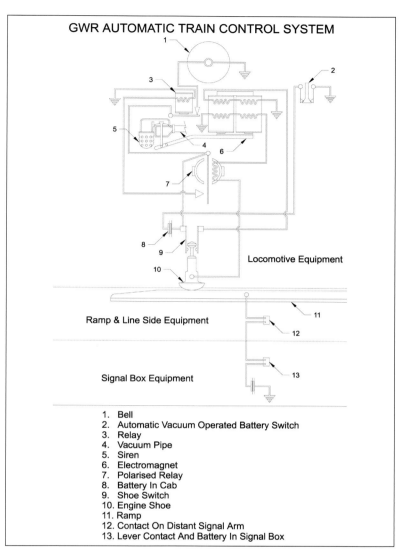

GWR AUTOMATIC TRAIN CONTROL SYSTEM

Locomotive Equipment

Ramp & Line Side Equipment

Signal Box Equipment

1. Bell
2. Automatic Vacuum Operated Battery Switch
3. Relay
4. Vacuum Pipe
5. Siren
6. Electromagnet
7. Polarised Relay
8. Battery In Cab
9. Shoe Switch
10. Engine Shoe
11. Ramp
12. Contact On Distant Signal Arm
13. Lever Contact And Battery In Signal Box

before being sent back to their cab with their metaphorical tails between their legs.

The ATC also had an automatic shut off-system included that, when the locomotive had been at rest for more than half an hour, shut it off to conserve battery power. It was restarted by a switch operated by the vacuum system of the locomotive. When vacuum was restored to the train pipe and reservoir by the driver the system was switched back on. This system also failed to safe, and if it wasn't working the very first ramp the loco went over essentially caused a signal at danger response and stopped the train. While this seems fairly basic to us in our electronic era, we have to remember that this is a system that was conceived and implemented without the use of electronics. This makes it a truly remarkable achievement by any measure.

ABOVE GWR ATC gear. *(Author's Drawing)*

Chapter Five

The crew's view

Life with the Castles

The driver and fireman had set duties in various documents published by both the GWR and BR, and the rest of this chapter sets out in narrative form what is described as ideal practice in those publications.

OPPOSITE No 4079 is cleaned at Swindon shed in March 1964 after 12 to 18 months in stock standing outside in all weathers. The rank of cleaner was the first step on the ladder to driver, but sadly few of these young men are likely to have been in railway employ much longer, due to dieselisation. *(Collection of Sir William McAlpine)*

The crew will have arrived in good time to prepare the locomotive for that day's turn. There is a strict hierarchy on the footplate and the driver is in charge of the locomotive, therefore his safety and that of his fireman and locomotive is his responsibility. He will ensure that both his checks and preparations and those done by his mate are completed correctly. The crew will have first consulted the shed's notice boards to pick up the required information about their journey, including their locomotive and turn allocation, any special traffic notices (such as engineering work being carried out) and, indeed, anything else pertinent to the safe and efficient running of the railway. This completed, the crew would then split up and carry out their individual preparations. The fireman would make his way to the tool stores to obtain the small tools, supplies and keys needed to run the locomotive. He would then

proceed to the engine. Let us imagine he is walking up to a gleaming *Pendennis Castle* and her duty today is to haul an express train. No 4079 is in good mechanical order and has just received a wash-out, so the engine will perform – it is now down to the careful preparation and handling of the crew to get the very best out of her.

As he approaches, the fireman will know that the engine is in steam as the shed crew will have ensured that she is hot, but the fire will not be anywhere near the condition which No 4079 needs to do her day's work. Before he attends to that, though, there are a number of other important checks that he must do. The most important of these is to check the safety equipment on the boiler. The gauge glass will be first, and he will close the top and bottom cocks using the top handle. He will then open the drain at the bottom. This will cause the water to disappear and clear the glass. Once shut again the cocks are reopened and the water should return to the same level. He will also test the two try cocks on the side to ensure that they operate as required.

He will then carry out an examination of the boiler, and begins with the firebox. His first check is the fire, and if the fire is in poor order, the water level is too low or the pressure is too low then he would have to immediately report this to both the driver and the running foreman. He will examine the fusible plugs, and check that the brick arch and deflector plate are in good order, and that the tubes are not leaking or blocked. He will then go underneath to inspect the ash pan to ensure the shed crews have done their job and it is clear that the damper doors are in working order and fit properly in their holes. He will then move on to the smokebox end of the boiler, ensuring the jumper top is operating and that it is free from char and soot. He will then wipe round the smokebox ring to ensure a seal can be obtained and the door can be shut tightly.

The fireman will then tend to the fire. If it is burning well, he will just maintain it until required for the departure, but if it is small or not very good then he will begin to add coal to build it up. The fire needs building today, so the fireman starts by sprinkling a few shovelfuls around the firebox to put a thin layer across the grate, and

BELOW Early in the morning of one of her main-line runs, No 5029 *Nunney Castle* has her fire brought round for the day's train by one of her support crew. *(Author)*

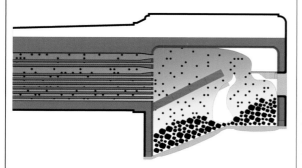

This represents a good, clean burning fire. All of the fuel is being fully burnt in the firebox and as a result, the locomotive is producing little or no visible smoke. There is an even layer of burning coal across the whole grate and there are no holes in the fire bed. The heat across the whole firebox is even and no stress is being imparted upon it. The fire will be white hot when the locomotive is working hard.

Here the fire has two problems. The first is that the fireman has allowed a hole to develop in the fire bed. The other issue is that the fire has become too thick. This means that there is not only coal in the firebox that is not burning but also that the air cannot get through the grate to assist in the complete combustion of all of the volatile compounds in the coal. This is leading to uneven heating of the firebox and the structures within it which can cause leaking and damage and poor coal consumption.

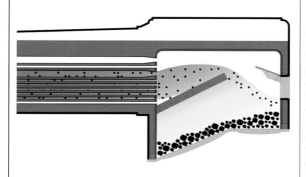

In this picture we can see that the baffle plate is at the wrong angle. This is causing uneven flow of the hot gasses from the fire. This means that the top and bottom tubes and the front or nose of the brick arch is not getting the full heat of the fire and therefore there is stress being imparted on the tubes, tube plate and inner firebox and causing leaking and damage. As with above, incomplete combustion of the coal and the volatile compounds given off when it is burnt will lead to soot building up in the boiler tubes.

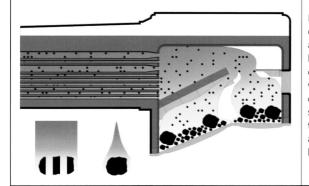

In this scenario, the fireman has used lumps of coal that are too large. This has the same effect as having too much coal in the firebox. Uneven heating causing mechanical stresses and poor combustion. The size of coal is fairly critical when firing and the rule of thumb was that crews were told to use lumps 'no larger than size of a man's fist'. As the inset diagram shows, the large lump on the right has far less surface area burning than the same lump that has been broken up into three pieces on the left.

LEFT The shape of fires, draughting and the effects on locomotive performance. *(Author)*

to help it burn the damper doors are opened and the blower is switched on. This will help promote proper combustion of the coal our fireman has just put in. Coal begins to burn at about 800°F (426.67°C), but temperatures of between 2,000°–2,500°F (1,093.3°–1,371.1°C) are required to really get the best from the fuel.

Coal has two main constituents – firstly the volatiles, which are given off as a gas when heated, and secondly the fixed solid materials that remain once the coal is burnt. At the higher temperatures, the hydrocarbons are split into carbon and hydrogen and, when burnt, become carbon dioxide and water vapour. If the fire is starved of oxygen some of the volatiles will escape up the chimney, producing black smoke. If too much air is introduced the smoke disappears and heat is lost. The ideal is to see light grey smoke at the chimney; that way a fireman can be assured that the coal is being completely consumed in the firebox. It is this that he will be working towards as he makes

up the fire. He will break up any large lumps to about the size of a man's fist. This gives a good amount of surface area to allow the volatiles to be released. As he adds coal, he will wait for that to catch before adding the next round, avoiding blacking out the fire and producing thick smoke in the shed.

The fire is slowly built up and any holes filled as he goes along. Once the fire has produced enough steam, the injectors are tested to ensure efficient operation. If they are not in good order the driver and foreman would require informing, and the attentions of fitters would be sought to see if they could be coaxed into life. Fortunately for us, No 4079 is in a good mood today. The fireman will also need to ensure that the loco has a full set of lamps (headlights, gauge glass lamp and a flare lamp) and will ensure that the wicks are trimmed, the lenses are clean and that the oil reservoirs were full. He will make sure that two red flags and a set of no less than 12 warning detonators (small explosive warning charges that are placed on the rail head and are triggered when a train rolls over them) are on board. He will then clean and tidy the footplate, using the pep pipe to hose things down, and wipe a hot, wet rag over the gauge glass so it can be read accurately. Finally he will ensure that the sanding gear is working and that the sandboxes are full.

While all this is going on, the driver would have made his way to the oil stores. There he would have collected the measures of the thinner lubrication oil and the thicker steam oil. He was supposed to fill the hydrostatic lubricator upon his return to the engine, but in practice many drivers put their oil can on the shelf above the firehole door to warm through and therefore become more liquid and easier to pour. He would make sure that the locomotive was in the optimum position, with the cranks in the right place to leave all the oil pots clear and free for filling. Once this was achieved, he would then make the locomotive safe. This would mean that the regulator was securely closed, that the reverser was locked in mid gear, the cylinder drain cocks were open and the tender handbrake was screwed hard on.

He will now work his way round the locomotive doing two important tasks. Firstly, he will be filling the well over 100 oil pots that

BELOW The coal stage at Didcot is the sole survivor of its type in full working order and is still used for its original purpose. There is a water tank above, the coal unloading deck in the middle and the wash and mess rooms for the men at the bottom. The ash pit where the locos were cleaned is to the left in this picture. Where your author stood to take the picture is where the empty ash wagons were loaded (again by hand) to remove the waste from the shed. The level of labour intensity demonstrated here provides a partial explanation for the demise of steam traction on BR. *(Author)*

are needed to keep the engine lubricated. He will also be carrying out an inspection of his mount to ensure that there are no defects that might cause a problem on today's run. As he goes round he will also be making sure that no oil pot is contaminated by water. This was particularly true of the axleboxes, and a large syringe would be used to draw off any water before adding fresh oil. He would start by going under the machine from front to back, ensuring that all of the motion is tight and lubricated, likewise the brake cylinder and trunnions, the loco-to-tender buffers and couplings and the water scoop (also ensuring that the scoop is secure and in the up position).

Next he makes his way down the driver's side from the rear to the front, across the front and then along the fireman's side, before returning to the cab, examining his fireman's work and then carrying out the last few checks. These begin with the vacuum brake system, checking its function and the function of the vacuum ejector – opening this carefully, to ensure that the soot and debris in the shed roof is not dislodged by the blast up the chimney. He will also start the lubricator working, setting the oil flow to the various parts to the correct rate by using the taps under the main lubricator body and generally ensuring its smooth operation. If it is in season, he will also check that the steam heat system is working. This requires opening the cock on the tender end of the loco and the Mason valve in the cab, to blow all of the condensate out of the system. The tender cock is then closed and the system inspected for good operation and steam-tightness. During this time the crew will also ensure that their billycans are full of tea and safely placed on the oil shelf above the firehole door to keep it hot!

The engine is now ready to move, but before they go they may need to top up the coal and water, and that means manoeuvring slowly and carefully to the correct parts of the shed. To blow the brakes off, the brake lever is pushed over to the off or running position on the right to start the ejector that fills the reservoir and then the train pipe. This blows the brakes off and allows the locomotive to move. Firstly she will go to the most convenient water crane, where the crew will fill the tank to the brim and then

ensure that the lid is properly closed to prevent the ingress of debris. Then to the coaling stage where the shed workmen will top up the coal load to maximum to ensure No 4079 gets to its destination with fuel to spare.

A point of minor irritation today is the fact that the locomotive is facing the wrong way, so a trip to the turntable is required. This would usually have been taken care of by shed staff, but unfortunately it hasn't been today. Using the hand levers in the shed limits they make their way to the turntable. It is a requirement that all locomotives stop before coming on to the turntable. This enables the crew to check that the table is aligned to the correct road and that the locks are in place to prevent it moving under the engine. Once they have moved slowly into position on the table and screwed the handbrake down, the locks are released and the two push bars are extended so that the crew can manually turn the engine. It sounds difficult, but if the engine is in the right place and the table is in good mechanical order and balanced it is surprisingly easy. They will never pull the bar in case the operator slips, when there is a possibility of being run over by the turntable. The loco is then moved off the table and makes its way to the shed exit road. They are bang on time and one of the crew will jump down to telephone or blow a whistle to indicate to the local signalman they are ready to proceed to their train.

Once the signal has dropped into the proceed position, the driver puts the locomotive into reverse gear and slowly traverses the complex trackwork that always marked out the entrance to a main terminus. This is where the fireman has to start a clever and skilful game. He needs to begin to build the fire to such a condition that it will supply the massive amount of heat required to power the Castle along the main line. However, it is not a good idea to get the fire to such a stage that the safety valves are lifting heavily and therefore wasting fuel and water, but the fire bed that is in there has to be thoroughly alight to produce the required temperature. Here is where all his skill and experience starts to show. The train of ten coaches has already been delivered to the platform by one of those most ubiquitous of machines, a GWR pannier tank. This engine has

ABOVE No 5051 *Earl Bathurst* on the turntable at Didcot. The only major authenticity issue with this image is the fact that the turntable is actually the one from the Southern Railway's line at Southampton Docks. *(Author)*

uncoupled from the train and has pulled forward to the buffer stops at the far end. Once the train has left, the pannier will pull out again and make its way back to the carriage sidings to pick up the next set of vehicles.

No 4079 will pull up to the coaches and then press up against the buffers in order to compress them in so that the fireman can climb down and connect up the screw link coupling, the vacuum hose and the steam heat hose,

LEFT The fireman of No 5050 *Earl of St Germans* arranges the two-lamp express head code at Exeter some time in the early 1960s.
(Frank Dumbleton)

ensuring the cock on the latter is turned to the on position. The fireman removes the white oil lamp from the bottom centre lamp iron on the tender and the red tail lamp from the lower centre iron on the front buffer beam. He replaces two white lamps on the two outer lamp irons of the front buffer beams that is the head code for express passenger trains. There may also be a metal frame containing a three-digit code on large metal plates on the smokebox door handle. The alphanumeric code indicated the service the train was on (*ie* 'the 8.15 to Bristol service').

At about five to ten minutes to departure time, the fireman would be working hard to ensure that the boiler is full and that the fire is ready to go. There were a number of different firing techniques and shapes that were used dependent upon the locomotive type and the work it was doing. The most familiar to be seen on a Castle was a thin layer of coal on the front sloping section of the grate while the rear flat section was kept thicker at the front and tailed off a little towards the firehole door. It would also be heaped slightly towards the centre line and tapered out slightly to the sides of the firebox. The action of the locomotive in motion would shake the fire and cause the coal to naturally work its way sideways and forward, and to keep the fire in good order the fireman would only have to ensure that the centre is filled and that no holes have appeared anywhere.

As the time for departure is reached, *Pendennis Castle*'s safety valves are just beginning to lift, with a very thin white feather of steam issuing from them. This indicates that the boiler is at its ideal condition, on or very close to the red line mark of 225psi on the cab gauge. This gives the driver the maximum amount of power to use. The green flag is waved and whistle blown by the guard and, after blowing the brakes off and checking that the cylinder drain cocks are open, the driver blows the whistle and opens the regulator. The locomotive is in full forward gear, so that the engine gives a loud bark as each of the exhaust beats is released up the chimney. With each blast the fire flashes to an incandescent white. As the engine leaves, it hauls the massive weight of its train out of the station.

ABOVE Although the loco is stationary and the view is from outside the cab, it wonderfully illustrates the very restricted view along the length of the boiler of No 4079. This is why looking out for signals and dangers on the road was a two-man job and why it was very important for the crew to be familiar with the route that they were traversing. *(Collection of Sir William McAlpine)*

After the first few revolutions of the wheels the drain cocks can be shut again. With careful feathering of the regulator, the driver ensures that the locomotive does not slip its wheels. As it is wet he will pump the sander lever until the engine finds her feet. Slowly, as the beats increase in speed, he will wind the reverser back toward mid gear in small increments. He has to find the narrow margin between using enough power to haul the train up to cruising speed while also making the most efficient use of the steam. As the locomotive is moving, the brake pump is taking care of the creation of vacuum for the braking system, and the draught from the chimney draws the fire so that the blower is almost shut but still in operation.

The driver will be using the expansive properties of the steam, and when he is up to a cruising speed of anywhere between 60–80mph (96.56–128.74kph) he will be using a cut-off in the 20% range. This permits a small amount of steam into the cylinders but allows it to expand and do its work before being ejected out the chimney. It also has to be remembered that it is far easier to maintain a speed once you are there rather than to climb to it, trying to overcome the weight of the vehicles.

The fireman will have turned the exhaust injector on and this will be keeping the boiler topped-up with a small but constant flow of water into the pressure vessel. He would not have been able to fire the engine as the locomotive was accelerating under full power, as at this time the firebox and brick arch are at their coldest in the journey, and they need to reach temperature. The fireman will close the firehole doors. This ensures the vast majority of the air for the fire is drawn through the grate and as a result is hot from the outset. Now

that the engine is not working as hard it is time for him to start firing the engine again. He will open the doors, and, by directing the stream of cold air being drawn in by the blast with the shovel, will inspect the condition of the fire. Where the fire bed has holes, they are filled first, and then any thin areas are built up. Any areas that are not burning to full temperature are left for now. He would then watch the chimney. There should be a five-second period in which the chimney shows light smoke. Once this period passes, the fireman shovels on another round and ensures that the fire is burning to the correct depth all over the grate. Once she is into her stride No 4079 will need firing in the 'little and often' fashion, with no more than about 12 shovelfuls per round. So the fireman's attention is split three ways, between the condition of the fire, the amount of water in the boiler – supplementing the flow from the exhaust injector when needed – and keeping an eye on the road to report signals and conditions to his driver.

BELOW No 7010 *Avondale Castle* takes a mail train through the famous water troughs at Goring in South Oxfordshire. *(Frank Dumbleton)*

As has been mentioned before, there was not enough water in a 4,000-gallon tender to make the long, non-stop runs that the Castles were expected to undertake. As a result the locomotive had to take water on the move. This is where the water scoop came into its own. The fireman would wait for the appropriate lineside indicators, which were a large white rectangular board with a black horizontal zigzag marking. He would then wind the scoop down so it was just skimming the surface of the water. If the water scoop was plunged deep into the trough the power of the jet entering the tender was such that it blew straight up and out of the mushroom vents, and soaked the entire footplate without picking up sufficient water, which could mean that the engine would not reach its destination without running out. However, assuming that the fireman was doing his job correctly the scoop could pick up a couple of thousand gallons (from half to three-quarters of a tank) along the approximately 500-yard (457.20m) length of the trough. The fireman was also required to get the scoop up before the end of the trough. Failure to do so would knock the end out of the trough, rip the thin metal scoop blade off the tender and cause a fireman a great deal of trouble...

All the time they were on the flat this state of affairs could be maintained, but despite Mr Brunel's attempt to keep his main line flat it wasn't practical to do so completely. Consequently there are times when conditions dictate that the locomotive has to work harder, so the fireman has to be ready for that and make sure that the fire is in exceptional condition at the point of the start of a climb. That means, ready to fire *before* this point to ensure that the coal is all burning fiercely at the given moment – and this is where the supreme route knowledge of both driver and fireman kicks in.

Drivers often took a liberal interpretation of the schedule, preferring to make up time on the easygoing sections of line so that the locomotive and fireman did not have to work as hard during the difficult sections of the road. There was only limited scope for this to happen, but as long as the train arrived at its destination(s) on time there would be no problem. The firing rate of even the best firemen would increase as the driver slowly wound the reverser to a higher cut-off and again put more power down to the wheels to overcome the obstacle. If the climb was severe and the load heavy a practice called 'mortgaging the boiler' was used. This was where the fireman would ensure that the boiler was full and the fire hot and would then turn off the injectors and anything else he could to conserve steam. This meant that as there was no fresh water going in, the water level would continue to drop, and there would come a point when the fireman would be forced to restart the

BELOW No 4079 on test on 25 February 1967. This is where the true skill of the fireman becomes apparent. The placing of coal in the correct place on the grate is hard enough while stationary. When travelling at over 70mph the loco and tender are moving about in separate rhythms, as is the fall plate between the two; add to this the onrushing air, the lack of side doors and the requirement to put one ton (0.9 tonne) of coal into the inferno per hour, and something of the magnitude of operating an express steam locomotive can be understood. *(Collection of Sir William McAlpine)*

injectors. If he mistimed this it would be on the climb, and the sudden influx of cold water and reduction in steam pressure could bring an engine to its knees, forcing it to either crawl or – embarrassingly – halt, when the fire and boiler would have to be brought round. The process was known as 'stopping a blow-up', and was obviously detrimental to schedules, particularly those of an important express of the type that *Pendennis Castle* is pulling today. If the fireman got it right, however, that point wasn't quite reached, and the downward slope on the other side of the gradient could be used for recovery.

The fireman would have tried not to fire the engine while the regulator was shut, and as the regulator was shut the blower was opened. This was to prevent the frightening problem known as a blowback. This is where fire enters the cab through the firehole doors, and is caused by a lack of enough air being drawn through the fire. It can be simply countered by having the regulator open or ensuring that the blower is turned up to the correct level. There are two types of blowback. The first is where the regulator is shut and the blower is not opened sufficiently. This causes air to be available towards the firehole door. The mix of this and the volatile gasses means that the fire goes towards the air source and out of it. This is known as a

non-explosive blowback. The second type is far more terrifying and also results from a lack of draught from either the exhaust or blower. This happens when a sudden inrush of air (as might be caused by going into a tunnel or under a bridge) momentarily stops combustion. The heat of the fire bed itself will reignite the volatile gas and air mix, causing what is known as an explosive blowback. This causes very rapid propagation of flames in all directions, including into the cab, which has obvious and very serious consequences for the crew.

Towards the end of the run the fireman will begin to work the fire down. This also requires a keen eye for detail and route knowledge, the balance here being between supplying the driver with enough steam to do the final section of the journey and not arriving on shed with a massive fire that is difficult to remove and wasteful of fuel. As the fire is worked down the boiler is kept topped up, and the engine would then glide into the station and come gently to a halt. The locomotive would then have been uncoupled and the lamps rearranged to display the light engine code. Another station pilot would come and collect the train and No 4079 will follow shortly after to the signal at the end of the platform to wait for the signal to change to release them back to the shed, as this is a

RIGHT As No 7035 *Ogmore Castle* demonstrates, it wasn't all glamorous express trains. At Newbury we see a Castle in charge of a mail train with some six-wheel milk tankers thrown in.
(Frank Dumbleton)

double home turn (*ie* the crew will overnight here and then return with No 4079 tomorrow).

Once back at the shed, the locomotive will first be put over the ash pit and the loco made safe. The fireman will fill the boiler to three-quarters full and then return the tools and equipment to the shed. The driver, meanwhile, was required to fill in an engine defect card to report any mechanical defects on the locomotive. Any defects where steam is escaping have to be reported accurately and may need to be tested to pinpoint the issue. Any defects with the ATC are obviously very serious, and required a separate defect card to be filled in. All the available information had to be reported on these cards, as the fitter may get to the engine when it is out of steam and will therefore be unable to test the loco himself. If the engine was in perfect order then a 'no defect' card had to be filled out.

The fire droppers will be next to work on the engine. The first job is to drop the fire. This means using a long-handled rake and shovel to remove the majority of the fire and to push any clinker and ash through the fire bars and into the ash pan. Once the firebox is mostly clear, the remaining bit of fire is spread around the grate to keep the firebox warm and the firehole doors are shut. The fire dropper checks that the damper doors are closed and then leaves the cab. He will open the smokebox door and shovel out any char and ash that has collected there. He will then sweep down the running plate to get rid of any spillage. This is not only good housekeeping but also stops the char being blown down into the motion, where it can act as quite an effective grinding paste!

With a wipe of the smokebox ring and door to ensure they seal, the smokebox door is closed. The final job here is to climb back into the cab, open the dampers and then clamber underneath with the long rake and clear out the ash pan. There are two sections to empty, one in front and one behind the rear driving wheel axle, and to prevent it flying around it will require damping down with water before it is raked. Once this is done the fire dropper will climb back into the cab to close the damper doors to prevent cold air getting to the firebox and causing stress and warping of the tubes and tubeplate. He will then start the live steam injector. This means that he can start the pep pipe and hose down the footplate. With the last remaining steam in the boiler, and taking care to drive very carefully so as not to cause a draught with the exhaust that entrails cold air into the firebox, the loco is moved to its position on shed by a shed pilot crew to rest for the night.

LEFT The end of the day in the early 1950s – except of course it isn't, it's No 5051 *Earl Bathurst* **and her stablemates at Didcot on 27 September 2008 recreating the scene.** (*Frank Dumbleton*)

Maintenance and main-line running

Get your spanners out

There were a number of maintenance and inspection tasks undertaken at the locomotives' home running shed. The system of maintenance was called MP11, and set out a number of different tasks that were required to be undertaken to keep the locomotives running safely and efficiently.

OPPOSITE The view in 'A' Shop at Swindon works in 1962 with some of the last steam locomotives being overhauled there nearing completion. Here we can see No 7026 *Tenby Castle* flanked by Hall Class No 4920 *Dumbleton Hall* and Modified Hall Class No 6971 *Athelhampton Hall.* (Frank Dumbleton)

119

MAINTENANCE AND MAIN-LINE RUNNING

Inspections were set according to either a time period or mileage completed. The full procedure is reproduced in Appendix 1 of this book; however, there are a number of key points that justify explanation here. Everyday inspections undertaken by the crews were supplemented, on large express locomotives like the Castles, with an 'X Day' examination. This was undertaken whenever a locomotive was due to pull a vacuum-fitted freight or passenger train, and was a simple visual inspection of the machine to ensure that it was fit to run. Beyond that there were a number of maintenance tasks that had to be carried out as follows.

Boiler washouts

Scale and mud-like deposits liberated from the water can build up in a boiler as it is being heated, and if left to accumulate can result in a blocked waterway which in turn leads to areas of platework heating up differently to others, causing stresses and damage to the pressure vessel. It also inhibits the boiler's ability to make steam efficiently. This has a detrimental effect on the performance of the engine and is therefore something the railways were keen to avoid. As a high-performance machine, therefore, boiler

washouts were performed on Castles after every four days of operation.

This was a two-stage procedure. Firstly the firebox and tubes were cleaned. This was hot work, as even though the fire had been thrown out the boiler was still at a high temperature. The cleaner gangs would brush the inside of the firebox and the brick arch clean of soot and ash, and the resultant detritus was then forced through the grate. The tubes were then cleaned out with either a brush on a rod or a steam lance connected to a steam supply in the shed or a nearby locomotive. This is why GWR-designed engines have the strange tap device on the front of their smokeboxes. If a tube was blocked the rod could be fitted with a special screw-type attachment that would be wound into the soot to break it up.

The second stage involved the boiler being drained down via the removal of the lower mud hole doors and some of the upper wash-out plugs, to allow air in to replace the water. When this had been done the rest of the plugs and doors were removed and a hot water supply from the stationary boiler in the shed was used to wash the mud and deposits from the boiler using a number of shaped hose fittings. The shed boilersmith would carry out his inspection of the unit and then it would be boxed up again, with the plugs and doors (with new lead joints) being refitted and the boiler refilled.

BELOW Another view of Swindon's 'A' Shop. At one point this was one of the largest covered spaces in the world, with 11.25 acres (45,500m²) of space in which to work on the locomotives. The frames of No 7001 *Denbigh Castle* can be seen in the distance. Swindon works was a massive affair that was almost self-contained and at its height employed 14,000 men. By 1960 this was just 5,000 men, and the works finally closed in the 1980s.
(Frank Dumbleton)

Inspection schedule

The inspections listed here were carried out periodically, and any faults discovered would have been rectified before the locomotive could re-enter service. There were inspections of the following components by the shed fitters, boilersmiths and ATC specialists on a monthly basis:

- Axleboxes (lubrication and keeps).
- Boiler (all).
- Bogie (frames).
- Brake gear (pull rods and pins, hangers and brackets and adjusting screws).
- Crossheads (all).
- Cylinders (all).
- Draw gear (all).
- Frames (all).
- Injectors (all).
- Flexible connections on engine and tender (all).
- Lubricator gear.
- Rods, connecting (oil cups).
- Rods, eccentric (bolts, nuts and split pins on jaw ends, shelves, straps, feet of cups, oil cups).
- Springing gear (springs).
- Water gauge frame (all).
- Water tank (water feed valves, tank lid hinge pins, level indicator).
- Wheels (axles, cranks, wheel centres and tyres).
- Air pump (all).
- ATC (all).
- Smokebox (blast pipe, jumper top).
- Vacuum brake (retaining valve – clean and oil).

In addition to the monthly schedule items, at two-monthly intervals the following items would also be checked:

- Brake gear (hand screws, safety chains, brake shafts and brackets).
- Buffers (all).
- Firehole doors (all).
- Rods, connecting (examine in position for fractures).
- Rods, coupling (examine in position for fractures).
- Sand gear (sand pipes).
- Smokebox (saddle and cylinder bolts, spark plates, steam pipes, superheater, ejector and blower ring, blast pipe and lubricator pipes and connections inside and outside smokebox).
- Steam valves, various (all).
- Whistles (whistle chains).
- Vacuum brake (pepperbox valve, ejector drip valve and vacuum cylinder).
- Speedometer (drive block in slotted rod).
- Tender (water scoop gear).
- Boiler (renew lead plugs, check expansion bracket and bolts and boiler keys).
- Boiler (examination by divisional boiler inspector).

In addition to the one- and two-monthly inspection schedules, every four months the following items were also inspected:

- Axleboxes (horn ways and faces).
- Sand gear (sand valves, rods, levers, brackets, pins etc and sandbox fitting bolts).
- Spring gear (tee hangers and pins, hangers and brackets, bolts, nuts and split pins).
- Axleboxes (bogie).
- Bogie (centre pin and block and control springs).
- Piston valves (all).

Added to the list at eight-month intervals were:
- Pistons (all).

And finally, at twelve-monthly intervals:
- Vacuum brake (retaining valve).

As you can see, there was a huge amount to keep track of, and this was done using a card index system at each shed. That this was achieved efficiently is all the more impressive to our modern eyes, used to the luxury of spreadsheets and electronic devices with automatic notification systems!

Regardless of these regular inspection checks, the wear and tear on locomotives eventually became such that they required a complete overhaul. There were various categories of overhaul and these were classified differently in the GWR and BR periods. Under the GWR they were classified (with codes) as:

- General (G).
- Heavy (H).
- Intermediate (I).
- Light (L).

After 1948 the LMS system became the adopted method, and the system became:

Heavy general (HG) – Boiler changed, all mechanical parts stripped and repaired or renewed as required to enable the engine to run to the next intermediate or general overhaul.
Intermediate (I) – Could be either Heavy (H) or Light (L) – see guidelines below. Boiler not changed but repairs carried out to it and all mechanical parts such as will ensure that mileage approximately equal to average for the class between consecutive general or intermediate repairs will be reached before the next scheduled general or intermediate repair.
Casual (C) – Could be either Heavy (H) or Light (L) – see guidelines below. Replace or repair those parts that have become defective due to failure or mishap, making engine unserviceable. No other work carried out on components.
Unclassified (U) or non-classified (NC) – Repairs defined as casual repairs required but not covered by Ministry of Transport Heavy or Light classification.

These repairs could be classified Light or Heavy by the Ministry of Transport under British Railways, like this:

Light repair
- Fitting new axle or axles on tender or engine.
- Removing and replacing 50 or more boiler tubes.
- Removing and replacing four or more superheater tubes.
- Taking down superheater header.
- Renewal of piston valve liners or piston valves.
- Fitting new tyres to one or more wheels.
- Turning up and fitting four or more wheels and refitting axleboxes.
- Complete overhaul of one or more valve gears.
- Fitting patch on boiler or firebox.
- Renewing 30 or more firebox stays.
- Fitting four or more new axleboxes or axlebox brasses.
- Welding, patching or straightening frame or renewing buffer beam.
- Re-boring cylinders or refacing ports.
- Removing and repairing the water tank(s).*

* With tender engines such as the Castle, this would have been done by swapping the tender rather than the locomotive being delayed from re-entering traffic by awaiting repairs to a specific tender. Tenders were easier and quicker to repair and would be dealt with on a separate production line. The next available tender was the one sent out with a finished locomotive.

Heavy repair
- Engine re-boilered.
- Boiler taken out of the frame for repair.

OR any two of the following:
- Fitting of new tyres to four or more wheels.
- Fitting new cylinders.
- Fitting new axle or axles on engine or tender.
- Re-tubing of boiler.
- Turning up wheels or refitting axleboxes, or motion and brake work stripped and overhauled. (These separate items taken together would *not* constitute a heavy repair.)
- Repairing of boiler on frame with not less than 50 stays renewed.

To determine when a locomotive was to be scheduled for one of the repairs (Casual and Unclassified excepted), a 'Locomotive Shopping Bureaux' was set up in each region that not only arranged the two-monthly major boiler inspection but also decided when a locomotive was to be stopped for work, and organised a slot in the works for the work to be undertaken. There were specific time periods before any locomotive could be considered for a slot in the locomotive works, and six weeks before that time a thorough inspection of the locomotive, while it was still in traffic, was carried out. The decision of the Bureaux could be either to return it to service for a specified amount of time or to send it to the works. This second course of action was taken if the engine was in such poor condition that it would be unable to undertake its allotted tasks, or if the engine was already out of traffic at its home shed because of failures that could not be remedied using the facilities there.

In 1951, the Castles were completing 87,400 miles (140,656.6km) between periodical repairs. They were far better than their only other real equivalents on the Western Region, the Kings, which were completing 79,000 miles

(127,138.2km) between workshop visits. As a case study, No 4079 *Pendennis Castle*'s record sheet shows that she visited Swindon works for all types of repair 40 times during the 40 years she was in service between 1924 and 1964, with a total recorded mileage to 1963 of 1,758,398 miles (2,829,867.3km). There were 23 heavy-type repairs in that time.

A heavy overhaul would have resulted in the locomotive being delivered to Swindon works and stripped to the frames. All the various component parts, including the motion, bearings, wheels etc, would have disappeared off to various corners of Swindon works to be repaired as required. It surprises some to know that the only original part of No 4079 that we can be certain of dating back to 1924 is her main frames, and that is true of most steam locomotives. The main frames are where the identity of the locomotive rests. We know for certain that her cylinders were changed at least three times in her life and that she had 18 changes of boiler and pulled no less than 37 different tenders. In a large class like the Castles there were always more boilers available than locomotives. This is because repairs on these units took far longer than anything else, so to speed up the process they were literally swapped when the time came.

To minimise lost revenue the whole of Swindon was geared to turning a machine around in the fastest possible time. It usually took about a month to refurbish a locomotive for a heavy general overhaul, and this was made possible by the multitude of highly skilled workers, the dedicated tooling and the decades of experience that Swindon works represented.

Today, all this has changed. Gone are the magnificent facilities, jigs, templates and machinery, and we are left with a smattering of the correct equipment and the requirement to be clever, ingenious, and to embrace as much modern technology as possible. As you

will have read, the Castle is a machine that in principle is fairly simple but in practice is fairly complex. Overhauls today are measured in years, not months, and prices have gone from the tens of thousands to build the engines in the first place to price tags for overhauls stretching into six figures. We do have certain advantages: we aren't pressed to get the locomotive back into service in quite the same way as Swindon was, and despite the price tags potentially being high we can reduce them

ABOVE An early morning at Bristol's Barton Hill depot sees No 5029 being awaken from her slumber, with her support coach out in front of her. *(Author)*

RIGHT The updated cab of No 5029 with the air brake pedestal from a Class 37 diesel and the 'oil/no oil' gauge associated with her new mechanical lubricator. Above the casing for the ATC is the AWS 'sunflower' indicator. *(Author)*

RIGHT The header unit for the radio housed in a modified tool box. The main GSMR radio equipment is on the rear of the tender. *(Author)*

by using volunteer labour to bring costs down. We may not have access to all of the patterns in the same way that Swindon did, but we can have one-use patterns made from polystyrene and cut by a computer-controlled machine, and can have parts cut by a water jet to such a degree of accuracy that little or no machining is required. In the future, whilst it will only get more expensive to keep these magnificent machines alive, progress in modern technology will mean that things we preservationists thought impossible even ten years ago are now becoming a reality. With a big locomotive like a Castle, though, there is one challenge left: to take her back on to the 'big railway'. To go main-line. That creates a whole set of new challenges, however.

The 21st-century main line is very different to the main line on which No 4079 started her career in 1924. The regulations and requirements are very stringent, and as a result only a few locomotives remain operational on the main line. Any locomotive that ventures out on to it has to be under a Vehicle Acceptance Body (VAB). During the progress of the overhaul process there will be a number of staged inspections and monitoring of paperwork and maintenance regimes and, if all goes well, the VAB will sign it off as fit to travel on the national network. A particular difference is the length of the boiler certificate. On preserved lines the maximum number of annual certificates is ten, whereas the theoretical limit on the main line is just seven. This can be extended, however, if the boiler has a new set of tubes fitted during the ticket at the right time to extend it to the full ten years. This is, of course, in agreement with the authorities and is very dependent on the condition of the pressure vessel at that time.

The other big difference is that the locomotive has to be fitted with a number of electronic devices to enable it to interact with the systems fitted on the national network. The first of these is the Train Protection & Warning System (TPWS). Fitting TPWS was made a requirement under the Railway Safety Regulations 1999, which decreed that by the end of 2003 all passenger train lines must be equipped with a train protection system. On the track there are a pair of TPWS aerials (known colloquially as 'toast racks') spaced between

4.4m and 36m apart, dependent upon the speed limit on the line. The first aerial is called the arming loop, and the second is known as the trigger loop. By registering the time it takes to pass between the two aerials, the system can work out the speed of the locomotive, and if the locomotive is approaching too fast the system will take over and apply the brakes, the aim being to stop the train before a collision can occur. In most places this means speeds up to 75mph (120.7kph) – the upper limit for an historic 'Castle' on the main line – but in key areas it can be set up to operate to 100mph (160kph). There is another set of loops directly at the signal, and if the signal is set at danger and a train passes it, it will stop it regardless of speed. The equipment fitted to the loco consists of the front and rear aerials, the electronic box housed in a watertight container, the driver's panel (a simple affair of just three buttons) and the dump valve, which is grafted into the vacuum pipe in the cab that leads below the driver's brake handle. All of this is interconnected with wiring and pipe work that is suitably shielded from the rigours of the steam locomotive footplate.

OTMR (On Train Monitoring & Recording) is the locomotive equivalent of an aircraft black box. It monitors a number of functions such as boiler pressure, regulator setting (done through steam chest pressure), reverser setting and speed-applied brake pressures etc. A number of transducers and other sensors feed back into the electronic recording device that is mounted in a housing engineered to withstand the massive potential trauma it could endure if the train was in a major accident, including fire-

ABOVE AND LEFT
The converted Mk 1 Brake coach No W35461 displays the workshop and spares and the kitchen areas. This mobile home from home keeps locos like No 5029 on the main line and gives the support crew a comfortable place to rest. *(Author)*

BELOW LEFT
Lubrication is undertaken at a station stop to make sure that the engine is kept topped up. *(Author)*

LEFT An old job done with new methods. Back in the steam era a driver would have checked if a bearing was running hot by touching it with the back of his hand. Today an infrared heat gun does the same job and records the result to monitor the engine's performance. *(Author)*

resistance, impact shock, static crush forces, immersion in water and magnetic fields. The system can also be used to download data to check on the performance and regulatory compliance of the crew.

The GSMR (Global System for Mobile Communications – Railway) system is the latest requirement at the time of writing. This is a radio system that has been specifically developed by a number of European partners for railway communication, and guarantees performance at speeds up to 310mph (500kph) without any communication loss. It will replace the approximately 30 different systems that existed prior to its introduction in Europe and creates a group standard across the continent. It offers a secure platform for communication of both voice and data between the locomotive and signal controllers and any other authorised agency. It can enable group voice communication and can be linked to facilities such as emergency services, cargo tracking, on-train CCTV and passenger information services as well. On board, the locomotive requires a power source (usually batteries on a steam loco), the header unit (the radio/human interface, placed in the tender toolboxes of most GWR locomotives on the main line) and the transmitter/receiver

LEFT One of the less glamorous jobs is cleaning the clinker from the fire. No matter how good a fireman is, how good the coal is and how much non-combustible material it contains is down to Mother Nature. If there are a lot of such compounds they can form a glass-like layer under the fire and it all has to be got rid of. There is only one way to do it – break it up with a series of different size and shape chisels and get it out with a long-handled shovel. *(Author)*

unit (placed at the rear of the tender in a special housing).

Other difficulties can be encountered due to the sheer lack of steam-related infrastructure left on the national rail network. There are a few turntables left, but little in the way of machinery or equipment capable of dispensing coal and water to a hungry and thirsty locomotive.

Before every run, the engine will undergo what is known as an FTR (Fitness To Run) examination. The locomotive will be in steam and at full working pressure, with all systems active to their operation can be checked. The examination will be an independant one, carried out by a person nominated by the VAB as a competent individual to carry out the testing. Once complete, it provides a limited period for the locomotive and coach to run on the national railway network infrastructure. The locomotive's number is entered into TOPS (Total Operations Processing System – a computer system for managing locomotives and rolling stock) for 72 hours upon the completion of the paperwork. The TOPS number is not what the locomotive carried in historical service, and indeed not what is carried on the cab sides. For example No 5051 *Earl Bathurst* is
No 98751. Usually the last two digits of the number would be the last two digits of the cab side number.

Once this is complete and signed off, the locomotive has its fire cleaned and then reduced to a level that will see it burn slowly through the night to keep the locomotive hot but not to cause the safety valves to lift and waste fuel and water. The support crew is up and active many hours before the locomotive is required to leave the depot. The tender tank will be filled, the fire built up to full strength, the boiler is taken up to near its working pressure, all the oil pots are filled and all the batteries for the electronics are topped up to fully charged ready for the official crew to drive her out. There could be a number of water and coal stops along the way, and the support crew will be there making sure the needs of the engine are satisfied. They will also monitor the performance of the engine, which could mean taking timings from the support coach or taking temperature readings of bearings with an infrared thermometer gun.

At its destination the loco will usually be turned (either on a table or on a triangle of track, which could result in quite a long journey in itself) and oiled, coaled, watered and have its fire cleaned. The return journey gets the happy passengers back to their station, but the support crew's job is not over. The disposal procedure has to be gone through and the locomotive needs to be attended to for perhaps another couple of hours. It is a very time-consuming and difficult process, being a support crew member, so the next time you see a Castle (or any other steam engine, for that matter) charging along the main line, or have the privilege of a ride on one, spare a thought for those few greasy, dirty and tired souls in the less glamorous-looking coach. They are the reason why it is there.

BELOW The aim of the exercise – No 5029 stands ready to go at Bristol Temple Meads station ready to perform again. *(Author)*

Epilogue

The legend continues

Well, there we are: a single design that, with modification, served its railway from 1906 until the last one was withdrawn in 1965 not because it was life expired, or indeed

unable to do its job any longer, but rather due to a change in policy that removed all of its kind from the railway. It was a wholesale slaughter that wasted locomotives with a projected 30-plus years' lifespan by scrapping them after barely 13 years' service. It was an ignominious end to the Stars, Castles and Kings that had

BELOW **No 4079 in steam in the 1960s.** *(Frank Dumbleton)*

reigned with style, precision and grace and, it has to be said, without the need to resort to building bigger and bigger locomotives as time went on and traffic levels increased. As a locomotive type, the Castle was designed for fairly light traffic loads but was more than capable of coping with far heavier and more demanding trains. Both Collett and Churchward would have been right to be satisfied, and indeed very proud, of the way the Star and Castle classes evolved way beyond the expectations of their original designs.

Eight Castles have been preserved (along with a Star and three Kings). All but two of these machines have steamed in preservation, and at the time of writing only one remains in the condition in which it left Barry Scrapyard. This alone goes some way towards demonstrating the affection for and popularity of these truly remarkable machines in the hearts of railway enthusiasts. They are magnificent, elegant, powerful and impressive. They are both technological achievements and timeless classics. They have been driven by people from all walks of life, from the average man in the street to royalty, and have operated to great acclaim on two continents. Few machines can claim to have enjoyed the long-term success of the Castles and their four-cylinder brethren. Their standardised parts and the wisdom of their Wiltshire engineers kept them not only current and useful but also efficient and cost-effective. Their weight of numbers helped too, and by the end of steam they were able to traverse the vast majority of the ex-GWR system – only the former Cambrian route main line eluded them.

They did have their shortcomings – the valve gear is a nightmare to work on if you have less than four elbows and wrists per arm, the ash pans are horrible things to clean out (especially if there is no pit in which to do it), and the cabs, to modern eyes at least, are draughty, uncomfortable and unpleasant. But if we translate that to the railway enthusiast it means they are challenging and interesting, with many charming traits including a cab that puts you in the heart of the action, and provides a memorable experience for the crew and footplate riders alike.

The Castles were effectively removed from

ABOVE Your author at work on No 4079 and dreaming of future main-line runs... *(Frank Dumbleton)*

everyday service on British Railways many decades ago, and with every passing year the memory of their time in service is fading from the collective consciousness. Despite this, many of the volunteers that restore, maintain and look after these machines are too young to have seen them during that period. I myself missed the last BR steam service by about seven years, but I am still compelled to work towards my ultimate goal, to see my project locomotive steam again, to charm, entice, inspire and capture the imagination of future generations. I am just one link in the great chain of people who, during her lifetime, have worked on No 4079. Hundreds of people have been involved in designing, building, driving, maintaining and overhauling her, and I will not be the last. My name will undoubtedly be forgotten, but the locomotive will continue on for future generations. My small contribution enables those enthusiasts in days yet to come to enjoy *Pendennis Castle*. It is quite an honour when you think about it, and in the meantime I and my team will be having a great deal of fun and excitement with the engine, and we hope that others will get the same measure of enjoyment from her that we do.

Long live the Castles!

Drew Fermor

Appendix 1

Maintenance schedule for Castle Class locomotives

This is based upon extracts from circular No 6763, dated December 1947.

General instructions

The following schedule gives the period at which each part of every engine, boiler and tender should be examined by the shed maintenance staffs, and defines the procedure to be adopted when carrying out such examinations, including any duties falling on the shed and footplate staffs where such apply.

The period set out in this schedule for the examination of engine parts are the maximum allowable between successive examinations. Where local circumstances make it necessary, shorter periods between examinations may be laid down by the Divisional Locomotive Superintendent, but no extension of the periods laid down in the circular should be undertaken without the matter being referred to and agreed by headquarters. A copy of the instructions from headquarters agreeing to extended periods of examination must be filed in the master copy at Swindon, in the Divisional Office copy and the Shed copy of the places concerned.

The list of examinations due to be carried out monthly includes only those that are essential at that period. A more general examination of the engine is to take place every two months. Examinations of valves and/or pistons, with the examinations of other parts done at that same time, are arranged at periods to suit their being carried out in all cases, with the two-monthly examinations. All mechanical examinations due at a given date (except those in respect of the ATC apparatus) must be done at one stoppage of the engine, and this stoppage should, whenever possible, coincide with the Divisional Boiler Inspectors' examination of the boiler, if this is then due.

	Detail	Procedure	Period
Air pump.	Valves.	See that check nuts and split pins are secure. Correct lift of valves ⅛in minimum and 5⁄32in maximum.	Monthly.
	Ram.	Examine connection to pump arm on crosshead and see that nut and cotter are secure.	
	Cylinder.	Examine studs and nuts on covers and fixing bolts in barrel flanges.	
	Arm on crosshead.	Examine nuts, bolts and split pins. Examine arm for flaws and tightness of securing bolts. Examine oil lubrication pipe to barrel.	
ATC gear.	Battery.	Change.	Monthly (by ATC Electrician).
	Shoe switch.	Remove cover and clean contacts with a soft cloth.	
	Brake valve, siren disc and spindle hinge pin of valve electromagnet armature lever, bell, vacuum cut-out switch, clipping up and resetting gear.	Remove, examine and oil. Floating armature to be examined for freedom, height of brass pins. Resetting handle to be quite free.	
	Shoe height – unsprung type.	Adjust if above or below correct height of 2½in above rail level. Change shoe if ⅛in free lift on shoe without moving switch.	Monthly (by Fitters or as reported by ATC Electrician or Enginemen).
	Shoe height – sprung type.	Adjust if more than ¼in above or below correct height, after ensuring engine is at correct height. Examine shoe securing bolts and slipper piece for wear.	
	Relays.	If out of order, change cab apparatus.	Monthly (by ATC Electrician).

Axleboxes.	Keeps.	Siphon out and restore.	At each washout (to be carried out by Conciliation Staff).
		Examine nuts, bolts and studs.	Monthly and at lifting.
	Lubrication details.	Examine auxiliary oil feed boxes, pipe, unions, brackets and bolts. Check oil pipe connections to crowns and horns.	
		Clean and restore all oil wells in all auxiliary oil boxes and axlebox crowns.	Loose covers: At piston examination. Fixed covers: When lifted (to be carried out by Conciliation Staff except when at local repair shop).
	Crowns.	Make sure crown is secure in box.	When lifted.
	White metal in crowns.	Examine for fatigue.	
	Horn ways and faces, coupled wheels axleboxes.	Examine for lateral play using test strips. Report when ⅛in above standard clearance. Examine flanges for fractures and loose liners.	Four-monthly.
	Bogie axleboxes.	Report ¼in side play between wheel boss and axlebox face. (Except collared axles, report if ³⁄₁₆in). Side play report at ¹⁄₁₆in.	
Bogie.	Frames.	Examine for fractures and loose bolts.	Monthly.
	Centre pin and block control springs.	Examine for broken oil pipes and ensure that all bolts, etc, are secure.	Four-monthly.
		Report if centre pin or bush is more than ⅛in oval.	When bogie is out.
Boiler.	Expansion bracket studs, boiler keys.	Examine for slackness.	Two-monthly.
	IN CASE OF ANY DEFECT BECOMING SERIOUS, THE ATTENTION OF THE DIVISIONAL BOILER INSPECTOR MUST BE DRAWN TO THE MATTER, AFTER WHICH HE WILL EXAMINE AND REPORT TO THE DIVISIONAL SUPERINTENDENT'S OFFICE. NB: Divisional Boiler Inspectors' examinations take place two-monthly for boilers over 180psi.		
	Tubes.	Examine for leakages and cleanliness. NB: If one tube behind the header is found to be pitted through, all tubes behind the header are to be renewed.	At each washout.
	Crown plate stays.	Remove all deposits from around stay nuts. Scale to be removed from crown stays, waterside, to ascertain condition.	
	Copper plates in firebox.	Remove all deposits, report all cracks, bulging or thin flanges.	
	Washout plugs.	Examine plughole threads and re-tap if necessary.	
	Mud hole doors.	Examine for condition and fit, thread and nut also to be examined.	
	Ash pan and fittings.	Studs carrying ash pan to be specially examined. Damper doors and gear to be examined.	
	Grate rack and fire bars.	Any defective rack or bars to be renewed.	
	Brick arch.	Examine and repair or renew if defective.	
	Waterways and stays.	All firebox stays to be hammer tested, SPECIAL ATTENTION BEING GIVEN TO: Those in the top corner of each plate and those in positions in which it is known breakages are frequent. Make sure all waterways are clear.	Monthly.
	NB: Especial care to be taken to examine all accessible internal parts, using acetylene light and mirrors. Nuts to be renewed on nutted stays where necessary. ⅝in stays not to be reduced to ⁹⁄₁₆in without authority of Divisional Boiler Inspector. Deposit on steel stays waterside to be removed when grooving or fracture is suspected. Rivet heads of tubeplates, back plate, and crown plate waterside should be specially examined.		
	Smokebox and smokebox door.	Examine for air leaks. Threads on dart and handles to be examined.	
	Casing plates.	Examine where possible and remove any corrosion.	
	Lead plugs.	Examine lead. Examine hole threads and re-tap if necessary.	Monthly – NB: Renew plugs every two months.

Brake gear.	Brake shaft and brackets.	Examine for alignment. Report if ³⁄₃₂in slack in brackets.	Two-monthly.
	Handbrake screw.	Change nut and screw it thread is below ⅛ in thick. Examine cotter, split pins, column bolts and nuts and stop bracket where fitted.	
	Pull rod and pins.	Examine jaws and pins for excessive wear. Examine for loose, broken or missing bolts and split pins. No part of brake gear should be less than 3⅛ in above the rail.	Monthly.
	Safety chains.	Replace if missing or defective. Renew when ³⁄₁₆in worn in link.	
	Blocks.	Change if less than 1⅜ in thick or if or if 'spewing' off wheel.	As required.
	Hangers and brackets.	Examine for loose, broken or missing bolts and split pins.	Monthly and when blocks are changed.
	Adjusting screws.	Test for tightness and condition of thread. Replace key if missing.	
	Brake cylinder.	Report if cylinder or piston rod is 0.015in oval, tapered or scored.	Whenever cylinder is opened.
		Lubricate trunnions and brake shaft. (TO BE DONE BY CONCILIATION STAFF EXCEPT WHEN IN LOCAL REPAIR SHOP).	Monthly.
Buffers.	Heads.	Examine for flaws between head and stem.	Two-monthly.
	Springs.	Test buffer for broken spring by twisting head.	
	Fixing bolts.	Examine for tightness.	
Crossheads.	General.	Examine for fractures (report if clearance between crosshead & bars is more than ⅛in). Check motion bars for parallel.	Monthly.
	Crosshead air pump arm. Gudgeon pin. Slipper bolts.	Examine for loose or missing nuts, bolts and split pins. Examine gudgeon pin for fit in crosshead.	
Cylinders.	Covers, front.	Examine for fractures.	At piston examination.
	Covers, rear.	Test motion bar bolts for tightness.	Monthly.
	Covers, front and back.	Test nuts for tightness. Special attention to be given to front covers of four-cylinder engines. During factory or shed repair or new engine, nuts to be tightened after trial.	Two-monthly OR if covers have been re-jointed.
	Barrel.	Record wear and clearance of piston head. Examine barrel for fractures. Report when piston clearance exceeds ⁵⁄₃₂in. If cylinder or pistons reveal signs of rapid wear, make sure that oil is being delivered through the lubricator. The maximum permissible variation in the cylinder diameter out of round is 0.04in. If the cylinder exceeds the figure, the cylinder should be reported for re-boring. The variation should be obtained by measuring WITHIN THE RING SPACE the SMALLEST diameter and subtracting it from the greatest diameter whether in the same cross-section or not. It will usually be found WITHIN THE RING STROKE that the smallest diameter is horizontal about the middle of the cylinder and the largest is nearly vertical at the mouth. IF THE PISTON IS BEING RENEWED, THE MAXIMUM OUT OF ROUND SHOULD NOT EXCEED 0.031in.	At piston examination.
Cylinder cock gear.	Levers, rods, pins, brackets.	Examine for missing or defective parts.	At piston examination.
	Cylinder cocks.	Change if defective. Replace any missing pipes or unions.	
Drawgear.	Engine drag hooks and screw connections.	Oil screw connections (BY CONCILIATION STAFF). Change if screw connections strained in hook or thread worn or if follows: Minimum width of hook at centre line is 2½in; 1½in between eye and hook; ⅛in on bearing in buffer beam.	Monthly.
	Shackles.	Change if worn to: 1¼in at end; 1⅝in diameter hole at end; If strained.	
	Screws.	Change if more than ¹⁄₃₂in backlash in a new unit. Change if less than 1¹³⁄₁₆in diameter over round thread.	
	Intermediate draw gear between engines and tender.	Examine for play between intermediate buffers and rubbing plates. See all cotters are in link pins.	
		Examine draw bars for flaws and wear. Report if rubbing plates are ⅛in hollow. Examine drag box for loose rivets, plate distortion or excessive corrosion.	Whenever engine and tender are uncoupled.

Firehole doors.	Handle gear.	Make sure that all pins are secure and doors slide freely.	Two-monthly.
Flexible connections on engine and tender.	Water pipes. Vacuum pipes. Steam heating pipes.	Examine for defective pipes and leakage at unions and joints.	Monthly.
Frames.	Frame plates.	Examine for fractures. If fractured, report to DSO and submit sketch showing position and extent of fracture.	Monthly.
	Framing brackets.	Examine for fractures. Boilersmiths to examine for loose rivets. Any defects noticed which do not require immediate attention to be noted for observation.	Two-monthly.
	Four-cylinder engine valve gear carrying brackets and bolts.	Examine for fractured brackets and report any to DSO. Examine securing bolts for slackness.	
	Horn ties.	Examine for looseness. See that split pins are secure.	
	Cylinder bolts.	Examine for slackness and broken bolts. If steam pipe joints continually reported, remove gangway plates for close examination of all bolts in saddle.	
	Horn blocks.	Examine for loose bolts and fractures. Check clearance over tops of axleboxes, to gauge supplied.	
Injectors.	Cones and clacks.	Examine and change or re-lap as necessary. Maximum clearance of cage above diameter of clack $\frac{1}{16}$in.	Monthly.
	Coal watering pipe and cock feed bags and pipes. Grease separators. Drip valves and water valves.	Examine for loose, worn or defective parts.	
	Non-return valves in exhaust injector steam pipes.	Check all union nuts for tightness.	
Lubricator gear.	Strainers.	Change if clogged.	Monthly.
	Three-way condensing cock.	Check for freedom of movement.	
	Sight-fed lubricator.	Examine for cleanliness. (TO BE DONE BY CONCILIATION STAFF EXCEPT WHEN IN LOCAL REPAIR SHOP).	At valve examination.
	'J' valve.	Make sure valve is workable.	
	Pipes, nipples and unions.	Check soundness of joints.	
	Cylinder and valve feeds.	See that oil holes in cylinder barrels and valve bushes are clear.	
	'W' valve and bullet catch gear.	Uncouple rod and see that valve is clean and has correct lift ($\frac{1}{8}$in) with regulator in drifting position. See that bullet catch is workable and secure.	Four-monthly.
	Oil spray nozzles in steam pipes.	Remove and clean.	At piston examination.
Pistons.	At all piston examinations, the following details must also be examined in accordance with the procedures set out in this schedule: Cylinders, cylinder cock gear, connecting and coupling rods, oil spray nozzles in steam pipes.		
	Piston heads.	Check clearance in bore. Report if $\frac{5}{16}$in or over. Examine for flaws.	Eight-monthly.
	Piston rings.	Change if $\frac{3}{8}$in or less thick.	
	Piston rods.	See that the cotter in key is bearing against the crosshead. Examine end cone for flaws.	
	Glands – piston and valve spindle.	Examine split and cone rings and packing cone for fractures. See that studs are secure and have good threads.	Eight-monthly or when glands reported blowing.
Reversing gear.	Screw thread, nut handle and catch. Bracket, bolts and nuts. Foundation bolts.	Examine for loose or defective parts.	Eight-monthly.
	Bridle rod joint bolts, pins and split pins.	Examine for loose or defective parts.	
	Weigh shaft arms, brackets and bolts, nuts and split pins.	Examine for loose or defective parts.	

Rods, connecting.	Rods.	ALL BENT RODS MUST BE SENT TO THE FACTORY FOR REPAIR. To be examined in position as far as is possible for fractures.	Two-monthly.
	Large ends.	Inside: Re-metal when metal shows signs of fracture on face. Outside: Re-metal if clearance on pins is 0.025in or more or if metal is fractured. Renew bush if found loose in rod.	At piston examination.
	Small ends.	Report if side play is ⅟₁₆in or more.	
	Pads and restrictor plugs.	Examine pads and remove restrictor plugs for cleaning.	
	Keys, set bolts, cotters, etc.	Examine for fit. Examine threads on bolts and fit of bolts in strap. Make sure cotter is a good fit against strap.	
	Large end keys, inside connecting rods.	Clearance between key and strap: Front (rod side) ⅟₁₆in; Rear (brasses side) ⅛in.	
	Bushes.	Large end: Remove crank pin washer and take wear with feelers. Re-metal if clearance on pin is 0.025in or more or if metal is fractured or renew if it is found loose in rod. Small end: Remove bush and examine rod eye end for fractures.	
	Oil cups.	To be examined for loose covers. Re-trim and restore (BY CONCILIATION STAFF, except when in local repair shop).	When rods are removed.

BELOW Here we see maintenance in action around the turntable at Swindon Shed in March 1964. The not to be moved board indicates that shed staff are at work under the locomotive. No. 4079 Pendennis Castle was in the company that day of '2884' Class No. 3802 (which survives in preservation) and 10XX 'County' Class locomotive No. 1011 County of Chester.
(Collection of Sir William McAlpine)

Rods, coupling.	Rods, bushes, etc.	To be examined in position as far as possible for fractures.	Two-monthly.
	BENT RODS: RODS MUST BE SENT TO FACTORY FOR REPAIR. Cranks must be quartered and detailed report of the results obtained sent to Swindon.		When reported.
	To be completely dismantled and examined for fractures.		When dismantled.
	Remove crank pin washer, check clearances on pin with feelers. Re-metal if clearance is 0.025in or more or if metal is fractured. Renew bush if found loose in rod. Examine pads and remove restrictor for cleaning.		At piston examination.
	Joint pins.	Examine for fit and tightness of fastening. Report if pin 0.020in slack in bush.	
Rods, eccentric.	Sheave bolts, nuts and split pins.	Examine for tightness.	Monthly.
	Strap joint and bolts, rod foot and bolts, nuts and split pins.	Examine for tightness. See that split pins bear on nuts. TURNED WASHERS OF $\frac{1}{16}$in and upwards to be used if necessary.	
	Jaw and pins, nuts and split pins.	Examine for tightness.	
	Oil cups.	Re-trim and restore. (TO BE DONE BY CONCILIATION STAFF EXCEPT WHEN IN LOCAL REPAIR SHOP.)	
	Sheaves.	Examine for side play between straps and sheaves. Report at above $\frac{3}{32}$in.	Valve examination.
	Straps.	Re-line and re-bore at $\frac{1}{16}$in slack on diameter. Examine pads and restrictors.	
Safety valves.	Complete.	Examine in steam for leaks at seat joint. See that blow-off pressure is not above correct working pressure or more than 5psi less by pressure gauge in engine.	When reported.
		Examine in position. Dismantle and examine all parts.	At top feed examination.
Sand gear.	Sand pipes.	See that sand is being delivered to rail at correct position and that pipes are secure. Ends of pipes to be not less than $2\frac{1}{2}$in above rail level.	Two-monthly.
	Sand valves, rods and levers, brackets and pins, etc.	Examine for worn or defective parts.	Four-monthly.
	Sandbox fixing bolts.	Examine for tightness.	
Smokebox.	Blast pipe.	Jumper top: examine for carbon deposit and clean if necessary. Make sure jumper is free. Check jumper stop's lugs for wear and nuts for tightness. Examine seat joint studs and nuts.	Monthly.
	Saddle bolts, cylinder bolts.	Examine for loose or broken bolts.	Two-monthly.
	Spark plates.	See that plates are easily removed and replaced. See that safety brackets are secure and undated.	
	Steam pipes.	Examine in steam for leakage.	
	Superheater.	Examine in steam for leakage.	
	Ejector and blower ring.	See that holes are clear. Examine blower pipe for defects and union for tightness.	
	Lubricator pipes and connections inside and outside smokebox.	Check for soundness of joints, etc.	
	Chimney.	Check alignment.	When reported for persistent bad steaming or high coal consumption.
Speedometer.	Drive rod in slotted block.	Examine for wear. Build up by welding or change block when $\frac{1}{16}$in or more slack in slot.	Two-monthly.
Spring gear.	Complete.	Dismantle and examine.	When engine reported riding roughly.
	Springs.	Examine for broken plates.	Monthly.
	Tee hangers and pins.	See that split pins are secure.	Four-monthly.
	Hangers, nuts and split pins.	Examine for worn or defective parts.	
	Brackets, bolts and nuts.	Examine for worn or defective parts.	
	NB: The normal running heights from rail to top of footplate for Castle with new tyres are: Front buffer plate: 4ft $2\frac{1}{4}$in; Rear buffer plate: 5ft $7\frac{1}{4}$in.		

Steam valves (various).	Ejector, blower, steam heating, lubricator, warning whistles, injector, blow down cock.	Examine when engine is dead for worn spindle threads and loose or defective parts.	Two-monthly.
Tender.	Axleboxes, brake gear, spring gear, draw gear, vacuum pipes, etc.	See corresponding engine parts.	See corresponding engine parts.
	Water feed valves.	See that water flows freely.	Monthly.
	Tank lid hinge pins.	Examine for looseness.	
	Test cocks.	Operate and see that water flows freely when tank is full.	
	Level indicator gear.	See that indicator is operating.	
		Examine for worn or defective parts.	When reported.
	Tanks.	To be cleaned out and examined.	According to local water conditions.
	Water scoop.	After ascertaining that axlebox clearance is correct, lower scoop and check distance of edge below rail. The correct distance with 2,000 gallons of water and 4 tons of coal is: 1½in below rail for a 4,000-gallon tender; 1in for all other tender types. Care must be taken when water scoops are changed that the type of scoop fitted to 4,000-gallon tenders is not fitted to any other type of tender and vice versa. When adjustments are necessary to the scoops and the tender is at the correct height, the adjustment must be made with the liner at the top portion of the scoop. The correct height for standard GWR Castle tenders from rail measured from front and back buffer plates on new tyres is 4ft 4½in front and back.	Two-monthly.
	Water scoop gear.	Examine for worn or defective parts. Report if shaft is ⅛in worn in brackets.	
Top feed gear.	General.	Remove safety valves. Clean trays, clacks and pipes.	According to local water conditions.
Vacuum brakes.	Pepperbox valve.	Test for opening at 25in vacuum. Change if defective.	Two-monthly.
	Ejector drip valve.	Remove, clean and replace.	Two-monthly (daily in frosty weather).
	Vacuum cylinder.	Examine gland and test for leakage. Oil trunnion brackets.	Two-monthly.
		When a vacuum cylinder is dismantled, interior surface should be examined. If badly rusted or corroded, cylinder should be changed. If water is present, source should be traced to ensure cylinder being dry.	When reported.
	Retaining valve.	A vacuum must be blown up and the brakes applied. If the needle of the vacuum gauge shows that an undue leakage is taking place into the reservoir, the retaining valve must be temporarily blanked off. If this stops the leakage, the valve is defective and must be changed. If it does not the leak must be elsewhere and the brake must be examined and the defect found and remedied. In all cases the retaining valve should be cleaned and oiled when the test is made. If one of the new pattern valves should fail and only the old type is available to replace it, one of these can be used by removing the pepperbox valve and substituting a blank.	12 months or when reported.
		Clean and oil. Flexible connection, check all unions for tightness.	Monthly.
	Moderating valve.	Check that ball is in position.	When reported.

Valves.	At all valve examination the following details must also be examined in accordance with this schedule: Lubricator gear; Valve gear; Reversing gear; Eccentric rods. For procedure to be adopted see Appendix 2.		Four-monthly.
	Piston valve spindles.	Spindles or renewable spindle sleeves where fitted will need renewal when worn to $\frac{1}{16}$in out of round. When spindles or spindle sleeves require renewal, the valves complete must be sent to Swindon and the gland packing rings sent therewith. Where facilities exist however, the spindles may be ground locally, the diameter to be reduced in steps of $\frac{1}{32}$in and new bushes obtained from Divisional Piston Valve Stores. Spindles must not be ground below 1 $\frac{5}{8}$in diameter.	
	Glands.	Packing to be renewed.	When valves are examined.
Valve gear.	Four-cylinder engines: Adjusting screws and connections.	Dismantle and examine for tightness.	At valve examination.
	Combination lever.	Examine for worn or defective parts.	
	Quadrant link, lifting link.	Examine for worn or defective parts. Report when block is 0.030in slack in link.	
	Rocking arm, rocking arm brackets, all nuts, bolts and split pins.	Report when there is a cumulative clearance of $\frac{1}{4}$in between eccentric and valve spindle (ie $\frac{1}{4}$in loss of travel in valve gear).	
Water gauge frame.	Complete.	Remove test plugs in front of gauge, cap above gauge glass and caps at top and bottom of gauge. Test rod $\frac{1}{4}$in square to be passed through all passages. See that test cocks blow through cocks and pipes are clear. See that shut-off cocks, glands and levers are in perfect working order.	Monthly.
Wheels.	Axles – crank.	Built-up cranks to be examined for looseness. Dowels to be examined.	Monthly.
	Wheel centres.	Examine spokes and rims for fractures. Test key ring for tightness. Report if defective.	
	Axles – straight.	Axles to be examined for flaws. Report if defective.	When engine is lifted.
Tyres.	There are two types of wheel flange profiles on a Castle Class locomotive, Thick and Thin (see Appendix 3 for details). These are arranged per axle thus: Loco: Thick, Thick, Thick, Thin, Thick; Tender: Thick, Thick, Thick.		
	Flanges.	See that depth and thickness are within limits on the gauge provided. Report if these limits are likely to be exceeded in the next month.	Monthly.
	Tread.	Report if tread shows $\frac{3}{16}$in or more hollow when compared with the standard profile gauge. NB: If flange is not at minimum depth, the profile gauge will not touch the tread at any point and this must be allowed for in measuring tread wear.	
	Tyres must be carefully examined for fractures, especially lip over key ring. Report if thickness of tyre is below 1$\frac{3}{4}$in for coupled wheels and 1$\frac{5}{8}$in for bogie and tender wheels. Tyres showing signs of movement must be reported and at the time of the examination, wheel centre should be marked with a centre punch and early subsequent examination made with a view to ascertaining whether the tyre has moved between the examinations. The fastening ring must be specially examined and if it is in a loose condition, the engine must be taken out of traffic. It is especially necessary that the ring be tight at two ends.		
Whistles.	Chains.	Make sure all chains are sound and secure at each end and that the valve works freely when the chain is pulled.	Two-monthly.

Appendix 2

Valve examination procedure

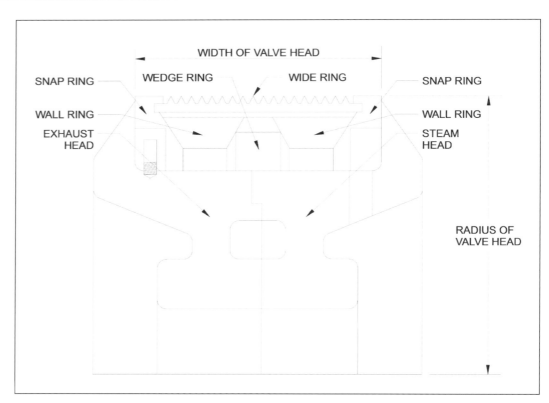

General

The above diagram shows a section through a piston valve and indicates the correct name for each part. There are three nominal diameters of piston valve in service, viz 8in, 9in and 10in, and nominal diameter exists in two or more widths of valve head, according to the class of engine in which the valve is running. The difference in widths of valve of the same diameter are made by varying the widths of the wide ring and the wall rings, but snap rings and wedge rings are the same width no matter what class of engine they may be in.

A) After withdrawing valves from the steam chests, take sizes of front bushes in steam chests and note out-of-round and out-of-parallel dimensions. Make a chalk mark inside the bush at its largest diameter. Wear in the bush must be calculated from its nearest nominal boring size, *ie* the wear is the difference between the largest dimensions of the bush (excluding port bars) and the valve nominal size. Castle valve sleeves are new when bored to 9in. At re-boring these are increased at increments of 1/16in each time, until the final re-boring, which is 9⅜in. If the bush is out of parallel more than 0.030in but less than 0.040in, or if it is more than 0.010in but less than 0.015in out of round, report the engine for re-boring in the near future. If the bush is out of parallel more than 0.040in or out of round more than 0.015in then the engine must be stopped for immediate re-boring.

B) Take valves apart and clean if the engine is not being stopped for immediate re-boring. Rings must be cleaned by scraping, the grooves in the wide ring cleared using a hacksaw. On no account must rings be decarbonised by heat in an open fire.

C) Test exhaust snap rings for slackness, if any, by placing the front exhaust snap rings in the most worked part of the front bushes (*ie* the part with the chalk marks therein) and try around the ring with feelers. If more than 0.020in slack, all snap rings on that valve must be changed. *Scrap the old snap rings*.

D) Examine all wall rings and wedge rings. Any defective rings must be renewed. If the rivets in the joint place of the wedge rings have become loose, tighten them by careful riveting. (NB: Wide rings cannot be tested until new snap rings have been obtained and fitted.) *Scrap the old rings rejected*.

E) Fitting new rings. When the rings are received, separate the new snap rings from the new wide rings. Test each assembly for slackness between the heads. Care must be taken in carrying this out to tighten the spindle nut sufficiently to close the two heads properly together. If the old wide rings are reusable then *return the new ones to divisional store immediately. Do not retain for use in another engine*. Rings easily may be confused, and if retained at the depot may get mixed with others sent later for another engine. Endorse the label that was sent with the rings as 'Not required' and attach it to the new rings being returned. *If the old wide rings are not useable, scrap them. Do not retain for use on another engine.*

On no account must only one new snap ring be fitted to a valve. Renew all or none.

Try the edge of a ring on a surface plate when filing to ensure that it is kept flat. Do *not* grind rings on the carborundum or sandstone wheel. When fitting new rings, make sure that the wide ring is trimmed sufficiently. *It is important to ensure that the two heads do not grip the snap rings.*

When the valve is assembled, place a straight edge across the two snap rings. If necessary, file the wide ring until they are very slightly below the level of the snap rings. *Do not attempt the easing of any ring except wide rings*. Send old rings back to Divisional Stores in the boxes in which the new rings were sent. This scrap is valuable high-grade cast iron.

F) Reassembling valve. Give the nut securing the heads of the spindle a dressing of graphite grease in the threads and apply a thin coating to the taper pin before driving it into the hole. It is now permissible to insert a tinplate washer between the nut and the head in cases where the fitting of a new nut would delay the return to traffic of the engine, but this practice is to be regarded as expedient only and new washers will not be stocked. It must be clearly understood that only *one* washer may be used behind each nut.

Castles use 9in S8-type valves.		
Markings on piston valves.		
Type of ring	Diameter of ring	Class of valve
Snap ring	Nominal	8A
	Nominal + $\frac{1}{16}$in	8A1
	Nominal + $\frac{1}{8}$in	8A2
	Nominal + $\frac{3}{16}$in	8B3
	Nominal + $\frac{1}{4}$in	8B4
	Nominal + $\frac{5}{16}$in	8B5
	Nominal + $\frac{3}{8}$in	8B6
Wedge ring	To suit 'A' size snap rings	8A
	To suit 'B' size snap rings	8B
Wide ring	Nominal	S8A
	Nominal + $\frac{1}{16}$in	S8A1
	Nominal + $\frac{1}{8}$in	S8A2
	Nominal + $\frac{3}{16}$in	S8B3
	Nominal + $\frac{1}{4}$in	S8B4
	Nominal + $\frac{5}{16}$in	S8B5
	Nominal + $\frac{3}{8}$in	S8B6
Wall ring	To suit 'A' size snap rings	S8A
	To suit 'B' size snap rings	S8B

Appendix 3

Tyre profiles

Extracted from GWR drawing No 97774

4073 class loco and tender tyres are all to the 'Thick' profile, except the centre coupled driving wheels which are to be to the 'Thin' profile.

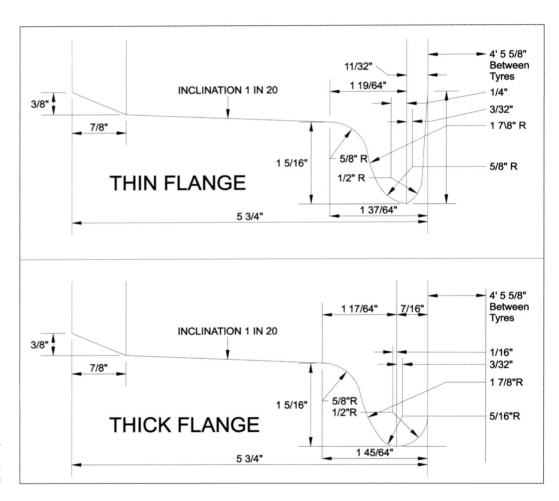

Appendix 4

Axlebox clearances

Method of measuring side play of horns and journals

Only one figure is required for each axle, which should be the total amount of side play of the axle relative to the frames. The maximum side play is obtained as shown in the diagram below and is a sum of the individual clearances of A, B, C and D.

The side flanges of the axleboxes are tapered, and therefore great care must be taken that clearances B and C are taken at the middle of the side flanges on the flat portion.

All clearance should be taken by means of the test strips provided.

Report for attention when the total lateral play is ⅛in or more *above* standard clearance.

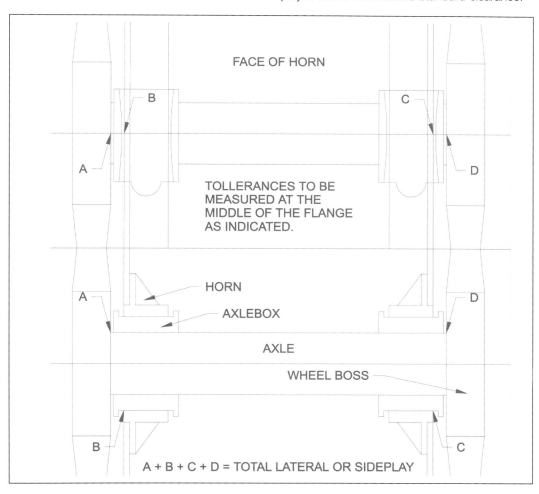

FACE OF HORN

B

C

A

D

TOLLERANCES TO BE
MEASURED AT THE
MIDDLE OF THE FLANGE
AS INDICATED.

A HORN

AXLEBOX D

AXLE

WHEEL BOSS

B C

A + B + C + D = TOTAL LATERAL OR SIDEPLAY

LEFT Measuring side play of horns and journals.
(Author's Drawing)

All castle axlebox measurements to be to 'easy fit' standards.
Easy fit on journals: 1/32in total clearance between box faces and wheel bosses.
Easy fit in horns: Coupled boxes 1/32in clearance side play, bogie boxes 3/64in clearance side play.
Bogie to have 2in clearance each way.

Appendix 5

GWR four-cylinder express passenger locomotive histories

This list includes the entire Star and King classes as well as the Castles, as there is much crossover of interest, and it gives a complete picture of top-link steam express motive power from the turn of the 20th century until dieselisation of the network in the mid-1960s on the GWR route.

Loco lot no.	1st loco no.	2nd loco no.	Build date	Class as built	1st name	2nd name (date)	3rd name (date)	Conversions (date)	Double chimney	Withdrawn	Notes/significant dates
161	40	4000 (Dec 1912)	April 1906	Prototype	—	North Star (Sept 1906)	—	Star (Nov 1909) Castle (Nov 1929)	—	July 1953	Prototype four-cylinder GWR engine built as an Atlantic. Superheater fitted from Nov 1909. Scissors valve gear until Castle conversion. Never fitted with fire iron tunnel.
171	111	—	Feb 1908	Prototype	The Great Bear	Viscount Churchill (Sept 1924)		Castle (Sept 1924)	—	July 1953	Built as sole GWR Pacific. Superheater fitted as built.
168	4001	—	Feb 1907	Star	Dog Star	—	—	—	—	Jan 1934	First true Star Class locomotive. Superheater fitted Jan 1911. Castle style outside steam pipes Oct 1930.
	4002	—	Mar 1907	Star	Evening Star	—	—	—	—	June 1953	Superheater fitted Aug 1909. Elbow outside steam pipes Dec 1929.
	4003	—	Feb 1907	Star	Lode Star	—	—	—	—	July 1951	Sole preserved Star, National Railway Museum collection. Superheater fitted May 1911. Elbow outside steam pipes May 1949.
	4004	—	Feb 1907	Star	Morning Star	—	—	—	—	Apr 1948	Superheater Fitted Jan 1911. Elbow outside steam pipes May 1946.
	4005	—	Feb 1907	Star	Polar Star	—	—	—	—	Nov 1934	Sent to LNWR 15–27 Aug 1910 for trials. Superheater fitted Feb 1911.
	4006	—	Apr 1907	Star	Red Star	—	—	—	—	Nov 1932	Superheater fitted Apr 1911.
	4007	—	Apr 1907	Star	Rising Star	Swallowfield Park (May 1937)	—	—	—	Sept 1951	Superheater fitted May 1911. Elbow outside steam pipes May 1947.
	4008	—	May1907	Star	Royal Star	—	—	—	—	June 1935	Superheater fitted Dec 1911. Elbow outside steam pipes July 1933.
	4009	100 A1 (Jan 1936)	May 1907	Star	Shooting Star	A1 Lloyds (Jan 1936)	—	Castle (Apr 1925)	—	May 1950	Superheater fitted Oct 1912. Only Castle with 2 number plates per side. Never fitted with fire iron tunnel. Oil burner Jan.1947–Sept 1948.
	4010	—	May 1907	Star	Western Star	—	—	—	—	Nov 1934	Superheater fitted May 1907.
173	4011	—	Mar 1908	Star	Knight of the Garter	—	—	—	—	Nov 1932	Superheater fitted May 1908.
	4012	—	Mar 1908	Star	Knight of the Thistle	—	—	—	—	Oct 1949	Superheater Jan 1911.
	4013	—	Mar 1908	Star	Knight of St Patrick	—	—	—	—	May 1950	Superheater fitted Dec 1910.
	4014	—	Mar 1908	Star	Knight of the Bath	—	—	—	—	June 1949	Superheater fitted Oct 1910. Elbow steam pipes Sept 1935.
	4015	—	Mar 1908	Star	Knight of St John	—	—	—	—	Feb 1951	Superheater fitted Sept 1910. Elbow steam pipes Dec 1948.
	4016	—	Apr 1908	Star	Knight of the Golden Fleece	The Somerset Light Infantry (Prince Albert's) (Jan 1938)	—	Castle (Oct 1925)	—	Sept 1951	Superheater fitted Mar 1909.
	4017	—	Apr 1908	Star	Knight of the Black Eagle	Knight of Liège (Aug 1914)	Knight of Liège (circa 1925)	—	—	Nov 1949	Superheater fitted Mar 1909. 2nd name change from French to Belgian spelling at political request.
	4018	—	Apr 1908	Star	Knight of the Grand Cross	—	—	—	—	Apr 1951	Superheater fitted Sept 1910. Elbow outside steam pipes May 1931.
	4019	—	May 1908	Star	Knight Templar	—	—	—	—	Oct 1951	Superheater fitted Jan 1910. Elbow outside steam pipes May 1948.
	4020	—	May 1908	Star	Knight Commander	—	—	—	—	Mar 1951	Superheater fitted Nov 1909. Elbow outside steam pipes Mar 1948.
178	4021	—	June 1909	Star	King Edward	The British Monarch (June 1927)	British Monarch (Oct 1927)	—	—	Oct 1952	Superheater fitted June 1909. Elbow outside steam pipes July 1948.
	4022	—	June 1909	Star	King William	The Belgian Monarch (June 1927)	Belgian Monarch (Oct 1927)	—	—	Feb 1952	Superheater fitted Oct 1910. Elbow outside steam pipes June 1948. Name removed May 1940.
	4023	—	June 1909	Star	King George	The Danish Monarch (July 1927)	Danish Monarch (Oct 1927)	—	—	July 1952	Superheater fitted Sept 1912. Name removed Nov 1940.
	4024	—	June 1909	Star	King James	The Dutch Monarch (Sept 1927)	Dutch Monarch (Nov 1927)	—	—	Feb 1935	Superheater fitted Sept 1912.
	4025	—	July 1909	Star	King Charles	Italian Monarch (Oct 1927)	—	—	—	Aug 1950	Superheater fitted Jan 1911. Name removed June 1940. Castle-style outside steam pipes Feb 1929.
	4026	—	Sept 1909	Star	King Richard	The Japanese Monarch (July 1927)	Japanese Monarch (Nov 1927)	—	—	Feb 1950	Superheater fitted May 1913. Name removed January 1941. Elbow outside steam pipes Oct 1932.
	4027	—	Sept 1909	Star	King Henry	The Norwegian Monarch (July 1927)	Norwegian Monarch (Nov 1927)	—	—	Oct 1934	Superheater fitted June 1912.
	4028	—	Sept 1909	Star	King John	The Romanian Monarch (July 1927)	Romanian Monarch (Nov 1927)	—	—	Nov 1951	Superheater fitted Sept 1911. Name removed Nov 1940.
	4029	—	Oct 1909	Star	King Stephen	The Spanish Monarch (July 1927)	Spanish Monarch (Nov 1927)	—	—	Nov 1934	Superheater fitted Apr 1911.
	4030	—	Oct 1909	Star	King Harold	The Swedish Monarch (July 1927)	Swedish Monarch (Nov 1927)	—	—	May 1950	Superheater fitted Jan 1913. Name removed Nov 1940.

Loco lot no.	1st loco no.	2nd loco no.	Build date	Class as built	1st name	2nd name (date)	3rd name (date)	Conversions (date)	Double chimney	Withdrawn	Notes/significant dates
180	4031	—	Nov 1909	Star	Queen Mary	—	—	—	—	June 1951	First GWR four-cylinder 4-6-0 to have superheater as built; all other engines follow suit. Elbow outside steam pipes Aug 1948.
	4032	—	Nov 1910	Star	Queen Alexandra	—	—	Castle (Apr 1926)	—	Sept 1951	
	4033	—	Nov 1910	Star	Queen Victoria	—	—	—	—	June 1951	Elbow outside steam pipes Apr 1940.
	4034	—	Nov 1910	Star	Queen Adelaide	—	—	—	—	Sept 1952	Elbow outside steam pipes June 1932.
	4035	—	Nov 1910	Star	Queen Charlotte	—	—	—	—	Oct 1951	Castle-style outside steam pipes Jan 1931.
	4036	—	Dec 1910	Star	Queen Elizabeth	—	—	—	—	Mar 1952	Elbow outside steam pipes July 1943.
	4037	—	Dec 1910	Star	Queen Philippa	The South Wales Borderers (Mar 1937)	—	Castle (June 1926)	—	Sept 1952	
	4038	—	Jan 1911	Star	Queen Berengaria	—	—	—	—	Apr 1952	Elbow outside steam pipes Aug 1932.
	4039	—	Feb 1911	Star	Queen Matilda	—	—	—	—	Nov 1950	Elbow outside steam pipes Dec 1948.
	4040	—	Mar 1911	Star	Queen Boadicea	—	—	—	—	June 1951	Castle-style outside steam pipes Feb 1930.
195	4041	—	June 1913	Star	Prince of Wales	—	—	—	—	Apr 1951	Elbow outside steam pipes Oct 1947.
	4042	—	May 1913	Star	Prince Albert	—	—	—	—	Nov 1951	Elbow outside steam pipes May 1948.
	4043	—	May 1913	Star	Prince Henry	—	—	—	—	Jan 1952	Castle-style outside steam pipes Oct 1931.
	4044	—	May 1913	Star	Prince George	—	—	—	—	Feb 1953	Elbow outside steam pipes Oct 1946.
	4045	—	June 1913	Star	Prince John	—	—	—	—	Nov 1950	Elbow outside steam pipes Jan 1946.
199	4046	—	May 1914	Star	Princess Mary	—	—	—	—	Nov 1951	Elbow outside steam pipes Jan 1949.
	4047	—	May 1914	Star	Princess Louise	—	—	—	—	July 1951	
	4048	—	May 1914	Star	Princess Victoria	Princess Mary (28 May 1922)	Princess Victoria (29 May 1922)	—	—	Jan 1953	Elbow outside steam pipes Aug 1932. Castle-style outside steam pipes Oct 1938. Temporary renaming carried out for Royal wedding.
	4049	—	May 1914	Star	Princess Maud	—	—	—	—	July 1953	Castle-style outside steam pipes Feb 1935.
	4050	—	June 1914	Star	Princess Alice	—	—	—	—	Feb 1952	Elbow outside steam pipes June 1946.
	4051	—	June 1914	Star	Princess Helena	—	—	—	—	Oct 1950	Castle-style outside steam pipes Dec 1944.
	4052	—	June 1914	Star	Princess Beatrice	—	—	—	—	June 1953	Castle-style outside steam pipes Apr 1939.
	4053	—	June 1914	Star	Princess Alexandra	—	—	—	—	July 1954	Castle-style outside steam pipes Oct 1933.
	4054	—	June 1914	Star	Princess Charlotte	—	—	—	—	Feb 1952	Elbow outside steam pipes Oct 1945.
	4055	—	July 1914	Star	Princess Sophia	—	—	—	—	Feb 1951	Castle-style outside steam pipes June 1945.
	4056	—	July 1914	Star	Princess Margaret	—	—	—	—	Oct 1957	Elbow outside steam pipes Aug 1949.
	4057	—	July 1914	Star	Princess Elizabeth	—	—	—	—	Feb 1952	Castle-style outside steam pipes Apr 1930.
	4058	—	July 1914	Star	Princess Augusta	—	—	—	—	Apr 1951	Elbow outside steam pipes Oct 1944.
	4059	—	July 1914	Star	Princess Patricia	—	—	—	—	Sept 1952	
	4060	—	July 1914	Star	Princess Eugenie	—	—	—	—	Oct 1952	Elbow outside steam pipes Dec 1930. Castle-style outside steam pipes Aug 1944.
217	4061	—	May 1922	Star	Glastonbury Abbey	—	—	—	—	Mar 1957	Elbow outside steam pipes July 1949.
	4062	—	May 1922	Star	Malmesbury Abbey	—	—	—	—	Nov 1956	Elbow outside steam pipes Mar 1930.
	4063	5083	Nov 1922	Star	Bath Abbey	—	—	Castle (June 1937)	Oct 1958	Jan 1959	Oil burner Dec 1946–Nov 1948.
	4064	5084	Dec 1922	Star	Reading Abbey	—	—	Castle (Apr 1937)	—	July 1962	Davies & Metcalf Lubricator circa 1956.
	4065	5085	Dec 1922	Star	Evesham Abbey	—	—	Castle (July 1937)	—	Feb 1964	
	4066	5086	Dec 1922	Star	Malvern Abbey	Sir Robert Home (May 1935–July 1927)	Viscount Horne (Aug 1937)	Castle (Dec 1937)	—	Nov 1958	
	4067	5087	Jan 1923	Star	Tintern Abbey	—	—	Castle (Nov 1940)	—	Aug 1963	
	4068	5088	Jan 1923	Star	Llanthony Abbey	—	—	Castle (Feb 1939)	June 1958	Sept 1962	
	4069	5089	Jan 1923	Star	Margam Abbey	Westminster Abbey (May 1923)	—	Castle (Oct 1939)	—	Nov 1964	
	4070	5090	Feb 1923	Star	Neath Abbey	Westminster Abbey (May 1923)	—	Castle (Apr 1939)	—	May 1962	Elbow outside steam pipes Mar 1937.
	4071	5091	Feb 1923	Star	Cleeve Abbey	—	—	Castle (Dec 1938)	—	Oct 1964	3,500-gallon tender for oil firing experiments in Oct 1946, then 4,000-gallon in 1947. Returned to coal burning in Nov 1948.
	4072	5092	Feb 1923	Star	Tresco Abbey	—	—	Castle (Apr 1938)	Oct 1961	July 1963	Last Star Class locomotive built.
224	4073	—	Aug 1923	Castle	Caerphilly Castle	—	—	—	—	May 1960	Prototype Castle, British Empire Exhibition Aug 1924. Preserved NRM. Collection. Originally fitted with bogie brakes.
	4074	—	Dec 1923	Castle	Caldicot Castle	—	—	—	Apr 1959	May 1963	April 1925, LNER/GWR trials competitor – GWR main line. Originally fitted with bogie brakes.
	4075	—	Jan 1924	Castle	Cardiff Castle	—	—	—	—	Nov 1961	Originally fitted with bogie brakes.
	4076	—	Feb 1924	Castle	Carmarthen Castle	—	—	—	—	Feb 1963	Originally fitted with bogie brakes.
	4077	—	Feb 1924	Castle	Chepstow Castle	—	—	—	—	Aug 1962	Originally fitted with bogie brakes.
	4078	—	Feb 1924	Castle	Pembroke Castle	—	—	—	—	July 1962	Originally fitted with bogie brakes.
	4079	—	Feb 1924	Castle	Pendennis Castle	—	—	—	—	May 1964	Originally fitted with bogie brakes. LNER/GWR trials competitor LNER main line. British Empire Exhibition Aug 1925 Preserved GWS Collection, Didcot.
	4080	—	Mar 1924	Castle	Powderham Castle	—	—	—	Aug 1958	Aug 1964	Originally fitted with bogie brakes.
	4081	—	Mar 1924	Castle	Warwick Castle	—	—	—	—	Jan 1963	Originally fitted with bogie brakes.
	4082	7013 (Feb 1952)	Apr 1924	Castle	Windsor Castle	Bristol Castle (Feb 1952)	—	—	—	Sept 1964	Last Castle Class locomotive built with bogie brakes – removed from all locomotives soon after. Name swap – see No 7013. Davies & Metcalf lubricator circa 1956.

Loco lot no.	1st loco no.	2nd loco no.	Build date	Class as built	1st name	2nd name (date)	3rd name (date)	Conversions (date)	Double chimney	Withdrawn	Notes/significant dates
232	4083	—	May 1925	Castle	Abbotsbury Castle	—	—	—	—	Dec 1961	
	4084	—	May 1925	Castle	Aberystwyth Castle	—	—	—	—	Oct 1960	
	4085	—	June 1925	Castle	Berkeley Castle	—	—	—	—	May 1962	The locomotive that ran down and killed G.J. Churchward 19 Dec 1933.
	4086	—	June 1925	Castle	Builth Castle	—	—	—	—	Apr 1962	
	4087	—	June 1925	Castle	Cardigan Castle	—	—	—	Feb 1958	Oct 1963	Davies & Metcalf lubricator circa 1956.
	4088	—	July 1925	Castle	Dartmouth Castle	—	—	—	May 1958	May 1964	
	4089	—	July 1925	Castle	Donnington Castle	—	—	—	—	Sept 1964	
	4090	—	July 1925	Castle	Dorchester Castle	—	—	—	July 1957	June 1963	
	4091	—	July 1925	Castle	Dudley Castle	—	—	—	—	Jan 1959	
	4092	—	Aug 1925	Castle	Dunraven Castle	—	—	—	—	Dec 1961	
234	4093	—	May 1926	Castle	Dunster Castle	—	—	—	Dec 1957	Sept 1964	First Castle with straight frames and wide version of fluted inside cylinder valve cover.
	4094	—	May 1926	Castle	Dynevor Castle	—	—	—	—	Mar 1962	
	4095	—	June 1926	Castle	Harlech Castle	—	—	—	—	Dec 1962	
	4096	—	June 1926	Castle	Highclere Castle	—	—	—	—	Jan 1963	
	4097	—	June 1926	Castle	Kenilworth Castle	—	—	—	June 1958	May 1960	
	4098	—	July 1926	Castle	Kidwelly Castle	—	—	—	—	Dec 1963	
	4099	—	Aug 1926	Castle	Kilgerran Castle	—	—	—	—	Sept 1962	
	5000	—	Sept 1926	Castle	Launceston Castle	—	—	—	—	Oct 1964	First Castle to pull Collett 4,000-gallon tender from new. All previous Castles use them later on. Sent to LMS on trials in Sept 1926.
	5001	—	Sept 1926	Castle	Llandovery Castle	—	—	—	June 1961	Feb 1962	Experimentally fitted with 6ft 6in driving wheels in 1931 for a few weeks to look at possible performance gains.
	5002	—	Sept 1926	Castle	Ludlow Castle	—	—	—	—	Sept 1962	
	5003	—	May 1927	Castle	Lulworth Castle	—	—	—	—	Aug 1962	
	5004	—	June 1927	Castle	Llanstephan Castle	—	—	—	—	Apr 1962	
	5005	—	June 1927	Castle	Manorbier Castle	—	—	—	—	Feb 1960	Last Castle to have porthole-style windows in the cab front. Later removed from all previous Castles. Streamlined in 1935 but casing removed soon after.
	5006	—	June 1927	Castle	Tregenna Castle	—	—	—	—	Apr 1962	Set speed records on the famous Cheltenham Flyer train in June 1932.
	5007	—	June 1927	Castle	Rougemont Castle	—	—	—	—	Sept 1962	
	5008	—	June 1927	Castle	Raglan Castle	—	—	—	Mar 1962	Sept 1962	
	5009	—	June 1927	Castle	Shrewsbury Castle	—	—	—	—	Oct 1960	
	5010	—	July 1927	Castle	Restormel Castle	—	—	—	—	Oct 1959	
	5011	—	July 1927	Castle	Tintagel Castle	—	—	—	—	Sept 1962	
	5012	—	July 1927	Castle	Berry Pomeroy Castle	—	—	—	—	Apr 1962	
280	5013	—	June 1932	Castle	Abergavenny Castle	—	—	—	—	July 1962	First Castle to have squared-off inside cylinder valve cover with curved front edge. Also fitted with five glass lubricators and fire iron tunnel; earlier Castles later retrofitted.
	5014	—	June 1932	Castle	Goodrich Castle	—	—	—	—	Feb 1965	
	5015	—	July 1932	Castle	Kingswear Castle	—	—	—	—	Apr 1963	
	5016	—	July 1932	Castle	Montgomery Castle	—	—	—	Feb 1960	Sept 1962	
	5017	—	July 1932	Castle	St Donat's Castle	The Gloucester Regiment 28th, 61st (Apr 1954)	—	—	—	Sept 1962	
	5018	—	July 1932	Castle	St Mawes Castle	—	—	—	—	Mar 1964	
	5019	—	July 1932	Castle	Treago Castle	—	—	—	Feb 1961	Sept 1964	
	5020	—	July 1932	Castle	Trematon Castle	—	—	—	—	Nov 1962	
	5021	—	Aug 1932	Castle	Whittington Castle	—	—	—	—	Sept 1962	
	5022	—	Aug 1932	Castle	Wigmore Castle	—	—	—	Feb 1959	June 1963	Last Castle to have ATC shoe under the cab. Later locos have unit fitted to bogie.
295	5023	—	Apr 1934	Castle	Brecon Castle	—	—	—	—	Feb 1963	First loco to have top lamp iron on smokebox door. Earlier engines subsequently have it moved from smokebox top.
	5024	—	Apr 1934	Castle	Carew Castle	—	—	—	—	May 1962	
	5025	—	Apr 1934	Castle	Chirk Castle	—	—	—	—	Nov 1962	
	5026	—	Apr 1934	Castle	Criccieth Castle	—	—	—	Oct 1959	Nov 1964	
	5027	—	Apr 1934	Castle	Farleigh Castle	—	—	—	Apr 1961	Nov 1962	
	5028	—	May 1934	Castle	Llantilio Castle	—	—	—	—	May 1962	
	5029	—	May 1934	Castle	Nunney Castle	—	—	—	—	Dec 1963	Barry Scrapyard, May 1964. Rescued for preservation in May 1976. Now part of the main line fleet of the Royal Scot & General Trust.
	5030	—	May 1934	Castle	Shirburn Castle	—	—	—	—	Sept 1962	
	5031	—	May 1934	Castle	Totnes Castle	—	—	—	June 1959	Oct 1963	
	5032	—	May 1934	Castle	Usk Castle	—	—	—	May 1959	Sept 1962	
296	5033	—	May 1935	Castle	Broughton Castle	—	—	—	Oct 1960	Sept 1962	
	5034	—	May 1935	Castle	Corfe Castle	—	—	—	Feb 1960	Sept 1962	
	5035	—	May 1935	Castle	Coity Castle	—	—	—	—	May 1962	
	5036	—	May 1935	Castle	Lyonshall Castle	—	—	—	Dec 1960	Sept 1962	
	5037	—	May 1935	Castle	Monmouth Castle	—	—	—	—	Mar 1964	
	5038	—	June 1935	Castle	Morlais Castle	—	—	—	—	Sept 1963	
	5039	—	July 1935	Castle	Rhuddlan Castle	—	—	—	—	June 1963	Oil burner Dec 1946–Sep 1948.
	5040	—	July 1935	Castle	Stokesay Castle	—	—	—	—	Oct 1963	
	5041	—	July 1935	Castle	Tiverton Castle	—	—	—	—	Dec 1963	
	5042	—	July 1935	Castle	Winchester Castle	—	—	—	—	Jun. 1965	

Loco lot no.	1st loco no.	2nd loco no.	Build date	Class as built	1st name	2nd name (date)	3rd name (date)	Conversions (date)	Double chimney	Withdrawn	Notes/significant dates
303	5043	—	June 1936	Castle	Barbury Castle	Earl of Mount Edgcumbe (Oct 1937)	—	—	Oct 1958	Dec 1963	Barry Scrapyard, June 1964. Rescued for spare parts in 1973. Later, however, was restored in its own right and now a member of the Tyseley Loco Works main line fleet.
	5044	—	Mar 1936	Castle	Beverston Castle	Earl of Dunraven (Sept 1937)	—	—	—	Apr 1962	First Castle to be fitted with short chimney from new. Earlier engines later retrofitted.
	5045	—	Mar 1936	Castle	Bridgwater Castle	Earl of Dudley (Sept 1937)	—	—	—	Sept 1962	
	5046	—	Apr 1936	Castle	Clifford Castle	Earl Cawdor (Aug 1937)	—	—	—	Sept 1962	
	5047	—	Apr 1936	Castle	Compton Castle	Earl of Dartmouth (Aug 1937)	—	—	—	Sept 1962	
	5048	—	Apr 1936	Castle	Cranbrook Castle	Earl of Devon (Aug 1937)	—	—	—	Aug 1962	
	5049	—	Apr 1936	Castle	Denbigh Castle	Earl of Plymouth (Aug 1937)	—	—	Sept 1959	Mar 1963	
	5050	—	May 1936	Castle	Devizes Castle	Earl of St Germans (Aug 1937)	—	—	—	Aug 1963	
	5051	—	May 1936	Castle	Drysllwyn Castle	Earl Bathurst (Aug 1937)	—	—	—	May 1963	Barry Scrapyard, Oct 1963. Rescued for preservation in Mar 1969. Restored by 1979. GWS Collection, Didcot.
	5052	—	May 1936	Castle	Eastnor Castle	Earl of Radnor (July 1937)	—	—	—	Sept 1962	
	5053	—	May 1936	Castle	Bishop's Castle	Earl Cairns (July 1937)	—	—	—	July 1962	
	5054	—	June 1936	Castle	Lamphey Castle	Earl of Ducie (Sept 1937)	—	—	—	Nov 1964	
	5055	—	June 1936	Castle	Lydford Castle	Earl of Eldon (Aug 1937)	—	—	—	Oct 1964	
	5056	—	June 1936	Castle	Ogmore Castle	Earl of Powis (Sept 1937)	—	—	Oct 1960	Nov 1964	
	5057	—	June 1936	Castle	Penrice Castle	Earl Waldegrave (Oct 1937)	—	—	July 1958	Mar 1964	
	5058	—	May 1937	Castle	Newport Castle	Earl of Clancarty (Sept 1937)	—	—	—	Mar 1963	
	5059	—	May 1937	Castle	Powis Castle	Earl of St. Aldwyn (Oct 1937)	—	—	—	June 1962	
	5060	—	June 1937	Castle	Sarum Castle	Earl of Berkeley (Oct 1937)	—	—	July 1961	Apr 1963	
	5061	—	June 1937	Castle	Sudeley Castle	Earl of Birkenhead (Oct 1937)	—	—	Sept 1958	Sept 1962	
	5062	—	June 1937	Castle	Tenby Castle	Earl of Shaftsbury (Nov 1937)	—	—	—	Aug 1962	
	5063	—	June 1937	Castle	Thornbury Castle	Earl Baldwin (July 1937)	—	—	—	Feb 1963	
	5064	—	June 1937	Castle	Tretower Castle	Bishop's Castle (Sept 1937)	—	—	Sept 1958	Sept 1962	
	5065	—	July 1937	Castle	Upton Castle	Newport Castle (Sept 1937)	—	—	—	Jan 1963	
	5066	—	July 1937	Castle	Wardour Castle	Sir Felix Pole (Apr 1956)	—	—	Apr 1959	Sept 1962	
	5067	—	July 1937	Castle	St Fagans Castle	—	—	—	—	July 1962	
310	5068	—	June 1938	Castle	Beverston Castle	—	—	—	July 1959	Sept 1962	
	5069	—	June 1938	Castle	Isambard Kingdom Brunel	—	—	—	—	Feb 1962	
	5070	—	June 1938	Castle	Sir Daniel Gooch	—	—	—	—	Mar 1964	
	5071	—	June 1938	Castle	Clifford Castle	Spitfire (Sept 1940)	—	—	June 1959	Oct 1963	
	5072	—	June 1938	Castle	Compton Castle	Hurricane (Nov 1940)	—	—	—	Oct 1962	
	5073	—	July 1938	Castle	Cranbrook Castle	Blenheim (Jan 1941)	—	—	July 1959	Mar 1964	
	5074	—	July 1938	Castle	Denbigh Castle	Hampden (Jan 1941)	—	—	Sept 1961	May 1964	
	5075	—	Aug 1938	Castle	Devizes Castle	Wellington (Oct 1940)	—	—	—	Sept 1962	
	5076	—	Aug 1938	Castle	Drysllwyn Castle	Gladiator (Jan 1941)	—	—	—	Sept 1964	
	5077	—	Aug 1938	Castle	Eastnor Castle	Fairey Battle (Oct 1940)	—	—	—	July 1964	
	5078	—	May 1939	Castle	Lamphey Castle	Beaufort (Jan 1941)	—	—	Dec 1961	Nov 1962	
	5079	—	May 1939	Castle	Lydford Castle	Lysander (Nov 1940)	—	—	—	May 1960	Oil burner Jan 1947–Oct 1948.
	5080	—	May 1939	Castle	Ogmore Castle	Defiant (Jan 1941)	—	—	—	Apr 1963	Barry Scrapyard, Oct 1963. Rescued for spare parts in 1974. Later, however, was restored in its own right and now a member of the Tyseley Loco Works main line fleet.
	5081	—	May 1939	Castle	Penrice Castle	Lockheed Hudson (Jan 1941)	—	—	—	Oct 1963	
	5082	—	June 1939	Castle	Powis Castle	Swordfish (Jan 1941)	—	—	—	July 1962	
342	5093	—	June 1939	Castle	Upton Castle	—	—	—	—	Sept 1963	Fitted with heavy cadmium whistle chain in Aug 1954.
	5094	—	June 1939	Castle	Tretower Castle	—	—	—	June 1960	Sept 1964	
	5095	—	June 1939	Castle	Barbury Castle	—	—	—	Nov 1958	Aug 1962	
	5096	—	June 1939	Castle	Bridgwater Castle	—	—	—	Jan 1959	June 1964	
	5097	—	July 1939	Castle	Sarum Castle	—	—	—	June 1961	Mar 1963	Last Castle to have straight cab window handrail. Later engines had rail that curved up around window.
357	5098	—	May 1946	Castle	Clifford Castle	—	—	—	Jan 1959	June 1964	Originally intended as part of Lot No 342 but wartime restrictions cancelled the job. Built as Lot 357 instead. First Castle to have square valve cover and three-row superheaters.
	5099	—	May 1946	Castle	Compton Castle	—	—	—	—	Feb 1963	Originally intended as part of Lot No 342 but wartime restrictions cancelled the job. Built as Lot 357 instead.
243	6000	—	June 1927	King	King George V	—	—	—	Dec 1956	Dec 1962	Alfloc water treatment fitted 1954. To USA for B&ORR Centenary celebrations Aug 1927. Cab side medallions and brass bell still on loco. Preserved NRM collection.
	6001	—	July 1927	King	King Edward VII	—	—	—	Feb 1956	Sept 1962	Alfloc water treatment fitted in 1954. 1948 BR Interchange trials locomotive.
	6002	—	July 1927	King	King William IV	—	—	—	Mar 1956	Sept 1962	Alfloc water treatment fitted in 1954.
	6003	—	July 1927	King	King George IV	—	—	—	July 1958	June 1962	Accident at Midgham, Aug 1927 when bogie derailed. Prompted redesign of bogie springing on all 60XX class. Alfloc water treatment fitted in 1954.
	6004	—	July 1927	King	King George III	—	—	—	July 1958	June 1962	Alfloc water treatment fitted in 1954.
	6005	—	July 1927	King	King George II	—	—	—	July 1956	Nov 1962	Alfloc water treatment fitted in 1954.
	6006	—	Feb 1928	King	King George I	—	—	—	June 1956	Feb 1962	Alfloc water treatment fitted in 1954.
	6007	—	Mar 1928	King	King William III	—	—	—	—	Mar 1936	This locomotive was severely damaged and written off in the Shrivenham collision 15 Jan 1936 and condemned.
309	6007	—	Mar 1936	King	King William III	—	—	—	Sept 1956	Sept 1962	Replacement No 6007, built in Mar 1936 using components from the original and carrying same name and number Alfloc water treatment fitted in 1954.

Loco lot no.	1st loco no.	2nd loco no.	Build date	Class as built	1st name	2nd name (date)	3rd name (date)	Conversions (date)	Double chimney	Withdrawn	Notes/significant dates
243	6008	—	Mar 1928	King	King James II	—	—	—	Dec 1958	June 1962	Alfloc water treatment fitted in 1954.
	6009	—	Mar 1928	King	King Charles II	—	—	—	May 1956	Sept 1962	Alfloc water treatment fitted in 1954.
	6010	—	Apr 1928	King	King Charles I	—	—	—	Mar 1956	June 1962	Alfloc water treatment fitted in 1954.
	6011	—	Apr 1928	King	King James I	—	—	—	Mar 1956	Dec 1962	Alfloc water treatment fitted in 1954.
	6012	—	Apr 1928	King	King Edward VI	—	—	—	Feb 1958	Sept 1962	Alfloc water treatment fitted in 1954.
	6013	—	May 1928	King	King Henry VIII	—	—	—	June 1956	June 1962	Alfloc water treatment fitted in 1954.
	6014	—	May 1928	King	King Henry VII	—	—	—	Sept 1957	Sept 1962	Fitted with streamlining from Mar 1935. All removed by 1943 except wedge-shaped cab front. Alfloc water treatment fitted in 1954.
	6015	—	June 1928	King	King Richard III	—	—	—	Sept 1955	Sept 1962	Alfloc water treatment fitted in 1954.
	6016	—	June 1928	King	King Edward V	—	—	—	Jan 1958	Sept 1962	Alfloc water treatment fitted in 1954.
	6017	—	June 1928	King	King Edward IV	—	—	—	Dec 1955	July 1962	Alfloc water treatment fitted in 1954.
	6018	—	June 1928	King	King Henry VI	—	—	—	Mar 1958	Dec 1962	Alfloc water treatment fitted in 1954. 1948 BR Interchange trials locomotive.
	6019	—	July 1928	King	King Henry V	—	—	—	Apr 1957	Sept 1962	Alfloc water treatment fitted in 1954.
267	6020	—	May 1930	King	King Henry IV	—	—	—	Feb 1956	July 1962	Alfloc water treatment fitted in 1954.
	6021	—	June 1930	King	King Richard II	—	—	—	Mar 1957	Sept 1962	Alfloc water treatment fitted in 1954.
	6022	—	June 1930	King	King Edward III	—	—	—	May 1956	Sept 1962	Alfloc water treatment fitted in 1954.
	6023	—	June 1930	King	King Edward II	—	—	—	June 1957	June 1962	Alfloc water treatment fitted in 1954. Barry Scrapyard, 1962. Wheel set cut up in scrapyard accident, so restoration difficult. Rescued in 1984 and restored by GWS at Didcot by 2011.
	6024	—	June 1930	King	King Edward I	—	—	—	Mar 1957	June 1962	Alfloc water treatment fitted in 1954. Rescued for preservation in Mar 1973. Restored by 1989. Now part of the main line fleet of the Royal Scot & General Trust.
	6025	—	July 1930	King	King Henry III	—	—	—	Mar 1957	Dec 1962	Alfloc water treatment fitted in 1954.
	6026	—	July 1930	King	King John	—	—	—	Mar 1958	Sept 1962	Alfloc water treatment fitted in 1954.
	6027	—	July 1930	King	King Richard I	—	—	—	Aug 1956	Sept 1962	Alfloc water treatment fitted in 1954.
	6028	—	July 1930	King	King Henry II	King George VI (Jan 1937)	—	—	Jan 1957	Nov 1962	Alfloc water treatment fitted in 1954.
	6029	—	Aug 1930	King	King Stephen	King Edward VIII (May 1936)	—	—	Dec 1957	July 1962	Alfloc water treatment fitted in 1954. Final production King Class loco.
357	7000	—	May 1946	Castle	Viscount Portal	—	—	—	—	Dec 1963	
	7001	—	May 1946	Castle	Denbigh Castle	Sir James Milne (Feb 1948)	—	—	Sept 1960	Sept 1963	
	7002	—	June 1946	Castle	Devizes Castle	—	—	—	June 1961	Mar 1964	
	7003	—	June 1946	Castle	Elmley Castle	—	—	—	June 1960	Aug 1963	
	7004	—	June 1946	Castle	Eastnor Castle	—	—	—	Feb 1958	Jan 1964	
	7005	—	June 1946	Castle	Lamphey Castle	Sir Edward Elgar (Aug 1957)	—	—	—	Sept 1964	
	7006	—	June 1946	Castle	Lydford Castle	—	—	—	May 1960	Dec 1963	
	7007	—	July 1946	Castle	Ogmore Castle	Great Western (Jan 1948)	—	—	Mar 1961	Feb 1963	Last express passenger loco built by the GWR before nationalisation. First Castle to leave Swindon with Hawksworth tender.
367	7008	—	May 1948	Castle	Swansea Castle	—	—	—	June 1959	Sept 1964	
	7009	—	May 1948	Castle	Athelney Castle	—	—	—	—	Mar 1963	
	7010	—	June 1948	Castle	Avondale Castle	—	—	—	Oct 1960	Mar 1964	
	7011	—	June 1948	Castle	Banbury Castle	—	—	—	—	Feb 1965	
	7012	—	June 1948	Castle	Barry Castle	—	—	—	—	Nov 1964	
	7013	4082 (Feb 1952)	July 1948	Castle	Bristol Castle	Windsor Castle (Feb 1952)	—	—	May 1958	Feb 1965	Name swap due to No 4082 being in Swindon works at time of funeral of King George VI when that loco was requested to pull funeral train.
	7014	—	July 1948	Castle	Caerhays Castle	—	—	—	Feb 1959	Feb 1965	Davies & Metcalf lubricator circa 1956.
	7015	—	July 1948	Castle	Carn Brea Castle	—	—	—	June 1959	Apr 1963	
	7016	—	Aug 1948	Castle	Chester Castle	—	—	—	—	Nov 1962	
	7017	—	Aug 1948	Castle	G.J. Churchward	—	—	—	—	Feb 1963	The only Castle Class engine to have full-stops on its nameplate.
	7018	—	May 1949	Castle	Drysllwyn Castle	—	—	—	May 1956	Sept 1963	First Castle to receive the double chimney modification. Had uprated lubrication delivering 50% more oil too.
	7019	—	May 1949	Castle	Fowey Castle	—	—	—	Sept 1958	Sept 1964	
	7020	—	May 1949	Castle	Gloucester Castle	—	—	—	Feb 1961	Sept 1963	
	7021	—	June 1949	Castle	Haverfordwest Castle	—	—	—	Nov 1961	Sept 1963	
	7022	—	June 1949	Castle	Hereford Castle	—	—	—	Jan 1958	June 1965	
	7023	—	June 1949	Castle	Penrice Castle	—	—	—	May 1958	Feb 1965	
	7024	—	June 1949	Castle	Powis Castle	—	—	—	Mar 1959	Feb 1965	
	7025	—	Aug 1949	Castle	Sudeley Castle	—	—	—	—	Sept 1964	
	7026	—	Aug 1949	Castle	Tenby Castle	—	—	—	—	Oct 1964	
	7027	—	Aug 1949	Castle	Thornbury Castle	—	—	—	—	Dec 1963	Barry Scrapyard, May 1964. Rescued for preservation in Aug 1972. Initial restoration effort began at Tyseley, although later sold to Peter Waterman. Still unrestored.
	7028	—	May 1950	Castle	Cadbury Castle	—	—	—	Oct 1961	Dec 1963	
375	7029	—	May 1950	Castle	Clun Castle	—	—	—	Oct 1959	Dec 1965	Hauled the last steam-hauled services from Paddington to Banbury in June 1964. Preserved from service. A member of the Tyseley Loco Works main line fleet.
	7030	—	June 1950	Castle	Cranbrook Castle	—	—	—	July 1959	Feb 1963	
	7031	—	June 1950	Castle	Cromwell's Castle	—	—	—	—	July 1963	
	7032	—	June 1950	Castle	Denbigh Castle	—	—	—	Sept 1960	Sept 1964	
	7033	—	July 1950	Castle	Hartlebury Castle	—	—	—	July 1959	Jan 1963	
	7034	—	Aug 1950	Castle	Ince Castle	—	—	—	Dec 1959	June 1965	
	7035	—	Aug 1950	Castle	Ogmore Castle	—	—	—	Jan 1960	Aug 1964	
	7036	—	Aug 1950	Castle	Taunton Castle	—	—	—	Jan 1960	Sept 1963	
	7037	—	Aug 1950	Castle	Swindon	—	—	—	—	Mar 1963	The last Castle Class built and the last GWR-designed express passenger engine built. Named by HRH Princess (later Queen) Elizabeth.

Appendix 6

No 4079 *Pendennis Castle* engine history sheets

Published in their original form here for the first time are the engine history sheets for *Pendennis Castle*. These records were kept for every locomotive and are now to be found at the Public Records Office in Kew, London. The exception is those for No 4079, which were given to Mike Higson when he preserved her in 1965. They are now part of the Great Western Trust's collection at Didcot.

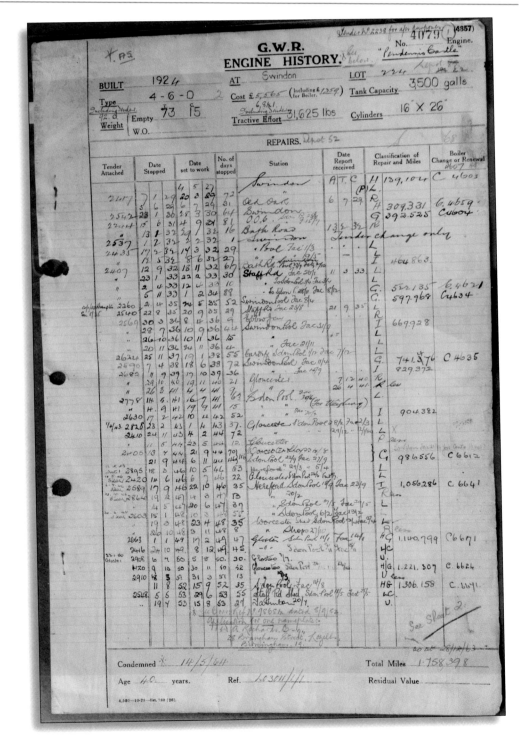

(Frank Dumbleton)

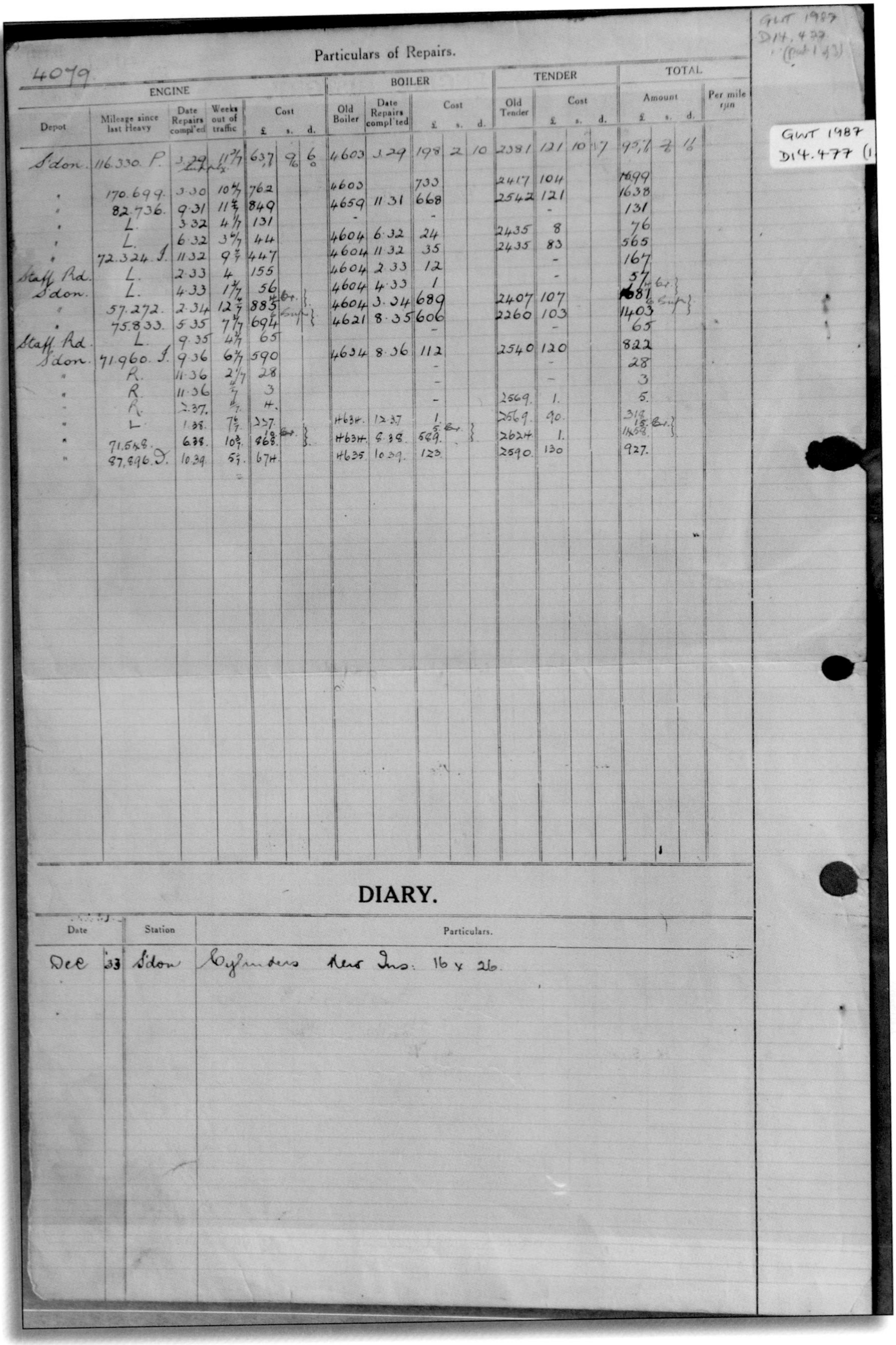

GWT 1987
D14.477 (1

4079

Particulars of Repairs.

ENGINE							BOILER					TENDER				TOTAL			
Depot	Mileage since last Heavy	Date Repairs compl'ed	Weeks out of traffic	Cost £	s.	d.	Old Boiler	Date Repairs compl'ted	Cost £	s.	d.	Old Tender	Cost £	s.	d.	Amount £	s.	d.	Per mile run
S'don.	116.330. P.	3.29	11 3/7	637	9	6	4603	3.29	198	2	10	2381	121	10	7	957	2	11	
"	170.699.	3.30	10 4/7	762			4603		733			2417	104			1699			
"	82.736.	9.31	11 4/7	849			4659	11.31	668			2542	121			1638			
"	L.	3.32	4 1/7	131			-		-				-			131			
"	L.	6.32	3 6/7	44			4604	6.32	24			2435	8			76			
"	72.324. I.	11.32	9 4/7	447			4604	11.32	35			2435	83			565			
Staff. Rd.	L.	2.33	4	155			4604	2.33	12				-			167			
S'don.	L.	4.33	1 1/7	56			4604	4.33	1				-			57			
"	57.272.	2.34	12 4/7	885 (4 Br.)			4604	3.34	689			2407	107			1681 (4 Br.)			
"	75.833.	5.35	7 1/7	694 (6 Sup.)			4621	8.35	606			2260	103			1403 (6 Sup.)			
Staff. Rd.	L.	9.35	4 1/7	65					-				-			65			
S'don.	71.960. I.	9.36	6 1/7	590			4634	8.36	112			2540	120			822			
"	R.	11.36	2 1/7	28					-				-			28			
"	R.	11.36	4/7	3					-				-			3			
"	R.	2.37.	4/7	4.					-			2569.	1.			5.			
"	L	1.38.	7 6/7	227.			4634.	12.37	1.			2569.	90.			318			
"	71.548.	6.38.	10 3/7	868. (10 Br.)			4634.	6.38.	569. (5 Br.)			2624	1.			1458. (15 Br.)			
"	87.896. I.	10.39.	5 1/7	674.			4635	10.39.	123.			2590.	130			927.			

DIARY.

Date		Station	Particulars.
Dec	'33	S'don	Cylinders New Ins: 16 x 26.

(Frank Dumbleton)

BRITISH RAILWAYS (W.R.)
ENGINE HISTORY.

② No. 4079

GWR 1987
D14. 477 (243)

BUILT _____ AT _____

Type _____

LOT _____

Weight { Empty _____ t. ___ c. ___

W.O. _____

Cost £ _____

Including { Boiler £ _____ A.T.C.£ _____ £ _____

Tank Capacity _____

Tractive Effort _____

Cylinders _____

REPAIRS

C.6671

Tender Attached	Date Stopped	Station	To Factory			Date set to work	No. of days stopped	Classification of Repair and Miles	Boiler Change or Renewal
			Station	Pool	Shops				
	25 11 53	Staff Rd Shed				10 12 53	15	U	
2653	28 1 53	" " "	1don	15 2	14 2	30 3 54	61	HI 1,373,850	C.4624
	4 10 54	Tyseley Shops.				21 10 54	17	U	
2846	16 5 55	Swindon Pool	Fac		18.5	21 6 55	36	HI 1442193	C 4608
Sdon tast 19/9/56 2584	26 4 56	Staff Rd Shed	Sdon	14.5	25.6	19 9 56	146	H6 1888699	C 6645
	30 9 57	Bath Rd.	Sdon	8.10	10 10	28 11 57	59	H6 1545683	C 6686 HD
Sdon 29 9 59. 2559	22 3 58	O.O.G.				28 3 58	6	U 620	
	27 7 59	Cardiff	Sdon	31.7	6.8	29 7 59	64	HG 1.622469	C 6681
Sdon 20 10 61 2390	EXT.		Sdon	25.8	30.8	20 10 61	56	HI 1.720.523	C 6672
	3 12 62	Swindon Shed				17 12 62	144	U	
OOC 8/5/64 2913	12 3 64	"				1 4 64	20	U	37875

Trailers dislodged following speed of 97 m/h on Shotten Bfd falder to W.O/B 9/5/64

as at 28/12/63

CONDEMNED _____

Age _____ years.   Authority _____

TOTAL MILES 1,758,398

Residual Value £ _____

(Frank Dumbleton)

Appendix 7

Pendennis Castle (x3)

ABOVE AND BELOW
Class 57, 57604, and the frame of 4079 (with original nameplate) at Didcot to mark the 175th anniversary of the Great Western Railway in 2010.
(Frank Dumbleton/GWS)

No 4079 was not the first or the last locomotive to bear the name *Pendennis Castle*. The first was Duke of Cornwall Class locomotive No 3253 which left the works in 1895 – some 28 years before No 4079. When the decision was taken to name the new express passenger class after Castles, any other locomotive that was still in existence that carried a name which could lead it to being confused with one of Collett's new wonder machines had it removed. After No 4079 was withdrawn, the GWR main line was bereft of a *Pendennis Castle* for around 40 years, until 2004 when First Great Western (FGW) accepted delivery of four Class 57 diesel locomotives from Brush Traction. These were bought to haul the Night Riviera sleeper service, and FGW decided to reuse names that were originally on 4073 Class engines that reflected the Cornish destination of the service. As a result, No 57604 became *Pendennis Castle* the third.

To mark the 175th anniversary of the Great Western Railway in 2010, FGW and the Great Western Society joined forces to design a special livery for No 57604 that mimicked as far as was possible the green GWR express passenger scheme as used by the Castles. This included such details as GWR-style crests, brass number plates and nameplates, the red dot and letter D route and power marking and fully lined-out body sides. This was unveiled in the presence of the under-overhaul No 4079 in June of that year. As a special touch, one of 4079's original nameplates was extracted from the museum safe (the plates she is usually seen with are replicas, as the originals are very valuable) and put on the engine's frames. This is significant, because Swindon – forever the thrifty establishment – reused the letters from No 3253 to make No 4079's nameplates. This meant that in a sense, all three engines were represented there in some way or another. Over 115 years of railway tradition and history were on display at Didcot that day.

Appendix 8

Painting of locomotives, engines and tenders, 1 July 1947

Priming Paint (one coat).	All steel and iron work except bright parts and boiler.
Stopping.	Making good all bad places after priming.
Black Oil Paint and varnish mixture (two coats).	Reversing rod. Frames. Wheels (new engines only). Ground of number plates around figures.
Black Oil Paint (two coats). Varnish (one coat).	Hanging bars. Strap plates. Ground of nameplates around letters. Cylinder cleating.
Priming Paint or Tar-Base Paint (one coat).	Boiler complete, outside.
Tar-Base Paint (one coat).	Wheels on repaired engines.
Smokestack Black (two coats). Smokestack Black (one coat).	Smokebox wrapper, door and fittings, handrail, chimney (except copper cap), saddle and outside steam pipe casings. Splasher tops. Cab roof (outside). Lamp irons. Buffer plungers and couplings. Inside of tool boxes. Four-cone ejector and pipe. Tender coal space and fittings. Side-tank tops and fittings. Bunker coal space, shelf and front plate. Firebox back. Footplate. All parts below footplate such as brake work, pipes, sand and cylinder cock gear, etc.
Engine Green Paint (two coats). Varnish (two coats).	Boiler cleating, handrails and brackets. Clackbox covers. Dome cover. Safety valve casing (except on engines that have chimneys fitted with polished copper caps). Cab sides, front and back (inside and outside). Cab roof (inside). Splasher fronts. Lower part of nameplates between brass beading and splasher. Tank sides and fronts (except on pannier tanks finishing at front of smokebox, in which case the fronts are painted with smokestack black). Tops of pannier and saddle tanks and fittings. Toolboxes (outside). Tender tank sides and back (given a coat of Grey priming coat before the Green is applied).
Chinese Red Paint (one coat). Varnish (one coat).	Buffer plates and buffer cases.
Venetian Red Paint (one coat).	All plates inside frames between smokebox and firebox. Eccentric rods. Crank axle. Regulator handle (except handgrip).
Polished brass.	Safety valve cover on engines having chimneys with polished copper caps. Splasher beadings. Vertical cab beading. Number plate border and figure faces. Nameplate letter faces and beadings. Cab window frames.
Polished copper.	Chimney cap.
Bright steel.	Connecting and coupling rods. Motion details. Handles in cab. Vertical handrails on cab and tender.
Linings, engine Only the following classes: 4000, Stars 4073, Castles 6000, Kings 1000, Counties 2900, Saints 4901, Halls	**Cab sides** – ⅛in orange line 3in from cab beading, following contour of cab sides; 1in black line ½in from orange line and another ⅛in orange line ½in beyond black line. Note: On the 'County' class the lower cab lines commence at 6in above footplate to coincide with tender lining. **Number plates** – ⅛in orange line ½in from polished border. *Splasher fronts* – ½in black line from footplate and around splasher with ⅛in orange line ½in away from black line. **Boiler cleating bands** – 1in black line with ⅛in orange line each side and ½in away. **Hanging bars and frames** – ⅛in orange line ½in from edge. **Buffer plates. Nameplates (lower part)** – Edged with ½in black line and ⅛in orange line ½in away from black line. **Outside cylinder cleating** – Two ⅛in orange lines 1in apart, set 1½in in from front and back cleating covers, forming panel with base line about 4in up from bottom, and top line 4in down from hanging bar. Note: Black lines to be painted with Black Oil Paint.

Linings, tenders for lined engines.	
4,000-gallon tender with flush bottom tank and flared sides.	**Tank sides and back** – Outside ⅛in orange line, 7in from black beading at top and sides, 4in up from top edge of bottom angle iron at footplate, forming panels with 5in radii at corners. 1in black line ½in from orange line and another ⅛in orange line ½in inside black line. No lining on coal plates.
4,000-gallon tender with flush bottom tank and straight sides.	**Tank sides (including coal plates) and back** – Outside ⅛in orange line 6in from black beading and top of footplate, following contour of plates. 1in black line ½in from orange line and another ⅛in orange line ½in inside black line.
3,500-gallon tender with well bottom tank.	**Tank sides and back** – Outside ⅛in orange line 6in from black beading at top and sides, 5in up from top edge of bottom angle iron at footplate, forming panels with 5in radii at corners. 1in black line ½in from orange line and another ⅛in orange line ½in inside black line. **Coal plates** – Outside ⅛in orange line 3in from black beading following contour of plates. 1in black line ½in from orange line and another ⅛in orange line ½in inside black line. Note: Beading around lined tenders painted black. Hanging bars, frames and buffer plates lines same as engine. Black lines to be painted with Black Oil Paint.
Lettering (transfers).	**For tenders of named engines** – 9in letters G.W. with centres 7ft 0in apart and with coat of arms between. **For all other tenders and all tank engines** – 9in letters G.W.R with centres 3ft 6in apart. Note: The letters and coat of arms to be arranged as nearly as possible in the centre of the tender or tanks sides but to be clear of all rivet heads.
Figuring (transfers).	**For engine buffer plates** – 6in figures of the engine number to be carried on the front buffer plates of all tender engines and on both buffer plates of all tank engines. The number to be placed between coupling hook and buffer on the right-hand side of the buffer plate as viewed from the track. Note: The whole of the lining, lettering and numbering to be completed before the final coat of varnish is applied.

The priming paint to consist of an iron oxide/red lead/linseed oil mixture formulated in such a manner that it falls within the limit specified for leadless painting as defined in the 'Vehicle Painting Regulations, 1925'.

The stopping to consist of a mixture of pigments, linseed oil, varnish gums and thinners of suitable quality for the purpose.

The Black Oil paint to consist of a mixture of ivory drop black or other suitable black pigment, linseed oil and the necessary driers and thinners.

The varnish to be best Engine Body Varnish.

The Black Oil Paint and varnish mixture to consist of Black Oil Paint and varnish as defined above, the proportion of varnish being not less than four times that of the linseed oil in the paint.

The Tar-Base Paint to consist of a mixture of dehydrated coal-tar, coal-tar pitch and heavy coal-tar naphtha formulated in such a manner as to give an opaque tough film of good substance.

The Engine Green Paint to consist of a mixture of pigments containing not more than 5% of lead compounds expressed as PbO, linseed oil, varnish and the necessary driers and thinners, the proportion of varnish being not less than twice that of the linseed oil.

The Chinese Red Paint to consist of Chinese red pigment, gold size and white spirit.

The Venetian Red Paint to consist of iron oxide pigment, linseed oil, varnish and the necessary driers and thinners, the proportion of varnish being not less than that of the linseed oil.

The transfers for letters and figures are to be obtained 'As supplied to the G.W.R.' from:
Messrs Eagle Transfer Company
Deritend
Birmingham
Or
Messrs Tearne & Sons Ltd
All Saints Road
Birmingham, 18

Appendix 9

Places of interest

Didcot Railway Centre

Didcot Railway Station, Didcot,
Oxfordshire, OX11 7NJ
Website www.didcotrailwaycentre.org.uk
Tel +44 (0) 1235 817200

Didcot Railway Centre is the home of
the Great Western Society. The society
was set up by four young gentlemen in
1962 to preserve Auto Tank No 1466
and Auto Trailer No 213. It has grown
to be the largest collection of GWR
locomotives, rolling stock and exhibits
anywhere in the world, and is based
in the last fully operational main line
steam loco shed in the UK. It is home
to No 4079 *Pendennis Castle*, No 5051
Drysllwyn Castle/Earl Bathurst and No
6023 *King Edward II*. There are regular
demonstrations of steam locomotives
and a collection of GWR buildings,
structures, signalling and the only
operational section of Brunel's original
7ft 0¼in gauge track left in the world.
It is open regularly throughout the year
and details can be found either on the
website or by calling the centre. Some of
the locomotives are main-line registered
and haul tours as well as visiting various
other heritage railways around the UK.

National Railway Museum

Leeman Road, York, North Yorkshire,
YO26 4XJ
Tel +44 (0) 8448 153139
and
'Locomotion', Shildon, Co Durham,
DL4 1PQ
Tel +44 (0) 1388 771448
Website www.nrm.org.uk

The National Railway Museum is the
world's premier national collection of
railway vehicles. Amongst its many
treasures are City Class No 3440 *City
of Truro*, Star Class No 4003 *Lode
Star* and King No 6000 *King George
V*. The NRM collection is also home
to No 92220 *Evening Star*, No 4468
Mallard and No 4079's great rival No
4472 *Flying Scotsman*. The engines
are displayed at various sites around
the UK as well as the two museums,
and the current location of any exhibit
should be checked before travelling.

STEAM Museum of the Great Western Railway

Fire Fly Avenue, Swindon, SN2 2EY
Website www.steam-museum.org.uk
Tel +44 (0) 1235 817200

The NRM also owns No 4073
Caerphilly Castle, but this is on
permanent display at STEAM in
Swindon. She is usually in the company
of one of the other major Swindon-built
exhibits from the national collection,
as well as a number of other GWR
locomotives and items of rolling stock.

Tyseley Locomotive Works/ Vintage Trains

670 Warwick Road, Tyseley,
Birmingham, B11 2HL
Website www.tyseleylocoworks.co.uk
Tel +44 (0) 1217084960

Tyseley own three locomotives of
interest to readers of this book –
Castles No 5043 *Earl of Mount
Edgcumbe*, No 5080 *Defiant* and No
7029 *Clun Castle*. The locomotives are
not on regular public display and are
sometimes loaned to other venues for
display, but there are open days at the
locomotive works throughout the year.
Vintage trains run many tours out on
the main line using the Tyseley-based
machines, which also include Hall and
pannier tank-type locomotives, and
tickets for these trains can be booked
using the above contact information.

Royal Scot Locomotive & General Trust/Locomotive Services/No 5029 Nunney Castle

Railway Yard, Collett Way, Great
Western Industrial Estate, Southall,
Middlesex, UB2 4SE
Websites www.royalscot.org.uk
www.iconsofsteam.com
www.5029nunneycastle.co.uk

The Royal Scot Locomotive & General
Trust was formed in 2009 to protect for
the long-term, steam trains capable of
hauling passenger trains on both the
main line and heritage railways. It is the
custodian of No 6024 *King Edward I*,
and Locomotive Services also look after
No 5029 *Nunney Castle*. These engines
are not on regular public display but
any of the websites will be able to give
details regarding the locations of any
of their engines and their upcoming
rail tours and appearances on heritage
lines around the UK.

At the time of writing the sole
unrestored Castle Class locomotive No
7027 *Thornbury Castle* is stored out
of sight at Crewe, with an uncertain
immediate future. It is the fervent hope
of many, your author included, that
this last of the remaining four-cylinder
GWR fleet will one day undergo full
restoration.

Index